NEW ORLEANS ARCHITECTURE

VOLUME V

The Esplanade Ridge

704 Esplanade

NEW ORLEANS ARCHITECTURE

VOLUME V:

The Esplanade Ridge

Authors:
MARY LOUISE CHRISTOVICH
SALLY KITTREDGE EVANS
ROULHAC TOLEDANO

Photographs by
BETSY SWANSON

PELICAN PUBLISHING COMPANY
GRETNA 1995

*The word "Pelican" and the depiction of a pelican
are trademarks of Pelican Publishing Company, Inc.,
and are registered in the U.S. Patent and Trademark Office.*

Library of Congress Cataloging in Publication Data (Revised)

Friends of the Cabildo
    New Orleans Architecture.
    Vol. 5 compiled by M. L. Christovich, S. K. Evans, and
    R. Toledano. includes bibliographies.
    CONTENTS: v. 1. The Lower Garden District.—v. 2. The
American Sector (Faubourg St. Mary)—v. 3. The
Cemeteries.—v. 4. The Creole Faubourgs.
    1. Architecture—Louisiana—New Orleans. 2. New
Orleans—Buildings. I. Wilson, Samuel, 1911–   II. Chris-
tovich, Mary Louise, ed. III. Toledano, Roulhac, ed. IV. Title.
NA735.N4F74 1971   720′ .9663′35   72–172272
ISBN 0–911116–51–6 (v. 1)

Manufactured in Singapore

Published by Pelican Publishing Company, Inc.
1101 Monroe Street, Gretna, Louisiana 70053

DEDICATION

This book is dedicated to the memory of Jacob Haight Morrison (1905–1974), a man who dedicated his life to the preservation of historic buildings.

On October 5, 1974, Mary and Jake Morrison received the Crowninshield Award, given each year by the National Trust for Historic Preservation to outstanding preservationists. On this occasion, I wrote to them: "Two more modest and deserving people than you are not in our ken; and it is but fitting that you receive this, preservation's most prestigious prize, for your selfless devotion to the cause through the years." Just two months after receiving the award, Jake Morrison died, and the preservation movement at large, and in New Orleans in particular, lost one of its most valued voices. A member of the New Orleans bar, Jake, as a volunteer, wrote briefs and appeared in court countless times to stem the rising tide of those who would mutilate, destroy, neglect, or commercialize the old buildings in the Vieux Carré. He fought the legal battles house by house; then in 1957 he published *Historic Preservation Law* which was not only a compendium of state laws and municipal statutes, ordinances and enactments concerning the preservation of historic structures and a record of court decisions, but contained his observations as a lawyer concerning the cases cited. In 1965 he revised the book, and it was published and distributed by the National Trust for Historic Preservation. In 1972 he published a supplement to this "lawyer's arsenal," and *Historic Preservation Law* is now the standard work on the subject.

Jake lived in his beloved Vieux Carré for thirty-six years, where he tirelessly organized and administered many organizations to reinforce his effort to save and preserve the old quarter. He was a founding member, wrote the charter, and for three years was president of the powerful Vieux Carré Property Owners and Associates; he remained their legal adviser for twenty-five years. He drafted the charter of the Friends of the Cabildo and served as president, 1957–1958; he took an active interest in the New Orleans Spring Fiesta, the Vieux Carré Restoration Association, and was a founding member and early chairman of the Louisiana Council for the Vieux Carré.

The preservation movement owes a great debt to Jake Morrison for his perspicacity and his pioneering voice in a field that has matured greatly in the last few years. Jake reminds one of Shakespeare's words: "His life was gentle, and the elements so mixed in him that nature might stand up and say to all the world, 'This was a man!'"

LEONARD V. HUBER

1707 Esplanade

CONTENTS

Luling Mansion

FOREWORD

The first volume of the Friends of the Cabildo architectural series appeared in 1971. Acknowledging the extraordinarily good advice of the late dean John L. Lawrence of Tulane University, who stressed the importance of the printed word, the Louisiana State Museum volunteers—the Friends of the Cabildo—have now completed a fifth book on the architectural history of New Orleans neighborhoods. The American Associations of State and Local History, the foremost organization in its field, has recognized the Friends' effort by granting a special award for this series.

The original survey that produced *The Lower Garden District, Volume I,* was based on Dr. Bernard Lemann's study executed for the Regional Planning Commission in 1967. Private neighborhood organizations and the Historic District Commission continue the collection of data on this historic area and support its preservation and twentieth-century adaptation.

The square between Howard Avenue, Iberville, the Riverfront, and Claiborne, covered in *Volume II: The American Sector,* was resurveyed for a growth planning study by the Pittsburgh architectural firm of Wallace and McHoag. Key historic spaces were specified as were those destined for new development. The city has recognized the importance of the American Sector, which it calls the Central Business District.

The fate of thirty-one nineteenth-century New Orleans cemeteries remains precarious. Their history and inventory were traced in *Volume III: The Cemeteries.* Only strong and unified forces can produce necessary legislation to protect these architecturally and historically important landmarks. Individual cemetery owners must provide sufficient safeguards against vandalism, and the city must assist by daily periodic patrols to assure personal safety during visitations.

Volume IV, The Creole Faubourgs, included the history and documentation of six "suburbs" below the Vieux Carré. Neighborhood organizations have acquired National Register status for large portions of this section; they have encouraged the city and federal governments to relandscape Washington Square; and they have promoted the rehabilitation of thousands of brick and frame residences. The results are a positive recycling of an early nineteenth-century city extension.

This fifth volume, *The Esplanade Ridge,* differs from the past books in a significant way. It is the history of the entire length of one street from the Mississippi River to Bayou St. John. The presentation and format are those of a running text, including not only eighteenth- and nineteenth-century history and title descriptions, but strong recommendations to remedy the assessed architectural and environmental errors. Past and present history is so integrated that the reader can visualize the land from open field to its present state.

Sally Kittredge Evans devoted two years to link the chain of titles of one hundred residences, and the essence of her effort is found in this text.

Roulhac Toledano's special talent for assimilating historic facts made possible the orientation of the eighteenth-century history with the Charles Zimpel map of 1834, which was the cornerstone of the entire dissertation. Mary Louise Christovich wrote the text, incorporating the observations of the other two authors. Faubourgs St. John and Pontchartrain were accurately described by Roulhac Toledano in the section covering Broad to the bayou. An essay on City Park by Sally Evans concludes the text. Included are the photographs of Betsy Swanson who has recorded the pictorial inventory in each of the five Friends of the Cabildo volumes.

By the inclusion of detailed and documented evidence such as specific notarial acts for each property on which title work was done, the authors have aspired to give owners or interested persons an opportunity to continue their building research. All known archival drawings of avenue structures are included, most with attendant floor plans, making possible restorations by "analogy." Color reproductions are not used in this section; however the text includes exterior paint and trim suggestions.

Many persons shared in the research and compilation of this work over a three-year period. Aline Morris of the Louisiana State Museum library has propelled all five volumes with a bibliography, including every book, article, and document known to her through all available resources. Her assistant, Rose Lambert, has cross-referenced and provided clues available from the Tulane University and the New Orleans Public libraries. Constant on-the-spot telephone queries at the museum library are answered by these ladies who keep always a watchful eye for "new" and pertinent information. Robert Mcdonald, director of the Louisiana State Museum, encouraged every department within his institution to further the intricate investigation. John Kemp of the archives division, along with Ghislaine Pleasanton, Vaughn Glasgow, and Bert Harter of the curatorial staff, searched and supplied archival, card file, and photographic material.

Boyd Cruise, director emeritus of the Historic New Orleans Collection, by providing the Zimpel survey of 1834 and hundreds of Esplanade research cards, gave the direction for the running text form of *Volume V*. The entire staff at HNOC, led by its director and past president of the Friends of the Cabildo, Stanton M. Frazar, supplied over seventy building titles from the Vieux Carré survey. Bonnie Bernius, Ann Lewis, Rosanne McCaffrey, John Mahé, Renee Peck, and Dode Platou were constantly on call. Kenneth Urguhart, HNOC librarian, generously gave from his family files, information never previously published concerning the Fisk family. Linda Faucheux, HNOC archivist, read the text and offered many helpful suggestions.

Colin Hamer, at the New Orleans Public Library, has led his staff in the Louisiana Division by assisting this project as he has for each of the four previously published volumes. Jean Jones and Wayne Everhard gave telephone research assistance and mailed reams of photoduplicated follow-up information.

Ann Gwyn, head of the Tulane University Library Special Collections, was always helpful and her assistant Bill Cullison gave invaluable aid and personal attention to the reproduction of the Sanborn and Robinson insurance maps; he stood by to lend last-minute verifications of a myriad of dates and cross references.

The New Orleans Notarial Archives is our home base, the place where the true story of title ownership and building contracts is unraveled. Guy Wootan, archives director, and his staff have provided a special corner for the Friends' researchers and helped them in every way. Ernest and Irving Crayton, Stephen Broussard, Peter Borrello, and Harold Hand are great folk with whom to work. Volunteer Lucinda Robin Woody coordinated much of the Notarial Archives research for the Friends of the Cabildo.

The present authors and past coauthors Samuel Wilson, Jr., Bernard Lemann, Leonard Huber, Peggy McDowell, Betsy Swanson, and Pat Holden are volunteers who donate their talents not only to the sections they write, but to the gathering of general data for each volume. Their only compensation is knowledge of the tremendous and tangible success that the architectural series has had for the city of New Orleans.

Nonetheless, the series is expensive for the nonprofit Friends of the Cabildo organization, and we most gratefully extend our appreciation for the large contribution by Joseph C. Canizaro. His continued support will provide the foundation for at least two more volumes planned for the series.

William H. Henderson and Stanley F. Diefenthal contributed sums that assisted in the vast expenditure for a complete photographic inventory of the Esplanade Ridge, 1976. The New Orleans Bicentennial Committee gave a donation and included this publication as a bicentennial issue.

The thousands of hours of research and complete compilation of data result in a readable survey of the subject only when augmented with pictures. The eight-year untiring efforts of photographer Betsy Swanson with this project have exhibited talent, accuracy, and devotion. Mr. and Mrs. Ronald Rizzo of Esplanade Avenue made it possible for Betsy to photograph at least twenty-five interiors. Joseph Swanson has supplied the sectional maps for the first, second, and fourth volumes and individual street graphs for Volume V.

Friends of the Cabildo secretary Alison Kimball Hoagland has reached far beyond the role of typist by supporting research efforts and by working overtime nights and weekends.

If we have omitted the names of some friends who have assisted along the way, we beg their forgiveness, and we try to include in the following list all our wonderful associates and board members of the Friends of the Cabildo.

Among board members, we express our appreciation to Wayne J. Bienvenu, Mrs. A. Thomas Bremermann, Mrs. Charles A. Capps, Miss Roger Clay, Glen Conrad, Mrs. Silas Cunningham, Jr., Mrs. John Dart, Jr., Mrs. Authur Q. Davis, Ben F. Erlanger, Gordon Edwin, Thomas B. Favrot, Stanton M. Frazar, Mrs. L. Austin Fontenot, Jr., Waldo François, Steve Gasperecz, Jr., Leo Haspel, Dr. and Mrs. Jack Holden, Leonard Huber, and Harnett Kane.

Also, Mrs. M. D. Kostmayer, Jr., Henry Krotzer, Jr., Bernard Lemann, Mrs. Lee D. McLean, Mrs. LeLand Montgomery, Stephen Moses, Paul Morphy, Jr., Mrs. Herbert O'Donnell, David Plater, Patricia Rittiner, Mrs. A. L. Schlesinger, Jr., J. Parker Schneidau, Mrs. Harry C. Stahel, Mrs. Duncan Strachan III, Mrs. Bert Turner, Mrs. Morgan Whitney, and Samuel Wilson, Jr.

We are grateful to our researchers: Louise Castell Ainsworth, Bonnie Baird, Bonnie Bernius, Dr. Robert Bush, Michael Mossy Christovich, C. Edgar Cloutier, William Cresson, Boyd Cruise, Charles L. Dufour, Hillary Ervin, Rosemarie Fowler, Chris Freidrichs, Sherwood Gagliano, Patricia Gay, Mr. and Mrs. Edmond Grosz, Marie Elise Grote, Sandra Cason Grossel-Rosse, Marie Cornelius Laan, Ann Lewis, John Mahé, Ann Maylie, Rosanne McCaffrey, Nettie Moise, Wiley L. Mossy, Sr., Maud O'Bryan, David Perrin, J. Waldo Pitkin, Dr. George Ronstrom, Leon Sarpy, Helen Schneidau, Bobbie Sontheimer, Martha Anne Swaze, Fred Toledano, Kenneth Urquhart, Sidney Villeré, Rudolph H. Waldo, Johnny Walker, and Lucinda Robin Woody, and Mrs. Joseph Swanson, Jr.

Joseph C. Canizaro, Stanley F. Diefenthal, and Mr. and Mrs. William H. Henderson were generous in their financial contributions, and we thank them heartily.

We are rewarded with the special talents of photographers Robin von Breton Derbes and Poco Sloss. For consultation at the city engineer's office we thank Blaise Carriere; for her help on archival drawing restorations we thank Phyllis Hudson; and we thank Katherine W. Barnett for her assistance in copyreading.

ELIZABETH PHARR MORAN, President
Friends of the Cabildo, Inc.

1347 Esplanade

INTRODUCTION

This is the story of a street. It begins in 1810, moves slowly along short distances, gains momentum in mid-century, and finally bursts forward to link the Mississippi River to Bayou St. John. It is a green strip with double rows of trees. It is a thoroughfare that made its way through plantations to a fortification replete with moat and glacis, finally to become a luxurious avenue. It is *the Esplanade Ridge.*

Here is the Esplanade that was; the Esplanade that is; the Esplanade that could be. Unlike most streets, every inch of its progress was involved in legal battles, political entanglements, and dalliances of private owners. The first seven blocks—the City Commons—were, from 1742 to 1792, a private plantation that was operated by five different owners. During the next half century the street was to bisect no fewer than thirty-three plantations or habitations from Rampart to Bayou St. John. Its existence is a monument to municipal tenacity. Every proposal, purchase, and improvement required the approval of the mayor and two municipalities, for the length of the street in 1837 divided the First Municipality (representing the upriver side) from Third (controlling the downriver side). The center of the neutral ground (median) is the vertical demarcation. The street's present psychological division into four succeeding segments reflects the difficult land acquisitions. First came the river to Rampart portion, then Rampart to Claiborne, followed by city property purchases from Claiborne and Broad, pushing through to Bayou St. John.

The development of the Esplanade was made possible by the passage of the 1807 act of the United States Congress giving title to the city for the land from rue Levee (N. Peters Street) to rue Rampart. This cleared the way for the subdivision of the area, by the city, into a wide street cut parallel to Barracks, the last street of the Vieux Carré. Lots with a depth of at least a hundred feet flanked the new street as indicated in a plan executed by Jacques Tanesse in 1810. The space included the first seven blocks which had been the old fortifications and the lower City Commons, a width of two arpents, twelve toises (one arpent equals about 192 feet; a toise is 6.4 feet), and for the next twenty-five years it would be involved in litigations brought by individuals claiming title to the land.

Prior to, during, and long after the Tanesse survey, these suits and countersuits persisted. Nevertheless, the thirty-seven lots on the upriver side of the new street and the thirty on the downriver side between Decatur and Rampart were sold by the City Corporation, and hundreds of new owners built, lived on, and transferred the property. Houses were being advertised for sale and described as early as January 16, 1811; the *Louisiana Courier* then refers to "the Esplanade" in one of the first documented references: "To be sold . . . a very elegant new house belonging to Mr. Chais at the corner of Condé [Chârtres] Street and of the Esplanade of the Fort St. Charles." John Gourjon, Jr., who built 833 Esplanade, probably the earliest extant building, sold to his father in 1811 and described the house as "a main house thirty-six feet long, built of colombage, and covered with 'bardeaux' [shingle roof]" divided into three rooms "with galerie on the street." The *Courier's* ad defined *Esplanade* as that military space separating the fortification from the first houses of the city. Indeed, the early land sales most often described the lots as facing Promenade Publique (Public Road), which was the nomenclature for any public undedicated roadway.

New Orleans' unique topography inspired the term *ridge.* Stretching 3.3 miles between the Mississippi River and Bayou St. John, the roadway moves in a northerly direction over land once filled by Mississippi River overflow. As these waters would recede, bayous were formed, as were bank deposits, similar to the high sections of the city's natural river levees. The north-south ridge, about two feet above Gulf level, crossed first the high land created by the Bayou Sauvage (Gentilly) waterway and then that of Bayou St. John which intersected Metairie Ridge, then known as Bayou Chapitoulas. This high land is approximately two blocks in width on either side of Bayou Road, the ancient Indian portage leading from Bayou St. John to the river. It was desirable land for settlement because of its elevation, as evidenced by early maps depicting three-arpent-deep concessions along each side, with swamps beyond. Essentially, the ridge provided the eighteenth-century link between Lake Pontchartrain and the old city. When Joseph Pilié surveyed this habitable land in 1822 and planned a parallel roadway along the entire course of the ridge, he christened it the Esplanade Prolongment.

Esplanade Ridge, used also as a unifying architectural term in this volume, refers specifically to a double-level brick or frame side-hall house with galleries, built from the mid-nineteenth century. Such three-bay houses may employ various decorative exterior styles: Greek Revival, Classic, Italianate, or High Victorian. Often identical and always extravagant millwork, plaster, and marble mantels may be seen in houses built in the 1850–1900 period. Even earlier houses were decorated to comply with Esplanade Ridge fashion. Their opulent interior decor often contrasts with the relatively chaste and simple exteriors.

Esplanade, more than all other avenues, is bound along its entire length by historic neighborhoods, the Vieux Carré, Marigny, Tremé, New Marigny, Faubourgs St. John and Pontchartrain. It also cut across the earliest French concessions of Antoine Rivard Lavigne, Marc Antoine Hubert, Louis Cesaire LeBreton, Chevalier Charles de Morand, and Le Sénéchal Dauberville. The Spanish colonials, many of whom acquired portions of land from early Frenchmen or Spanish land grants, were among the most distinguished citizens: Andrés Almonester y Roxas, the noted philanthropist and royal notary, with an insatiable appetite for land; Antonio Ramis, a colonial from Majorca; and Nicolas Vidal, acting Spanish governor.

The avenue is anchored at each end by cultural entities: the United States Mint at the river's edge, St. Louis Cemetery III, Bayou St. John, City Park, and the New Orleans Museum of Art. The lives of the political, the powerful, and the very rich mingled with those of the modest clerk and cottage-owner and included activities from one point of the avenue to the other. P. G. T. Beauregard, educated as an engineer at West Point, was employed in 1854 to repair the Mint building. At that time he and his wife, née Caroline Deslonde, lived at 1028 Esplanade in the former William Nott residence. He later died at 1631 in a home at the corner of Esplanade and Derbigny. An equestrian statue executed by the noted sculptor Alexander Doyle honors Beauregard's memory at the street's farthest point before the entrance to City Park.

As the street opened and improvements continued, many who first occupied the river-to-Rampart segment moved farther out: Cyprien Dufour's family, in 1810, owned 820, built number 1707 in midcentury, and by the year 1870 constructed another spacious dwelling near the bayou in the 2700 block of Esplanade; Felix Pinson, architect, built in the 400, 1000, and 1100 blocks for commission and investment.

Churches were seldom part of the Esplanade context. Three remain: Episcopal St. Anna's is the oldest congregation, dating from 1843; the Third Presbyterian built in 1924 stands near Broad Street, and, finally, the Roman Catholic Our Lady of the Rosary, designed in 1924 by Rathbone De Buys, is near the bayou.

A number of private schools flourished along or near the Esplanade. Madame Egerie Vatinel's opened at 604 Esplanade in 1860 and continued through the early

932 Esplanade

1824 Esplanade

1824 Esplanade

twentieth century, acquiring the elevated title of Vatinel's University "which offered a veritable degree in life as well as learning through its sixth grade curriculum." Its special forte, aside from that of formal education, was preparing children for their first communion. The nineteenth-century school tradition in the Vieux Carré section was continued at number 714 when Mrs. Edna H. Wilson opened La Petite Ecole in 1949; it moved in 1969 to 535 Barracks and continues its operation from that address. Just around the Dauphine corner of the avenue at 1308, Guillot Institute provided musical training under the Misses Valsinas' care. The New Orleans College occupied a frame building adjacent to the present 935 Esplanade and is shown in a notarial archival drawing by C. A. de Armas, 1857, as a frame two-story structure. Behind 1002 Esplanade, the Washington Institute for Negro children continued until the turn of the century.

In 1895 the Ursuline nuns owned a lovely Baroque structure on the corner of Esplanade and Rampart. They sold this building and others in the 1100 block in 1897 to the Brothers of the Sacred Heart, who conducted a school for boys known as St. Aloysius High School. All traces of these buildings on this land have disappeared.

Many an Esplanade Avenue child received his education at the Guesnon-Surgi-Rapier school founded in 1875 in a house built in 1841 by Louis Surgi, architect and owner at 1523 Governor Nicholls. The French school taught English as a secondary language and continued until 1937. The Cenas school, established in 1875, continued until 1910, under the tutelage of Louisa, Hilary, Margaret, Clarisse, and Frances Cenas at the corner of Esplanade and Claiborne, number 1601. Samuel Jamison, builder, had contracted with Mrs. Margaret Cenas on June 27, 1877, to build a two-story brick back building at Esplanade and Claiborne for a schoolhouse for $4,650.

Straight University, the forerunner of Dillard University, was founded on the site of 1631 Esplanade in 1869 and moved to Canal Street in 1878. Clark's school stood nearby on Derbigny where today a public school is dedicated to Joseph F. Clark.

632 Esplanade

Farther toward Broad Street, from 1880 to 1895 the Markey-Picard Institute educated young boys and girls in what was formerly the Musson home at number 2306. Near the end of Bayou Road, Guillaume Bellanger had a boarding school from 1834 to 1841. The *Courier* of July 13, 1834, advertised: "The building is a new and spacious brick house, the second story whereof contains dormitories, which are cool in summer, and comfortable in winter. The several classes are taught in the spacious halls erected in the centre of a quiet and retired lot of a depth of 540 feet, and which is appropriated to the recreations of the pupils; also a Basin dug out in the interior of the establishment so as to facilitate the wholesome and frequent use of baths to the students . . . it is located near the city, and may be said to be in the middle of the field."

A McDonogh public school built as Esplanade Girls High occupies the even side of the spacious 2400 block which was the site of two mid–nineteenth-century mansions belonging to W. H. Vredenbergh and Neville Soulé. The four-story brick school was designed in 1911 by E. A. Christy during Mayor Martin Behrman's administration. Another public school, McDonogh 28, stands on the site of the third Esplanade Avenue residence of the Cyprien Dufour family in the 2700 downriver square. The school's attractive entrance is on North White Street. Our Lady of the Rosary School faces Bayou St. John on Moss Street, but its schoolyard runs through to Esplanade as does the nearby New Orleans Recreation Department playground dedicated to Henry C. Desmare.

Esplanade is a storehouse of nineteenth-century architectural types and styles, blending the earliest with the mid- and late-Classic Esplanade Ridge dwelling. Every decade of the 1800s is represented in the Esplanade collection including the French colonial, creole-style, and American-style frame and brick townhouses, along with the Louisiana plantation type, Italianate-Victorian, Second Empire, Edwardian, and City Beautiful styles culminating in Mission Revival. There are few shotguns, making notable the three gingerbread cottages in the 1900 block. There are no fewer than 190 extant houses built prior to 1900 as compared to half that many on St. Charles Avenue and the handful on the other remaining strip avenues. Only two French colonial-type houses—that is six rooms with cabinet galleries—remain from the 1810 development. Facing one another across the Promenade Publique or the Esplanade at 830 and 833, they now reflect continuing stylistic changes and alterations. This original type was often referred to as a mansion dwelling, whereas the more prevalent four-room brick-between-post cottage now known as a creole cottage was simply "une maison." Property titles, archival drawings, newspaper and plan descriptions reveal that these four-room creole cottages were the most popular original structures, particularly between the river and Claiborne on both sides of the Esplanade. Seven early documented examples remain at numbers 638, 1029, and 1032, and across Rampart at 1308, 1338, 1500, and 1518. During these development years until 1820, Esplanade served mainly as a back field for some major complexes along Barracks Street. The importance of Esplanade as a residential strip had not been recognized, and the property owners most often remained oriented toward the old city.

The economy of the city prospered in the 1830s despite two yellow fever and cholera epidemics and emerged in 1835 with a thirst for building and expansion. The Esplanade between Decatur and Rampart blossomed. It was paved at least to Royal, new brick banquettes were laid, and gas lamps hung at the street corners. Across Rampart and the flagstone intersection, the present 1100 block was filled with creole cottages and two major establishments by Spanish colonial architect Felix Pinson.

632 Esplanade

These faced the single-lane street Julia, which ended just a few paces farther into the fields of Jean Mager and J. B. Plauché. It took many years for the city to buy the Mager property and to widen Julia and extend it into the Esplanade. Several landowners farther on refused to sell until the city met their price, and it was 1841 before Esplanade finally reached a few blocks above Claiborne, which itself was no more than a grassy field. Mr. Cruzat, city recorder, in a message to the mayor that same year, reported that it was mandatory to devise a means of draining Esplanade Street, for it was inundated in rainy weather from Rampart to Johnson. They concluded that a ditch had to be dug on Claiborne and that a bridge had to be constructed over the whole width of the street at Esplanade's intersection.

By the mid-1850s the wealth and subsequent cultural influence of American society dominated the architectural expression of the entire city. The sons of the earliest Creoles, whose families continued to speak French and retain their amalgamated European and local customs, had built and lived in structures of the most pronounced Anglo-American style.

The Esplanade during this period progressed to a definable architectural character and its residents to a rich life style. Massive homes crowded its edges. Whether designed in wood or brick, the houses were lavishly decorated with mixtures of Greek orders attendant to revival interpretation and Victorian scroll brackets, projections, and quoins.

Activities remained for the most part attached to the Vieux Carré for business, entertainment, and religious observance. Then St. Augustine's Church on Governor Nicholls, designed in 1844 by Jacques De Pouilly, began syphoning attendance from the St. Louis Cathedral. Presbyterians wooed their flock to Washington Square in Faubourg Marigny to attend services in the Third Presbyterian, designed by Henry Howard in 1858. Since the businesses, schools, churches, restaurants, markets, and promenades were available at any point, the society along Esplanade was essentially an ambulatory one. The boundaries of its world could be reached on foot.

Mrs. B. H. B. Latrobe, wife of America's father of professional architects and initiator of Greek Revival in the United States, wrote a letter as early as September of 1820 describing a walk to her home in Marigny across the Esplanade:

> There is a space from the Levee which bounds the river to the fronts of the houses four times as wide as Baltimore Street. Nothing but common warehouses. Now and then an old Spanish house, a great mass of buildings surrounded by a high wall and trees overhanging; this is the Convent Cathedral. On the Levee near the water sat a woman selling oranges as big as John's head almost, four for a fippenny bit. Peas, bun, apples etc. A jargon assailed me equal to Babel its-self. We walked rapidly along. My head was really confused with the newness of the scene, the whole way between the city and our house being filled up with houses in the midst of large gardens with the river in front. But to describe our residence will be to describe them all, tho' many houses are larger than ours, but all on the same plan.

Later generations remembered, as children, expeditions from the river all the way to Gayarré Place, 2200 block of Esplanade, where the treat was to dip their hands in the fountain's water and return home along the trolley track. Gayarré Place once had not only this attractive cast-iron fountain, but also a twisted iron shaft decorated with owls, ducks, and geese. Many years ago was posed the unanswered question, what has happened to these ornaments? A George François Mugnier photograph of 1895 records "the way it was."

Gayarré Place was just one of six small triangular parks that developed as a result of the Esplanade prolongment and resultant realignment of properties. Beyond

Gayarré Place. (Courtesy Louisiana State Museum)

Gayarré Place is Kruschnidt Park, presently undergoing rehabilitation by the Parkway Commission. Esplanade passes to the left of this area, near the 2400 block, the original site of the old Indian Market, later called Place Bretonne and used as a public market until after World War II. A building contract before J. Cuvillier, January 6, 1838, was signed between Joseph A. Bellanger and Laurent Cordier, builders, with the Third Municipality for the construction of the Breton Market on Bayou Road for $5,400. DeSoto Park, Capdieville Park, Alcée Fortier Park, and other unnamed, undedicated triangles were donated by adjoining property owners. They were landscaped by the city in the late nineteenth century for public enjoyment and are welcomed twentieth-century green spaces.

A *Picayune* article dated May 4, 1852, described the Esplanade:

On a fine afternoon the bright faces at windows and doors, the gay, well-dressed children on sidewalks and green, numerous flower gardens, broad river shipping, and a tower on the opposite bank glittering in the sun, made handsome Esplanade a delightful picture. It was lined with some of the finest residences, and its double row of forest trees in the centre, formed a long arch of bright, thick verdure. Promenaders got country quiet, coolness and vegetation, united with close neighborhood advantages—though persons on horseback sometimes trotted or galloped along the neutral ground, endangering the large numbers of little children who every afternoon assembled there. Residents wanted to extend it about half a mile to Broad, and make it unequaled for promenades and exercises.

Then came the transportation system. Where the inhabitants once walked, they then rode. The "foot" of Elysian Fields converged at Levee (N. Peters) with the lower Esplanade and made available to its populace the Pontchartrain railroad. The river edge of the avenue bustled with port, market, and transportation activities. The Morgan Line depot connected the avenue to the Gulf of Mexico by boat. A ferry crossed to Algiers Point, making convenient many a pleasant Sunday family outing across the river. The Mexican Gulf railway ran from St. Claude near Esplanade to Proctorville in Plaquemines Parish. The Esplanade and Bayou Bridge Line streetcar ran from 1863 to 1913, predated only by the Rampart-Esplanade railroad in 1861 and the Rodriguez Bayou Road omnibus in 1857. The Esplanade line, a part of the New Orleans City railroad, had its carbarn and turn-around across from the St. Louis Cemetery in the 3400 block of Esplanade, facilitating many a Sunday visit to the cemetery. From Esplanade and the bayou, as early as 1859, boats pulled by mules glided along the Bayou St. John banks to Lake Pontchartrain. Since Esplanade served as a major artery from the river to the Bayou and thence to Lake Pontchartrain, residents were situated with recreation available via parks, restaurants, and pleasure gardens in each direction. Prior to the establishment of City Park, pleasure gardens, first Tivoli and then Magnolia, stood on sites of early plantations at the bayou. These and later resorts at Spanish Fort and West End were a pleasant alternative for a Sunday promenade.

Ornamental neutral-ground iron posts supported chains that lined the streetcar tracks. These adornments disappeared, as the *Daily States* reported on March 11, 1880, "the ornamental iron posts . . . protecting the neutral ground in Esplanade street are being taken up by the state Railroad Company." Buses and cars replaced the streetcars, and finally the tracks themselves were removed. Promenaders now return along the rows of trees as the Parkway Commission extends a gravel walkway from Galvez toward the river. The trees, which were young sycamores in the 1840s and 1850s, were largely replaced through the years with live oaks and elms, but occasionally a one-hundred-year-old sycamore survives.

Prominent names in local architectural history fill the records of homes along

632 Esplanade

Esplanade Ridge. There are four documented houses designed by Henry Howard, major works by James Gallier, Sr., and James, Jr., William Fitzner, Alexander Castaing, and the Frerets, both William and James. Established names in the builders' trades include Little and Middlemiss, Hubert Gerard, Nicholas Duru, Louis Folliet, Alexander H. Sampson, and the noted family of builders, Louis and Joseph Dolliole, free men of color. Surveyors of note played a prominent role in the Esplanade growth. Jacques Tanesse, Joseph Pilié, Barthelemy Lafon, Nicholas de Finiels, Eugene Surgi, Louis Bringier, and A. Bourgerol subdivided the habitations through which Esplanade was carved.

Conceived as a nineteenth-century transportation link, pursued as a major real estate development for the Vieux Carré overflow and altered socioeconomic life style, the Esplanade Ridge reflects important architectural expressions paradoxical in uniformity and individualism. It is beautiful, it is grand, it is shabby and often frayed; it is struggling for new definition and survival. The variety of its beauties are herein revealed with the story of the New Orleanians who created them.

NEW ORLEANS ARCHITECTURE

VOLUME V

The Esplanade Ridge

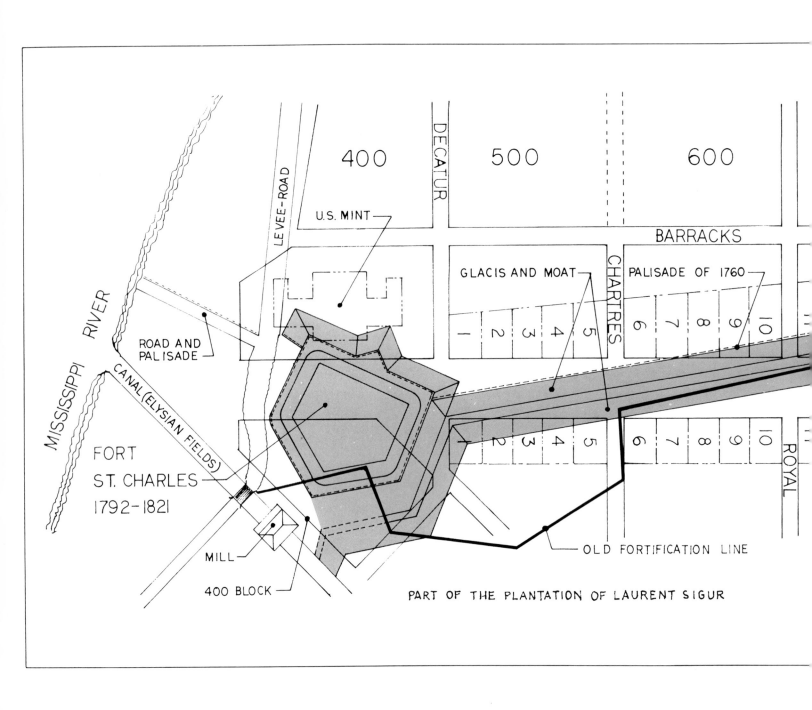

400

500

600

DECATUR

U.S. MINT

BARRACKS

MISSISSIPPI RIVER

GLACIS AND MOAT

CHARTRES

PALISADE OF 1760

1 2 3 4 5 6 7 8 9 10

ROAD AND PALISADE

LEVEE-ROAD

CANAL (ELYSIAN FIELDS)

FORT ST. CHARLES 1792-1821

1 2 3 4 5 6 7 8 9 10

ROYAL

MILL

400 BLOCK

OLD FORTIFICATION LINE

PART OF THE PLANTATION OF LAURENT SIGUR

A MILITARY ESPLANADE

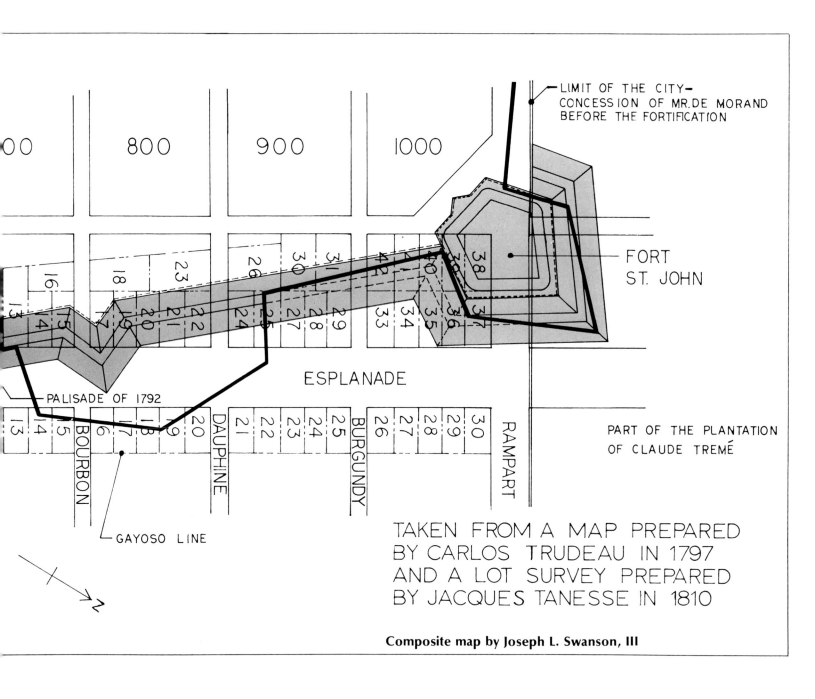

LIMIT OF THE CITY—
CONCESSION OF MR. DE MORAND
BEFORE THE FORTIFICATION

FORT
ST. JOHN

PART OF THE PLANTATION
OF CLAUDE TREMÉ

ESPLANADE

PALISADE OF 1792

GAYOSO LINE

BOURBON

DAUPHINE

BURGUNDY

RAMPART

800   900   1000

TAKEN FROM A MAP PREPARED
BY CARLOS TRUDEAU IN 1797
AND A LOT SURVEY PREPARED
BY JACQUES TANESSE IN 1810

Composite map by Joseph L. Swanson, III

Tanesse Map, 1816. (Courtesy Historic New Orleans Collection)

The City Commons—
A Military Esplanade

The colorful history of the City Commons dates from the 1721 French survey of New Orleans by LeBlond de la Tour. The plan was that of a fortified city and included land measuring three hundred paces from the breastworks of the town. By the laws of the Company of the Indies, which established the Louisiana colony, it was stipulated that no houses should be erected in this space "for the safety and defense of the towns." It was land "out of commerce, and belonged to the king, not to be alienated by his officers."

Jean Baptiste Bienville, the city's founder, established his original plantation just above the upper City Commons which measured from present Common to Iberville streets. During Bienville's early administration, the land around the early settlement was, for the most part, uncleared palmetto and cypress forests. Adrien de Pauger, the surveyor general after de la Tour's death in 1724, laid out the new city in a grid pattern down to Barracks Street, where the army barracks were established at the corner of Levee Street (N. Peters).

The Commons at that time was vacant above, below, and back of town toward Bayou St. John and measured a width of two arpents, twelve toises, uniformly around the city. Along the future military Esplanade or Promenade Publique it would comprise the present upper (Vieux Carré boundary) and lower (Faubourg Marigny) lots, incorporating the space of the present double street (Esplanade Avenue). Governor Etienne Perrier, during the French colonial period, barely used this land, and it was not until Governor Kerlerec, in 1760, had Bernard Deverges, surveyor to the crown, build the French fortification that there was any governmental encroachment into the two-arpent stretch.

By the time the Spanish had arrived in 1769, this lower or downriver Commons was included in the plantation holdings of Claude Joseph Villars Dubreuil and a subsequent owner, Jacques Delachaise. No one questioned their rights to the land, on which Dubreuil had established, before 1743, a sugarcane and wax myrtle plantation, with fifty acres being devoted to their cultivation. A large manor house and outbuildings were built directly on the Commons along with a lumberyard and brick kilns which employed the services of 260 slaves. Dubreuil, one of the most energetic, successful men of the French colonial period, had received not only the two arpents, twelve toises, width on the Commons, but an additional section of downriver property totaling seven arpents, eighteen toises, along the Mississippi, as a concession from French governor Pierre Regaud de Vaudreuil. If indeed, Vaudreuil and his intendant general, de Salmon, granted this Commons and the adjacent area downriver to Dubreuil, in exchange for an indigo factory and the buildings which Dubreuil constructed on the governor's plantation, the act was an extraordinarily rapid one, for Vaudreuil had arrived in the colony only two months earlier, in May, 1743. There is grave doubt that Governor Vaudreuil would have alienated, in any permanent fashion, the king's property.

In 1743 Dubreuil had purchased from the widow of Pierre Dreux, then the wife of

Pierre Voisin, another plantation below the Commons, described then in an act before notary J. B. Garic on July 21 as "a piece of land or plantation called La Brasserie [Brewery], situated auprès [close to] the city of New Orleans having six arpents frontage by forty arpents depth, bordering on one side by Mr. Darby [downriver] and on the other side by lands of the acquirer [Dubreuil], having been measured by surveyor Lassus and by the engineer Broutin." By April 7, 1745, Dubreuil had formally donated his upriver Chapitoulas plantation to his sons, Christophe and Claude. It is in that donation communiqué that Dubreuil mentions that Vaudreuil had given him "La Brasserie," which must have been a second one closer to town than the property of Widow Dreux. No record of the Vaudreuil concession of the seven arpents, eighteen toises, including the Commons has been discovered, but it may yet be found among the Vaudreuil Papers housed at the Huntington Library in San Marino, California. These illuminating documents were unknown or inaccessible to historians from 1755 until 1923, when they were purchased by Henry E. Huntington from the earls of Loudoun, the Campbell family of England. Dubreuil is mentioned in nine letters of a calendar and index of the personal and private records of Vaudreuil, royal governor of the French province of Louisiana, 1743–1753.

Dubreuil was obviously an indulgent father and grandfather, for in the marriage contract before notary J. B. Garic, April 16, 1748, he gave to Felicité Dubreuil, daughter of his deceased son, Louis Villars Dubreuil, in advance of her inheritance, the land of the Dreux-Dubreuil Brewery composed of six arpents front by forty arpents in depth. Felicité Dubreuil married Henri Amelot and lived on the riverfront plantation until it was inherited by her daughter Madame Daunois. The remaining Dubreuil plantation closer to the city is henceforth described as containing seven arpents and eighteen toises frontage (along the river) to a depth of the bayou (Sauvage) and the Chantilly (Gentilly), bound on the lower side by the property of Madame Amelot. These boundaries remain constant. The variable became the upper city limit, one contested by subsequent owners and their heirs.

An unsigned *Plan de Nouvelle Orléans*, March 1, 1753, affords visual proof of Dubreuil's occupancy of the Commons. He had built and fenced in five major buildings, sheds, and warehouses and installed the sawmill canal which was the precursor of the Marigny Canal and Elysian Fields. After Dubreuil's death in 1857, his son Villars Dubreuil, who lived in the house on the Commons, presented a statement at the auction of the family estate:

A plantation of the late Mr. Dubreuil, adjoining on one side the limits of this city, and on the other the plantation of Mr. Amelot, having seven arpents and eighteen toises front by all the depth, to the limits of the Bayou and of Chantilly, together with the principal house and other buildings, a saw-mill running four saws, another mill working pestles [for hulling rice] attached to the saw-mill, a sugar mill, a brick-yard with two kilns, containing each ninety thousand brick, five large sheds, a negro quarter, and generally all the buildings on the plantation, accessories and appurtenances, in the condition in which they are, and on the further condition that, inasmuch as the greater part of said buildings are constructed upon land which belongs to the king, and which he has reserved to himself, which land is not comprised in the above mentioned seven arpents and eighteen toises of front, it shall be free to the king to re-take that said portion of land which belongs to him whenever he shall think proper to do so; the purchaser removing previously all the buildings which are seated thereon . . . that to prevent reproaches and contestations on the part of the purchaser . . . [Mr. Villars] declares to us, in order to give through us a knowledge to bidders here present, and all others coming from one moment to another, that the house for which we are now receiving bids is situated upon land of the king, as well as all the other buildings between it and the city.

Plan de la Nouvelle Orléans, March 1, 1753.
(Courtesy Samuel Wilson, Jr.)

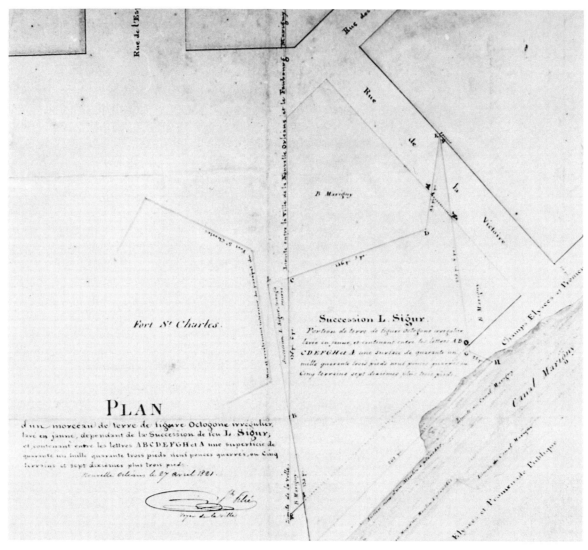

Plan of Fort St. Charles by Joseph Pilié, April 17, 1821. (Courtesy Notarial Archives, Plan book 100, folio 23)

Under these circumstances and with these considerations, Jacques Delachaise became the purchaser before notary J. B. Garic on December 18, 1758, and paid 130,000 livres for the land and buildings. On his death, the habitation was sold to Madame Maria Gauvrit de Monléon, and an inventory in the Louisiana State Museum archives translated by historian Samuel Wilson, Jr., reads as follows: "principal house of twenty-eight feet of length, sixteen of width, gallery front and rear, roofed with shingles, the said house consisting of a hall, a bedroom, a salon, a cabinet, an office, with a small lean-to attached . . . an old kitchen of posts in the ground, surrounded with stakes, .roofed with planks . . . an old pigeon côte . . . a sugar mill forming a polygon of eight sides, thirty-three feet from outside to outside, on brick pillars . . . two vaulted brick furnaces, linked together, in condition to contain 120,000 bricks each . . . a mill for planks."

This 1774 purchase act was lost, but on October 4, 1776, Dame Monléon sold the property to Antoine Gilbert St. Maxent, before Andrés Almonester, who recorded another lengthy description of the land and buildings with the usual measurement with the exception of the upper limit. It was stated clearly that Colonel St. Maxent bought land to the upper line, to the Gate of France, and the old fortification which served as the wall of the city; the frontage was still quoted at seven arpents, eighteen toises.

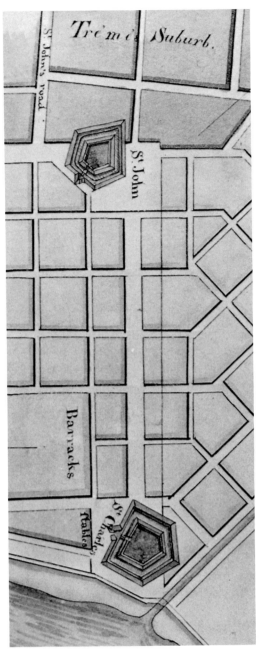

Plan of New Orleans, Barthelemy Lafon, 1814.
(Courtesy Historic New Orleans Collection)

The French fortifications which had been established on the Commons in 1760 were abandoned by 1780, as St. Maxent claimed that he was put into possession of the land on which they stood by Governor Bernardo Gàlvez and that he had built several houses in the soon-to-be disputed area. It is notable that by the time of his ownership the Dubreuil house on the Commons was replaced with a plantation house below the Commons, which became the famous Bernard Marigny mansion. St. Maxent sold the tract to Laurent Sigur in 1789 for $72,000, limiting it to the walls of the city and giving the frontage also as above.

The Spanish continued the practice of keeping the crown's right to land surrounding the city for the purpose of defense; however, when Alexandro O'Reilly took possession of the colony he placed the city limits only twenty toises into this Commons. It was exactly the line of French Governor Kerlerec, who in 1760 had engaged surveyor-engineer Bernard Deverges to build the French fortification.

No problems developed along the boundary from rue Levee to rue Rampart until in 1794, Baron de Carondelet, Spanish colonial governor, erected the Spanish fortification and entrenched into the land Sigur thought was included in his purchase. Gilberto Guillemard, the governor's engineer, moved the palisades, the ditches and military Esplanade into the center of the two arpents, twelve toises, said to be the City Commons, and extended the former Fort St. Charles as far as the Sigur sawmill. Sigur immediately sought an indemnity through the Spanish tribunal. Failing there, he sought redress from the St. Maxent heirs and requested a reduction of $25,575 from his mortgage loan with that family. The St. Maxent heirs formed a syndic which was represented by J. B. Labatut; they too sued the Spanish government but all their claims were denied.

The law suits continued long after the Louisiana Purchase. Thomas B. Robertson, commissioner of Land Office, and later governor of the state of Louisiana, declared in the *American State Papers* that this property was City Commons similar and of the same measure to that which bound the Jesuit's plantation, the original Bienville property (in part presently occupied by Canal Street), but the dissenting judge, Joshua Lewis, commented, "It is scarcely to be presumed that Dubreuil would have made establishments of such magnitude on lands known to be reserved by the King, when a few paces from it, he might have built on his own land and on a site equally eligible." Judge Lewis opined that the land "of the Commons" was a part of the estate of Dubreuil; that the French government "had the right to the use of the soil," but that the right of property remained in the individual with the soil reverting to the individual owner when no longer needed by the crown. Judge Lewis was overruled, and the Commons were confirmed along the line of the city. Despite the continuing lawsuit, Sigur exchanged a portion of the contested plantation for Philippe de Marigny's downriver plantation in 1798. This time, the plantation transferred measured only five arpents, six toises fronting on the river, by the limits of Nicholas Daunois, son-in-law of widow Amelot. The city reserved all the rights to the property taken by Baron de Carondelet, and Governor Gayoso de Lemos fixed the upper line of Marigny's property at two arpents, twelve toises, from the city limits.

One might think that the matter ended there, but well into December, 1850, Judge J. Preston of the Louisiana Supreme Court was pontificating in a case known as *Heirs of Villars [Dubreuil]* versus *J. M. Kennedy et al.* Kennedy was the superintendent of the United States Mint building which still occupies a portion of this once contested land. Judge Preston in a ten-page decision finally closed the issue by denying all claims by the plaintiffs. He did add:

And here it is proper to observe that if there was ever any pretense that this land was private property, the pretense belonged to Laurent Sigur, and not to the heirs of Dubreuil Vilars [sic]. For the district judge had demonstrated that if they sold a certain quantity of land by measurement, they sold seven arpents and eighteen toises, all that they ever possessed . . . they sold to their extreme boundaries, and parted with all their interest. . . . In consequence of the demand of Laurent Sigur for indemnification in 1797, Gayoso de Lemos, then governor of Louisiana, caused a thorough investigation to be made in order to ascertain the true line between Sigur's property and that belonging to the king. It was made in presence of persons of note, appointed on behalf of the Cabildo, in presence of Sigur, of course, and conducted by Trudeau. . . . After much examination, the line between the city and the plantation was ascertained and fixed at two arpents and twelve toises below Barracks street, about as nearly as we can judge one hundred feet below Esplanade street. Much notoriety was given to the proceedings; the line was established with great formality, and was subsequently known as Gayoso's Line. . . .

And the governor rejected the claim of Sigur for damages, on the ground that "neither he nor the persons from whom he held could have acquired any right on the ground within the lines of the old fortifications [meaning the 1760 French fortifications] although through error, inattention or indulgence, they might have been suffered to possess it. That with regard to the angles of Fort St. Charles, which might exceed the old fortifications, the plaintiff could not have a better title to an indemnity from the Government, because in all concessions made under the French Government, the king had always reserved the right of taking out of the lands granted the ground necessary for extending the fortifications of the city; a right to which the King of Spain has succeeded. . . ."

In consequence of the decision of the Spanish governor, Laurent Sigur refused to pay to the syndics of Col. St. Maxent, the whole price he had agreed to give for the plantation, on the ground that two arpents and twelve toises of the same belonged to the public and not to his vendor. He sued the syndics of St. Maxent for a proportional diminution of the price. This was the great occasion when all the old titles and plans were still in existence, also even living witnesses, and every means of ascertaining the exact truth, and when private interest to a large amount would have established the private right to the two arpents and twelve toises, if it had been possible. The contrary was established in the suit beyond all doubt. . . . And in 1800, the tribunal determined that . . . a diminution of $25,000 was allowed on the price of the purchase.

Considering the legal costs of suits covering a period of at least thirteen years, Laurent Sigur did not gain great monetary satisfaction from this settlement. Curiously, however, his daughter Françoise, widow of Sieur Christophe Marion and then wife of Jean de Bellievre of Baton Rouge, received $6,543 from the sale of land still involved in the auction of her father's estate. This wedge of land appears to have been acquired in February, 1818, by Barthelemy Lafon, well-known surveyor and iron-monger, and is recorded in a transfer of property before Philippe Pedesclaux on August 21, 1819.* It was the rear section of the present 400 block of Esplanade Avenue, along what was the Dubreuil-Marigny Canal and Moline (sawmill). According-ing to a 1797 Trudeau survey, introduced as proof in the act of sale of 1818, the Baron de Carondelet fortification at this point had pierced beyond the Commons and Laurent Sigur held the right of ownership. He received a $3,194 fee from the government for the use of the land. His battles for an individual's right to property received some financial return and redress; the heirs of Claude Villars Dubreuil and Gilbert St. Maxent did not fare so well.

* See Plan of Fort St. Charles, p. 7.

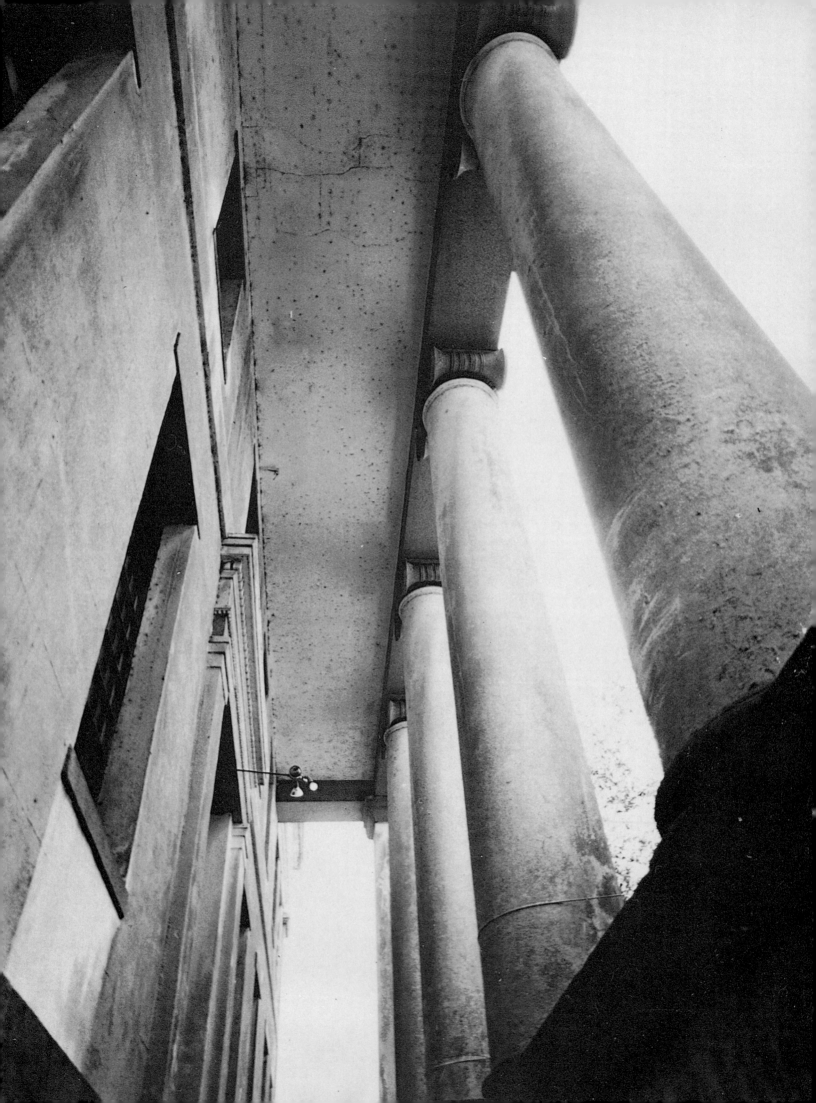

United States Mint

The United States Mint, at 400 Esplanade, designed in 1836 by Philadelphia architect William Strickland, occupies the site of the three former eighteenth-century military installations. The first and earliest was a protective moat which Governor Etienne de Perrier had dug in response to the panic created by the Natchez Massacre in 1729. Fearing a similar Indian attack, the citizens eagerly loaned their own laborers and immediately began to dig a moat around the city; as the Indian threat subsided, so did interest in the moat and fortifications. Governor Perrier wrote to the Count de Maurepas in 1731, "Some eight months ago I had work stopped on the ditch that I had begun around New Orleans. . . . Those who suggest that this work led to a great expense do not know the manner in which I had it done. . . . It cost the Company only the wheelbarrows and a few repairs to tools that were worn out on this work."*

The news of France's defeat by the English in Canada and its lost territory west of the Mississippi motivated Governor Kerlerec in 1760 to have Bernard Deverges, engineer in chief, design "a fortified enclosure of this town by a moat and a fence of palisades, conforming to the old plan of fortification." One must assume that Deverges followed the line of the Perrier ditch. He added wooden palisades around the entire city with bastions at five points. One bastion, identified as Chârtres Bastion (Fort St. Charles), positioned on the downriver side of the city at present North Peters and Esplanade, was directly across from the Claude Villars Dubreuil plantation according to a manuscript map of New Orleans by Lieutenant Philip Pittman. The barracks were placed behind this bastion on what later became known as Barracks Street. Because of the citizens' intense dislike of a palisade isolating the riverfront, the fence was removed from that area. The stockades, therefore, surrounded three sides of the city. Behind a glacis or sloping wall were built a banquette and a shallow ditch. A palisade was then erected outside, connecting the forts that stood at the four corners of the old city and one in the center of the rear or rampart line. Fort St. Louis was placed where the Customhouse now stands on Canal Street, Fort Bourgogne at Iberville and Rampart, Fort St. Ferdinand at Beauregard Square near the present Municipal Auditorium, and Fort St. Jean at Rampart and the present Esplanade.

By 1775 Luis de Unzaga, Spanish colonial governor, reported that "the fortress of this city is made of stockades . . . that are almost destroyed by decay and dampness of the soil. It is kept up only by continual repairs, to give the city the false appearance of a fortified city and obliging its neighbors to come in and go out through its gates." The gate at the Fort St. Charles was called the Gate of France; the Bayou Gate led to the Bayou Road from Fort St. Jean.

Spanish Governor Carondelet in 1792 learned that the Americans were planning to seize the city. Since the French palisade had fallen into ruin and most of it had disappeared by that year, Baron de Carondelet wrote on March 22, "I will work immediately to surround this city with a ditch, the dirt thrown on the side towards the city forming a kind of platform, which at the same time will serve as a parapet: I will also raise about five bastions, which I will build in the district with their good

* Translations by Samuel Wilson, Jr., *The Vieux Carré, New Orleans: Its Plan, Its Growth, Its Architecture* (New Orleans, 1968).

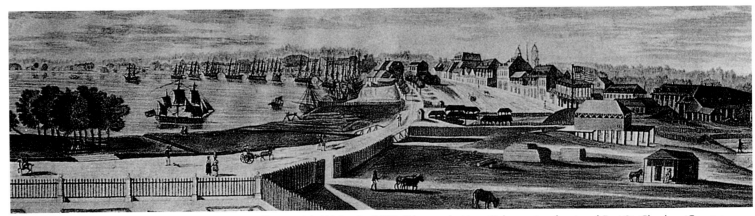

Boqueto de Woiserie, 1803, lithograph, New Orleans riverfront and Fort St. Charles. (Courtesy Historic New Orleans Collection)

parapets in order to defend the walls. In the ditch I will place a good paling [palisade] which will be above the water of the river, which water I can easily make flow into the ditch." Gilberto Guillemard, architect and engineer of the Cabildo, immediately planned the new fortifications, positioning the redoubts near the ancient Bernard Deverges system and giving each installation the Spanish version of the French names. The redoubt Fort San Carlos at the river, bounded by the Sigur plantation, extended past the Deverges French fortification over the City Commons and beyond into the former Dubreuil plantation then owned by Laurent Sigur. This corner redoubt was joined by a curtain wall or terraplein, moat, and glacis to Fort San Juan at the Rampart Street corner.

Eleven years later, Forts San Luis on Canal Street and San Carlos on the present Mint site were the only survivors of these fortifications. Terraced mounds of earth still surrounded the San Carlos redoubt, as seen in the Boqueto de Woiseri lithograph from the year of the Louisiana Transfer, 1803. Daniel Clark reported to James Madison, secretary of state, on September 8, 1803, that the Carondelet fortifications were "going fast to ruins," and "it would appear proper to throw the works into the ditches and thereby get rid of the stagnant water which occasions sickness." For the third time the ditches and remaining stockades were allowed to fill in and rot.

When the citizens were given Governor William C. C. Claiborne's approval to demolish the remaining stockade, they accomplished it overnight. On January 11, 1804, General James Wilkinson reported to Madison, "A few nights since, some person observed that the Governor or the General had given leave for the demolition of the stockade which surrounded the city, and by 8 o'clock the next morning, before the operation was noticed by our guards, which occupy the center of the city and the Forts St. Charles and St. Louis near the river, not one stick was left on a line of one and a half miles, and a house in one of the rear redoubts was razed to its foundation and the materials carried off." The property on which this series of military fortifications stood first belonged to the French and then the Spanish crown; according to terms of the Louisiana Purchase the land between Fort St. Charles and former Fort St. John at Rampart Street along the Esplanade or Promenade Publique belonged to the United States. Governor Claiborne wrote that "the Forts were delivered as national property, and I cannot recognize the claim of the city (to the former Commons) but through a judicial decision. I am however so strongly impressed with an opinion that the stagnant water which accumulates in the old fortifications must prove injurious to the health of the city and I cheerfully consent to the levelling of them all except those of Forts St. Charles and St. Louis [but] I have no objections to draining the ditches in [their] vicinity."

The city's claim to the land on which the ancient fortification stood was recognized by the 1807 act of Congress and was reconfirmed by similar acts in 1810 and 1811. The property acquired by these acts included old Fort San Carlos and all the land in and outside the palisade known as the military esplanade. This open space, which measured two arpents, twenty toises, was the much contested City Commons, today the Esplanade and its adjacent lots between Decatur and Rampart.

Fort St. Charles outlasted all the other forts and palisades. Even in its dilapidated state, it was commandeered in 1815 by General Andrew Jackson during the only bona fide foreign invasion of New Orleans. Under the leadership of the handsome young Irishman General Edward Pakenham, the British attacked the city, and Jackson manned the fort with two military detachments. Finally, in 1821, Fort St. Charles, which had become an unsightly dumping ground, was demolished, and in 1829 the land turned into a public square, planted with trees, and named Jackson Place, or Jackson Park, in honor of the hero of the Battle of New Orleans. In the final year of Jackson's term as president of the United States, a mint building at New Orleans was authorized by an act of Congress on March 3, 1835. The land was given from the city back to the federal government, and work was begun immediately.

Benjamin Latrobe's student William Strickland was engaged as the architect, and the task was completed three years later. The Philadelphia architect received numerous government contracts and his federal buildings remain landmarks in Charleston, Nashville, and Washington. He was one of eleven founders of the National Society of Architects in New York in 1836, and president of the society which was later reorganized as the American Institute of Architects. The Mint at New Orleans is one of Strickland's simpler designs, incorporating the Ionic portico, used also on the Naval Hospital and the Mint at Philadelphia. The strong structural sense, clear surfaces, the simplicity and restraint of the Mint building reflect Strickland's interpretation of the Greek Revival style, notable in his surviving architectural works.

Benjamin F. Fox, a master carpenter and joiner, and John Mitchell, a master mason and builder, appear to have been left in complete charge of the construction; it is not known whether Strickland made any inspection visits to New Orleans. The building contract before J. Cuvillier on August 22, 1835, is worth quoting because very few exterior alterations have occurred, and those of the interior are easily determined from the following specifications:

> The main building shall have a front of two hundred and eighty-two feet and a depth of eighty feet. . . . The height of three stories, resting on a sub-basement two feet and a basement to be eleven feet high . . . . The principal story to be sixteen feet; the whole of said building to be covered with a [Welsh] Slate-Roof. The brick work of the basement story is to be carried up three feet in thickness to the springing line of the groined arches . . . to be composed of paved or hard bricks nine inches in thickness, the rise four feet, and the spandrils to be filled up level with the top or crown of the arches. The basement is to be surmounted by a belting course of granite, one foot in height. . . . The principal story walls to be twenty seven inches in thickness and carried up ten feet. . . . The whole of this story flagged over with the exception of the rooms which will be laid over with boards one and a quarter inches in thickness . . . of best pine or cypress. . . . The columns of the pizzas [rear wings] for each story are to be cast iron ten inches in diameter, with a cap and base. . . . Each angle of the building is to contain a pilaster of granite two feet nine inches on each face, extending from the belting course to the underside of the Architrave. . . . Pilasters are to have plain moulded capitals of eighteen inches in depth. . . . There are to be four columns of three feet in diameter in front of the center building; these are to be flanked by antae or pilasters of two feet-nine inches square showing a single faced pilaster towards the columns. These columns are to be made of brick and rough cast; having stone bases and Capitals of the Ionic order . . . a flight of granite steps leading from the pavement to the

U. S. Mint Building. (Courtesy New Orleans Public Library)

floor of the principal story . . . to be six feet each in length in the clear. . . . The architrave to be of granite, two feet, two inches in height, by two feet, nine inches in width, extending across the whole front of the portico, breaking joint over the center of each Column; the frieze to be constructed with brick work and the cornice of wood. The portico to be covered on a level with the cornice, with a flat roof of copper or zinc. . . . Interior stairs to be three flights of stone and two of wood . . . with iron balusters . . . handrail of mahogany. . . . The whole of interior to be plastered with three coats . . . plain cornices at the ceilings of the principal stories . . . a rosette to be formed in the center hall opposite the central stairway, for the purpose of hanging a chandelier in each of the stories. . . . The whole of the exterior to be rough cast with good clear sand, washed and mixed with the best lime, trowelled and jointed . . . to correspond with that of the granite used in the porticos and pilasters . . . five foot wrought iron railing to surround entire lot on a granite wall two feet in height by fourteen in thickness; two wrought iron gateways eight feet wide . . . to be painted with three coats of paint.

The building cost $182,000 with $118,000 more spent for paving, fences, and installing machinery. James Gallier, Sr., a prominent New Orleans architect, obviously disdained the construction of the building without an architect's supervision and commented:

Several years before I reached New Orleans, plans and instructions had been sent from Washington to build a branch mint, and the construction of the building was confided to a carpenter and a bricklayer of the city. The floors were sustained upon groined brick arches, supported by square brick pillars; but the thrust of the arches having caused the abutments to give way, the arches began to sink at the crown, and the whole structure threatened to become soon a mass of ruin. I was called on

14

in a great hurry to devise some method of averting the danger. I caused to be inserted strong iron rods from outside to outside of the building in each direction; by shoring up the crowns of the arches and tightening up the rods, they having screw nuts and outside plates, the building was rendered perfectly secure and has remained so to the present time.

By 1854 repairs estimated at $25,000 were suggested by a young West Point engineer, Major P. G. T. Beauregard, in order to "fire proof" the building and reinforce it with iron beams. The roof was to be reslated, its frames strengthened, and a new garret floor installed. It was Captain Johnson K. Duncan, a retired West Pointer, who supervised the work and had a new smokestack built in the rear court-yard. The roof was not reslated but covered with a corrugated, galvanized iron, a new building material in 1856. By 1857 the repairs had reached $110,661; letters of explanation and recriminations flew back and forth between Washington and New Orleans. It appears that the entire renovation cost $127,972.73 and was completed in 1859. The exterior appearance was unaltered except that an iron verandah had been added on the river side of the building. The superintendent's apartment and several other apartments for officers and mint employees were within the wings. The New Orleans *Daily Crescent* on October 21, 1856, reported that "the branch Mint at the foot of Esplanade Street has received a new coat of brown stucco and undergone other improvements inside and out."

Eliza Ripley reported in her *Social Life in Old New Orleans*, published in 1912, that in the early 1850s:

I have never heard of a society ball in a United States mint building, before nor since, but the [Joseph] Kennedys, who gave this one, were a power in the social

A. R. Waud, pencil sketch, rear of United States Mint Building. (Courtesy Historic New Orleans Collection)

world at that time . . . and ambitious beyond their means. Rose and Josephine, the two oldest of quite a flock of daughters, were debutantes that winter. . . . The mint building was made ample for the gay festivities by utilizing committee rooms, offices and every apartment that could be diverted for the crowd's comfort . . . so, we wandered about corridors and spacious rooms, but never beyond the touch of a gendarme . . . officers, soldiers, policemen at every step. These precautions gave a regular regal air to the whole affair.

The Confederate forces requisitioned the Mint in 1861 and continued the operations for the sole benefit of the South until New Orleans fell to Union forces in 1862. The same Johnson K. Duncan, who had superintended the Mint repairs, now elevated to brigadier general of the Confederate army, surrendered to Admiral David Farragut, and New Orleans embarked on a course of occupation that curtailed its recovery and growth until long after Appomatox.

A New Orleans Confederate journal written by Mrs. Robert Dow Urquhart from her Esplanade home between April 24 and May 6, 1862, recorded, "They might have eventually been forced to surrender, for they could not hold the City without an army. Gen. Duncan gives as excuse that his men mutinied and he was forced to give up; Good officers make good men so it is said and had he enforced proper discipline this could not have happened. He has made as he says, 'honorable terms,' for himself and officers by which honorable terms he has sacrificed New Orleans. When he went down to the forts he swore never to leave them alive, and he ought to have kept his word."

William Mumford and several Confederate officers removed the United States flag which had been hoisted at the Mint while surrender negotiations were taking place. General Benjamin Franklin "Beast" Butler, with full intentions of bringing the city into submission, ordered Mumford to be hanged. General Allison Owen, architect in charge of the Mint building rehabilitation and reuse in 1930, in a speech outlining the history of the Mint, stated, "Mumford, a handsome man of 48, ascended the scaffold with a firm step. Captain Stafford of a negro regiment read the sentence. Mumford made a short address acknowledging and justifying his act. Stafford ordered the drums to beat and the trap was sprung."

On Friday, May 2, 1862, Mrs. Urquhart again wrote:

The Yankee soldiers in number about five thousand have entered the City and taken possession of the Mint, the Custom House, and other public buildings. Their entrance was quiet—no demonstrations of delight, or cheering for the Union, for they felt they were coming amongst a hostile and unwilling people. I am told they are the dirtiest, meanest looking set that were ever seen—nothing at all of the soldier in their appearance. Most of them have enlisted for their daily bread and care but little for the cause for which we are contending. I hear there is much dissatisfaction amongst them. They have completely surrounded Mr. Slocomb's, having encamped in Lafayette square and having taken possession of Lyceum Hall as a hospital for their sick. The windows of this building open directly on Mrs. Slocomb's house. Augusta tells me she can hear the cries and groans of the sick and dying. I feel thankful that we live so far downtown, for we are rarely ever annoyed even with a sight of their hated "blue coats."

Mrs. Urquhart continued on Sunday, May 4, "I did not go to church today, but the other members of the family did so. The Clergy it seems had agreed to leave out the first portion of the morning service so that they could not be forced to read the prayer for the President of the United States. I regret they did not as usual read the Prayer for *our* President, until ordered by Butler not to do so, but they I suppose desire to avoid difficulties. Dr. Leacock however read the prayer for deliverance from our enemies and in his sermon spoke his sentiments so." This diary is now in the Urquhart Collection, Manuscripts Division, Tulane University Library.

A. R. Waud's sketch in *Harpers Weekly*, owned by the Historic New Orleans Collection, illustrates the rear elevation of the Mint with the smokestack, prison watchtowers, and sentry stations in the late nineteenth century. The United States government reopened the Mint in 1878, and continued producing coins there until 1909. The Mint building was converted in 1932 to a federal prison by architects Diboll and Owen. Gervais Favrot was the contractor. Large prison dormitories and two cell blocks were installed in the rear wings; the old smokestack with its Egyptian design was removed. For the next twenty years, the building served as a veterans bureau, a public health service station, and a receiving station for the Coast Guard.

The federal General Services Administration advertised on July 26, 1965, that sealed bids were to be taken for the sale of the Mint building, but there were no acceptable bids. Through the efforts of the Friends of the Cabildo and many close to the Louisiana State Museum, action was taken to secure ownership of the building for the museum. This was accomplished in 1966 and now, ten years later, funds of $3.5 million are required to restore and preserve the 140-year-old structure.

The land on which the Mint stands has passed in ownership from the French to the Spanish to the American governments. Deeded by the latter to the city municipality, it was utilized shortly after statehood as an American garrison site during the Battle of New Orleans; forty-five years later it was occupied by the Confederacy and captured by federal troops. It became a city park before the federal government again acquired title in order to construct a national mint building. After almost 250 years, ownership has reverted to the state of Louisiana. Declared a National Historic Landmark by the federal government in 1975, the Mint building and site will continue to anchor the Esplanade.

The architectural firm of E. Eean McNaughton and Associates was selected in February, 1976, to execute plans for adapting the structure to serve as a center for visitors and tourists, educational exhibition area, and the State Museum Library and Archives. Dr. Bernard Lemann, Tulane University professor of Architecture, will be associated with the McNaughton firm. The building's exterior fabric will be preserved and its interior spaces renovated for modern usage only to the extent that such renovation does not destroy or detract from the building's historic architectural elements.

From the River to the Bayou

BLOCKS 400 THROUGH 3400

400 Block

Across from the Mint in the downriver 400 block of Esplanade is a small square bounded by Elysian Fields, North Peters, and Frenchmen. While Fort St. Charles sprawled in a disorderly manner over this river corner, it retarded the development of the square. Most of this small land area was covered by the walls and interior revetment of the fort's parapet. When the eighteenth-century fort was demolished and Jackson Park planned, the city continued its improvements by subdividing the remaining land of the Commons, which measured a minimum of a one-hundred-foot stretch along the front edge of the entire 400 block. The municipality purchased four lots of the Elysian Fields section inherited by Bernard Marigny from his father, Pierre. This sale was recorded by Michel de Armas, April 9, 1822. Another large portion of the Elysian Fields frontage previously had been sold to one R. F. Gallien Préval by Barthelemy Lafon, who had acquired it from the succession of Laurent Sigur.

A plan by the city surveyor, Joseph Pilié, April 27, 1821, shows the strange slice of land marked at eight points, A through H (see City Commons). It contained 41,043 feet, 9 inches, in superficial or square measurement. A 28-foot by 262-foot strip extended into the Marigny Canal overflow and over the upper side of Elysian Fields which was then known as the Champs Elysées. This land would be purchased by the city from Lafon to complete Elysian Fields Avenue, and there would also be a tiny cone-shaped piece for the city to acquire for rue de la Victoire (Decatur). Pilié divided the square into twenty-four lots for sale in 1822, an auction of the lots was held the same year, and many were purchased though few were immediately developed.

Lots 20 and 21, fronting on Esplanade on the Pilié plan, comprise the site of the present 435 Esplanade (Ruby Red's Restaurant), □* and the adjacent riverside sites were sold by the city to Louis Leroy for $2,000. In 1849 Leroy sold the vacant lots to Jean Baptiste Clovis Cadot. The properties remained in Cadot's possession until

sold by his estate on March 24, 1882, before notary O. Villeré, whose act described the properties as being "one square from Morgan's Louisiana and Texas Railroad Ferry." Ruby Red's, then number 17, was a "two story brick family residence, having a large room in the basement, three rooms and hall in the first story; two story brick building attached to main building, having three rooms on lower story and three rooms in upper; cistern, privy."

Next door was "a large and substantially constructed frame building, standing in the rear of said lot, elevated about ten feet from the soil on brick pillars, with some seven rooms, a front gallery running the whole length of the building which is nearly 64 feet long." J. B. Clovis Cadot's succession estate sold these properties to Frank Pericone, whose family retained them until 1920.

Adjacent to these properties on the river side, on a lot now occupied by 427 Esplanade □ stood a fine creole townhouse built in 1834 by New Orleans architect Felix Pinson for John Lawson Lewis, sheriff of Orleans Parish for years. Lewis purchased the thirty-two-foot lot from Maurice William Hoffman, who in 1832 was acting president of the Pontchartrain railroad. The Lewis house was one of the earliest buildings in the square and one of the most elegant. In a building contract dated 1834 before Felix Grima, Lewis and Pinson agreed upon the terms of the building's construction and attached the plans and elevations. The brick house had three arches below, with balcony and short windows with panels on the second level. It was a similar type to that constructed by La Compagnie des Architects the same year in the 2700 block of Chartres and to the three buildings still standing diagonally across Esplanade at 1331 Decatur. The creole townhouse floor plan included a side enclosed passage leading to rear stairs and a semi-enclosed loggia. Often, a graceful fanlight window illuminated both the loggia and the

*□ Symbol indicates placement of illustration in photo index.

18

second-floor landing. The house remained in the Lewis family until 1874, when it was sold to The Scandinavian Seamen's Friend Society. In 1880 it passed to the family of Captain Theodore Paderas and was municipal number 13 Esplanade.

A *Daily Picayune* article of October 19, 1895, gave a full account of the almost total destruction of this entire square. A blaze that started in the National Rice Mill became a half-million-dollar fire which reduced to ashes not only the mill but also the Lewis house which had become the Seamen's Bethel:

The mill, known as the Perseverance rice mill, was originally owned by Mr. Louis Ruch, who a little over three years ago sold it for $80,000 to the National Rice Company, of which Mr. Pembroke Jones is the president. The mill at that time was a large one, but shortly after its present owners gave out the contract to Messrs. Walker and Ralun to erect a much larger and more commodious structure. The building was not only an ornament to that section of the city, but gave employment to over 200 people. The building was of the modern type and occupied the entire front of

the upper part of Elysian Fields street except Mr. Knop's saloon, at the corner of South (North) Peters Street. The mill proper was a three-story-and-attic brick building annex and at the corner of Decatur Street and Elysian Fields, about forty feet from the mill proper, was the two-story frame warehouse, covered with corrugated iron. . . .

There is nothing left standing of the Lower Seamen's Bethel where the sailors were entertained for about seventeen years. Mrs. A. Watson, wife of Captain Watson, gave general attention to the institution, and was an earnest worker. It is thought to be the property of the Italian Evangelical Society, and rented for bethel purposes. It was a quaint looking little structure, which at one time was used as an Italian church. . . . Before it was given over to its present use a Rev. Dr. Pease used to conduct Sunday school there. . . .

The two-story brick building No. 421 Esplanade, owned by Albert Helm and occupied by M. Voorhies, notary public, was damaged to the extent of $3,000. . . . No. 419, a three-story brick building, owned by Theodore Paderas and occupied by the Esplanade street insurance patrol as an enginehouse . . . was partially destroyed. . . . No. 401 and 403 Esplanade street, a one-story

building used as a barroom, and attached to the building fronting on Peters street, is a three-story and a half brick building, owned by John B. Abadie and occupied by John Gloresich as a residence and restaurant and hotel, known as 'John's House.' The building has been a kind of a landmark to the traveling public, it being just across the street from the Southern Pacific depot.

St. Anna's church, established in 1847, stood at old number 5 Esplanade, "at the corner of Esplanade and the river." This building was either converted into one of the many commercial establishments that survived until the fire or demolished later, for in 1869 St. Anna's moved up the avenue to number 1313; it is presently utilizing the second building to be constructed on that site.

A section comprising the lower 400 block, referred to as being at the "foot" of Esplanade, has recently been sold by the Port-o-Call Corporation to the Joseph C. Canizaro interests for $462,000. In 1798 Laurent Sigur paid only $50,000 for land including this square and running downriver five arpents more.

500 Block

The 500 block of Esplanade, Vieux Carré or upriver side, begins with a group of French-style multilevel, commercial and residential buildings which face the riverfront at Decatur. These corner properties were once the edge and moat area of Fort St. Charles. Michel Anfoux bought this corner land from the city before M. de Armas, October 24, 1810, and erected at least two cottages during his six years of ownership. Anfoux lost the property at public auction, and the entire section was acquired by André Pierre Seguin. The property measured 152 feet along the Esplanade and was identified as lots 1 and 2 on the Jacques Tanesse plan of 1810.

Jean Baptiste Azereto, a Genoese entrepreneur active in real estate in the Vieux Carré, Marigny, and Tremé, reassembled lot 1 from two successions: the site of 504–506 from André Seguin and a lot sold by him to Augustin Duberque, 510. The present site of 516 is a vacant lot; 520 constitutes Tanesse lot 2 and was purchased from Seguin by Pierre Malochée in 1821, and held by his family until 1900.

The Azereto acquisition of 1822, before notary Lavergne, described one house as "bricked between posts with covered balcony facing Decatur, six rooms, kitchen with cov-

ered balcony and several other buildings." This house, probably the Anfoux creole cottage, was Spanish colonial in style. Azereto made it his residence and contracted with Jean Orelly, builder, in 1834 before Hughes Pedesclaux on October 17 to make repairs to the flat terraced roof of the main house and kitchen, and to raise the sections required on brick columns reinforced with cement. When the Citizens' Bank of Louisiana bought the lots and buildings from Azereto, notary F. Seghers on March 5, 1836, specified, "Une maison briques à l'étage couverte en terasse, une autre maison base en briques, cuisines en briques toutes autres appurtenances."

The Citizens' Bank demolished these buildings, the first on the site, and hired E. W. Sewell, builder, to construct a bank office and the present three stores which face Decatur and are numbered 1331, according to a building contract before C. Boudousquié, May 11, 1840. The specifications stipulated that the building fronts were to be made of lake brick with painted joints to imitate northern brick; all the ground floors, corridors, courts, and kitchens were to be paved with *asphaltum* put upon bricks laid flat. A cornice like that of the Fabric Store at Royal and Orleans (designed by architects Gurlie and Guillot) was given as a model

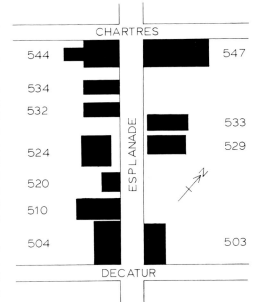

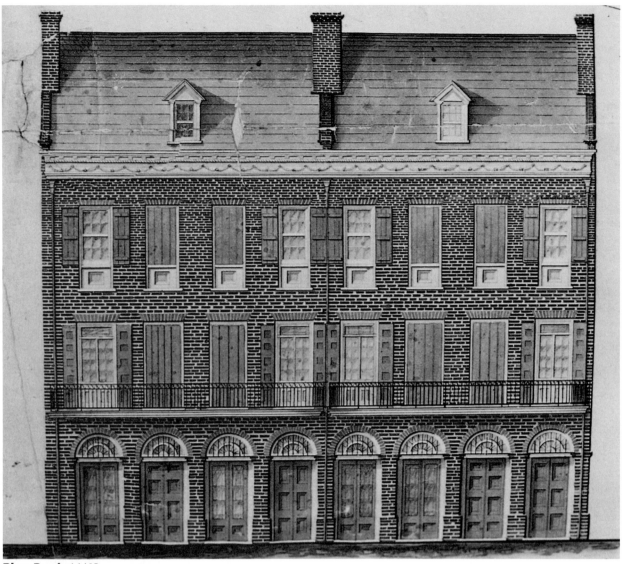

Plan Book 11/43

504

to use, and the millwork was to follow that of Mr. Soniat's on Hospital (Governor Nicholls) between Levee and Condé (Chârtres).

The bank entrance was to have a specially designed wooden door and two windows fronting the street were to be doubled and paneled with strong fastenings; a five-by-six-foot iron vault was also included. Citizens' Bank sold the stores two years after construction to Jean Mager, prominent investor along the Esplanade and in Faubourg Tremé. Felix Grima acquired them, by bequest, after Mager's death in 1845. An archival drawing by Mr. Harrison, civil engineer, dated April 19, 1845, illustrates two of these three, 3½-story brick buildings with the wood frieze having carved garlands and rope motifs with modillions. The original dormers and the shutter arrangement with lower panels are indicated as are splayed brick lintels at both upper levels. The second-level wrought-iron balcony survives today.

Used as rental property by subsequent owners Antoine Ernest Quertière and Jean Paul Lozes, this corner of Esplanade became "Donelson's Dime Museum," according to the *Mascot* of February 9, 1884. A marble mosaic with the name George A. Nami at the entrance reveals the long occupation and ownership of the Nami jewelry store. The original arched opening arrangement with grilles at the street level was changed into doors and plate-glass display windows. Comparison of the archival drawing with the extant buildings illustrates some unfortunate exterior changes: rough stucco, heavy vermiculated base, keystone lintels, and quoins.

The present house at 510 Esplanade, □ also a part of the original Azereto holdings, was described in an 1884 newsclipping as a "fine three story brick building having six rooms, two story brick kitchen with four rooms, water works, privies, etc. now renting at $25 per month." The Citizens' Bank, which constructed this residence in the late 1830s, sold it to Jean Mager, whose sister Madame Agathe Alexandrine Collard, living in France, inherited it in 1845. The Collard heirs held the property until 1884 and sold to Ramon Viosca, whose heirs sold to the Nami family. This is an early example of absentee landlordship, a travail that would afflict the Esplanade properties for many generations. The exterior exhibits a lack of maintenance, and there is slight foundation settling. The three-level iron balcony was probably added to the plain, undecorated façade which must have been penciled as were the three bank properties facing Decatur. The wooden lintels and sills are consistent with the pilastered frame entrance, and the structure,

510

524

with a minimum of exterior cosmetics, could be an outstanding visual addition to the street scene.*

The vacant lot at 516 is a part of the original Tanesse lot 2, and the twentieth-century house at 520 □ occupies the balance of that property. It is quite possible that an original creole cottage built here by Michel Anfoux when he owned this land to Decatur Street remained standing until 1901. A "brick filled" house directly on the banquette with an overhang and rear cabinet gallery was shown on the 1874 and 1896 Sanborn insurance maps. The Malochée family, who had bought the lot from A. Seguin in 1821 before M. Lafitte on August 16, held it for seventy-nine years, selling it in 1900 to Mrs. Theresa Reimer Seidel before notary E. J. Barnett.

Mrs. Seidel contracted with James J. Gazin to erect "one single raised frame slate-roofed dwelling with dependencies" (Mortgage Book 672/788, April 2, 1901). The scale and architectural simplicity of detail make this house compatible with other Esplanade Avenue structures. The filling in of the gallery is not appropriate and detracts from the original house, whose front had deep rustication and corner quoins.

Weysham-Ronstrom House

John Arnold Weysham bought the lot on which the house at 524 Esplanade stands in 1844 from the widow of John A. Mascey, Rosalie Fossier, as shown in L. Hermann's notarized act of sale of December 30. The lot had been improved soon after 1812 by Pierre Seguin who sold to Mascey, a bricklayer, in 1816 "a house of four rooms with fireplaces, galerie, cabinets and cave, brick between posts covered with tiles; in the yard a building of four rooms, two with fireplace covered with stakes (cypress shingles) and all other buildings on the lot" for a total of $4,900. Seguin had owned during this early time all the property to the Decatur Street corner.

On May 9, 1845, before L. Hermann, Weysham submitted specifications for a new home on his lot in order to secure a $5,000 loan from Cristobal Toledano, president of the Merchants Insurance Company. He "promised to build a brick dwelling house within eight months of the date of the mortgage." These specifications clarify that the house at 524 known today as the Ronstrom house did not incorporate an earlier house. Instructions were that the ground was to be cleared and graded, and in order to prevent dampness rising within

*Author John Dos Passos rented rooms here in 1924 while writing *Manhattan Transfer*.

the walls, the foundation was to have five layers of bricks, between which were laid courses of slate in cement. The yard and both "alleys" were paved in good lake bricks in a herringbone pattern. The roof was covered in the best slates, and the front and two sides of the house held copper gutters to carry off the water. The house was floored in yellow pine planks except in a basement section which had a floor of lake bricks.

This raised-basement masonry house has two rooms on each side of its forty-foot-long center hall, and the interior and exterior embellishments described in the specifications remain with minor changes: "The front Balcony with its gable to be made in a good looking stile [*sic*] . . . supported by four large well turned columns and to rest at their bottom on a row of slate slabs to be projected one inch over the Basement Wall, protected with a good looking iron railing between the columns [either never installed or changed to turned balusters], the Cornice around the House will be made in the best and proportioned manner, provided it being not less than Four feet in height."

In the interior, the double parlors have marble mantels with grates, and the two other rooms have "neat wooden mantels made and painted in imitation of Egyptian marble." Every room on the second floor was lathed and plastered on furred one-inch wooden strips, so the plastering would not be connected to the exterior brick walls. It was optimistically requested that the plastering carry a "warrant not to crack or fail in any manner." The exterior walls were plastered "in a rough casting manner with the upper walls in the best sharp sand mortar, but on the basement, with the best hydraulic cement. . . . All the wood and ironwork that is usually painted to have three coats of the best oil and paints, all the blinds to be painted with the best of French Green, the front door in imitation of mahogany, and all the inside white, and in the rear and back buildings in a lead color in Two Coats, all Glass to be bright Waterford, N.J. Cylinder and properly set in putty."

Weysham died in 1849, and his heirs lost the house at a sheriff's sale that same year, to the insurance company that had financed it. Merchants Insurance Company sold the house to Marie A. J. Palerne for $11,400. Madame Palerne was acting on behalf of her brother and sister-in-law, Vicomte Louis Amedée de Barjac, Madame de Barjac, and their two children, Celié Barjac, wife of Theodore Dromel, and Victoire Laure de Barjac.

The de Barjac family resided in the house for

forty-four years. Madame de Barjac was Celina Pauvert who married the vicomte in 1825, in New Orleans at the St. Louis Cathedral. Historically, she is associated with various charities and civic activities. Her daughter Celié Dromel and her husband Theodore lived with her in the house from the 1880s. Dromel, who was a representative of a French bank, Comptoir Nationale d'Escompt de Paris, was also active in local civic affairs and received a special citation from Emperor Maximilian of Mexico. His widow sold 524 Esplanade to Gaspar Cusachs at the time of her mother's death in 1893. A prominent president of the Louisiana Historical Society, Cusachs owned one of the city's most extensive libraries. He lived at 524 until his death in 1929. The Cusachs family retained ownership for the next ten years, selling in 1939 to the present owners, Dr. and Mrs. George Nelson Ronstrom, who continue the tradition of occupancy by a single family.

After thirty-eight years and constant rehabilitation, 524 Esplanade holds few secrets from the Ronstroms, both of whom have been prominent New Orleanians in their adopted city. Mrs. Ronstrom is the well-known newspaper columnist Maud O'Bryan, originally from Sulphur, Louisiana, and Dr. Ronstrom, from Chicago, has recently retired after holding a thirty-year post as professor of anatomy at the Louisiana State University Medical Center. At the time the Ronstroms purchased the house it had neither electricity nor plumbing; alterations to the original structure were minor. A fire in the attic shortly after 1929 had destroyed ceilings and damaged the roof. A fireplace in the back bedroom had to be bricked; its cypress mantel, exactly like the cypress one in the front bedroom, is still on the premises. The marble ones in the living room and dining room remain in place. The Cusachs heirs reported that their father removed the wooden entrance steps, replacing them with the present cement ones, and enclosed the back gallery with glass in 1900.

Various nonoriginal attachments to the rear of the house were removed by the Ronstroms, and cobblestones, probably from the Pierre Seguin 1812 period, were discovered by them in the patio. The rear of the interior center hall was enclosed for them by architect Morgan Hite and is designed as a French double door with a fanlight above. Architectural features include front jib windows and mantels as described in the original building contract. This American raised house with its center hall, imposing Greek Key entrance, denticulated portico, and cornice is a graceful, atypical Vieux Carré style of which only two others remain within the French Quarter: Le Carpentier-Beauregard house at 1113 Chartres and the house at 519 Dauphine.

Next down the Esplanade, there are two houses bearing the municipal numbers 530–32 and 534–36□ which occupy a sixty-five-foot frontage. These lots remained vacant in the early nineteenth century with the exception of a long carriage house which bordered a side property line and two 2-level service buildings in the rear. A garden also owned by the Weysham-de Barjac families occupied the site of 530–32, so that even though a turn-of-the-century structure now stands on the lot, it is the first in the history of the property. Brick side walls used to raise the house and adjustments made to the Victorian façade have cost this house architectural value. Its neighbor at 534–36 relates its history to the corner property at Chartres. The Sanborn map of 1896 shows a narrow house covering only sixteen feet of this lot. This present two-level Victorian double house with a gallery at the first level and deep balcony on the second level was built either by the Vaccaro brothers or Henry Seidel, Sr., between 1897 and 1903. Henry Seidel bought both lots 530–32 and 534–36 in 1903.

Tiblier-Cazenave House

Number 544 at the corner of Chartres is a large, imposing single-family residence. Today it represents a center-hall two-level brick house with step-gable side walls, ornate Italianate decorative motifs, and a cast-iron balcony supported over the banquette (sidewalk) by iron columns. Only the gable ends and six upper façade openings afford a clue to the true identity of the house, which in its original state must have resembled the two houses at 906 and 908 Esplanade. Built around 1860 for Claude Tiblier, this structure was a common-wall double townhouse having four windows on the upper level and two on the lower and adjacent doorways.

The history of this corner property at Chartres and Esplanade predates the present building; it was one of the first developed after the city sale in 1810. An ad in the *Louisiana Courier*, January 16, 1811, is slightly confusing because title research does not reveal a Mr. Chais as an owner; nevertheless, it does describe the extensive number of buildings which enhanced this property and which are thought to have survived until 1860. The 1811 ad states:

To be sold or rented in whole or partly. A very

elegant new house belonging to Mr. Chais at the corner of Condé street and of the Esplanade of the Fort St. Charles, fronting the little gate of the Barracks, consisting of six large rooms, four of which have chimneys with two large closets opening on the gallery, in which two beds can be placed. It contains, besides, two pantries and is divided into two yards: in the one which fronts Condé Street stand two large rooms with kitchen, two rooms or kitchen for the mansion house; and in the other yard fronting the Esplanade a lot of about sixty square feet with a large gate, a kitchen and rooms for servants, dove cote, hen roost, backyard, wells, and separate privies. The ground of the yard is very elevated and drained through channels. Its situation is very pleasant and wholesome, particularly in the spring, when the contemplated walk is established.

This complex was sold by the widow of the first recorded owner, Pierre André Engerran, in 1815 to Antoine Rocheville de Menard and by him to a free woman of color, Marie Louise Bremard. She sold to other free persons, one portion to Jean Baptiste Dinet and his sister, Marguerite, and another section of the lot to Philip Avegno. Both Avegno and Dinet sold to Marie Beaudequin, free woman of color, in 1823 before M. Lafitte and in 1830 before L. T. Caire, respectively. The succession of Marie

544

Beaudequin in 1854 indicated that the Enger-ran complex was still standing at the corner of Esplanade facing Chartres, for attached to the act of A. Mazureau, January 10, 1855, is a description of a lot sixty-five feet on Esplanade by sixty-one feet on Condé (Chartres): "ensemble une maison en bois, briquetée entre poteaux divisée en plusiers pièces. Cuisine haute en briques de quatre chambres, privées." François Gras bought this land in 1855 with the buildings from the Beaudequin estate. His own succession of 1860 repeated the earlier description, adding only that an annual and perpetual ground rent of 6 percent must be satisfied before selling the property.

Claude Tiblier, a French citizen active in New Orleans real estate, purchased this land in 1860 from the Gras succession and built the present houses which are incorporated into 544 Esplanade. Constructed as double brick two-story houses with attics and side gables, these buildings had a common wall which projected through the slate roof as indicated on the Sanborn map of 1897. The entrances on Esplanade were adjacent, and the houses did not have cast-iron trim or galleries.

When Tiblier died in 1875, his widow sold the corner house, numbered 546, to Mitchel Lion and the one next to it at 544 to the widow of Louis Arnaud Pepin. There were three intervening owners of 544 before Leon Arnaud Cazenave, the "Count" and famous New Orleans restaurateur, bought it on July 1, 1920, before E. Wegener. Five separate owners held the corner half, or 546, between 1875 and 1931. Sixty years after Claude Tiblier built both houses Cazenave brought them again into single ownership, and it was at this time that they were extensively remodeled. The "Count," it is said, designed the changes and had the common wall separating the houses removed and structural beams added. He introduced exterior manifestations of segmental plaster window tracings and placed one dormer in the center of the original two on the new roof. The entrance became a grand Italianate one with keystone and shell motifs. A cast-iron balcony across the entire front embellished it and covered the sidewalk, giving this house the appearance of a large single residence, perhaps of the 1880s period, recalling the Italianate Fitzner house across the street at 547 Esplanade. The alterations and total effects are successful and remain a complement to the Esplanade. Mrs. Germaine Cazenave Wells, daughter of the "Count," maintains this beautiful establishment and continues to operate Arnaud's Restaurant, founded by her father.

500 Block Downriver

When the Decatur corner Azereto creole cottages existed in the 1830s, the downriver 500 block, across the neutral ground, also had several similar houses. In François Sel's succession of 1837, there was recorded a row of gable-sided rentals, and a hip-roof frame cottage with an overhang, as seen in plan book 58, folio 6. These stood on the site of 529 and 533 Esplanade. A week before their auction sale they burned, and the property was sold as lots. The houses now standing had no connection with the Sel family. □ They were built by a wealthy cotton factor, John Hagan, for Lucy Cheatham, free woman of color, and bequeathed to her two sons, William A. and F. Cheatham. These attractive 1860s two-level brick houses are adorned and crested with cast-iron double balconies; shoulder-high front fences enclose the small gardens.

On the Decatur corner, Julien Lacroix, a free man of color who became a wealthy wholesale grocer, built a large brick structure, which was purported to be the mid-nineteenth-century "Louisiana Ball Room" where quadroon balls were held. A George François Mugnier photograph, housed in the Louisiana State Museum, registers the building, in 1895, as a masonry two-level, hip-roof store with a sidewalk overhang supported by iron columns. The Lacroix building, number 503, later became known to the city as Rougelot's dry goods and furniture store, and now has a mansard roof, Italianate architectural details, and first-level plate-glass windows. □

The Sanborn map of 1876 indicates that at least four frame buildings stood between the Julien Lacroix and Lucy Cheatham houses. The same map provides a hint that the twentieth-century house at 539 has the same placement of an earlier house and may indeed incorporate an earlier structure. The Chartres Street corner now contains a large late Italianate brick dwelling, 547, □ designed by William Fitzner and built by P. R. Middlemiss in 1879. The renovation of its neighbor across the avenue at 544 coordinates sculptural design effects and makes the two houses very compatible in scale and style.

600 Block

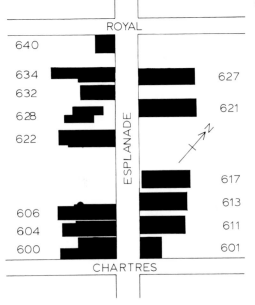

Research reveals that the downriver 600 block also abounded in creole cottages and the one which occupied the Chartres Street corner at 601 Esplanade □ was advertised for sale in 1866, indicating that commercialism was infiltrating the almost exclusively residential street in a modest way soon after the Civil War. It was described as a "large one story slate roofed house with a store at the corner; four large rooms, cabinet, and gallery." The early twentieth-century church building now standing here is the scale of the early cottage and has adapted to apartment conversion.

The second buildings to be constructed on this downriver side are predominantly two- and three-level common-wall brick houses appearing in the 1830s and 1840s like 611, 613, and 617. □ Architecturally similar to those built by Henry Raphael Denis across on the upriver Esplanade, they continue the urban style of building directly at the banquette; each continues the modish updating of the homes by the abundant 1850s cast-iron balcony ornamentation.

Next to the Lamothe House, which is 621, □ there stood, as late as 1925, a two-story brick house with three bays and a projecting cast-iron gallery. A photograph taken by Pops Whitesell at that time indicates that this was number 623, and its first floor housed a tobacco shop. A pencil sketch by Morris Henry Hobbs, in 1936, indicates that only the doorway remained of this two-level structure. Next to it, at 627, there was for some time a photography studio. Both the photograph and sketch are housed in the Historic New Orleans Collection.

In the same 600 block, Dr. Lewis Heerman purchased the corner property at Royal and Esplanade as early as 1814 and had Joseph Fernandez build several structures for the Navy Hospital which continued in existence until 1833, the time of the doctor's death. The Jacques Tanesse drawing from the Naval Records Collection of the Washington National Archives shows a two-story house on the corner having a tiled hip-roof, with a belvedere and front balcony. The parterre garden was on the side behind a plank fence and joined one-level, hip-roof buildings whose sites are presently occupied by 633,635, and 637. □ (See *New Orleans Architecture, Volume IV,* page 13.)

Denis-Morphy-Barnett Houses

The first owner of the three corner lots beginning the upriver 600 block of Esplanade was Antoine Mourlot, Sr., who purchased a 62-foot frontage on Esplanade that extended 101 feet on Chartres Street, August 7, 1811, before M. de Armas. Less than a year later Mourlot sold the property to Barbé Desdunes, free woman of color. Mourlot's remaining property toward Royal had "une petite chambre et une écurie en bois" when Jean Longpré collected the sites of the three present houses together from Mourlot and Barbé Desdunes in 1815. Longpré sold to Madame Victoire Delatte Visoso Espinosa in 1828, and in 1833 she sold to Henry Raphael Denis, an attorney who had the three present buildings (602, 604, 606) erected in 1834.

The property on which these three common-wall townhouses are built was described in the sale of November 16, 1833, before L. Caire, "A lot of ground situated at the corner of Esplanade and Chârtres measuring sixty-four feet front on Esplanade by one hundred nine feet fronting on Chartres bounded on one side by the property of Mrs. Espinosa and on the other side by that of Mr. Lafargue together with a ruinous frame house thereon." Denis sold the new townhouse at 604 to Alonzo Morphy, a judge and the father of the international chess champion Paul Morphy, before Felix Grima in April 14, 1835. Notary Grima purchased 606 for his own residence. Denis retained the corner (602 Esplanade) for himself. Morphy sold 604 to Pierre Pradat in 1836. Monsieur Pradat died, and his wife Elizabeth Ixilin sold the house to attorney Jean Baptiste Sauvinet on October 27, 1842, when the act of sale before C. Pollock described "the three story main brick dwelling house and out buildings, and generally all of the other buildings and improvements thereon." Across the street Sauvinet owned the two common-wall townhouses at 613–17 and the two single townhouses at 627 and 633 after having the four properties bequeathed him by his brother, Joseph Sauvinet.

Thereafter, number 604 had a series of owners every few years including the family of Charles Cavoroc, the wine merchant who had James Gallier build the cast-iron-front building for him at 111 Exchange Place. In 1860 Madame Egerie Vatinel opened a school for young ladies at 604, and seven years later Clorinde Vatinel bought the house before notary S. Magner. The Vatinel family retained ownership until 1925. More recently the home was known as the residence of Paul Ninas, well-known New Orleans artist, who bought the house in 1937, living there until his death in the 1960s. Ninas purchased the house from Dr. George B. Crozat, New Orleans orthodonist who restored Houmas plantation on the River Road.

602, 604, 606

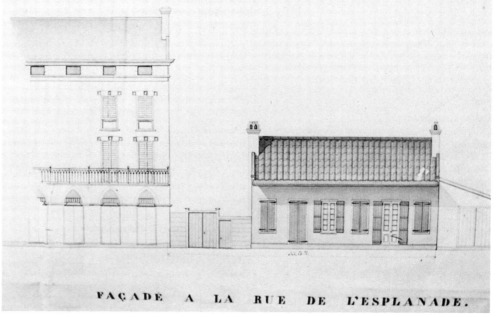

FAÇADE A LA RUE DE L'ESPLANADE.

Plan Book 22/32

Edith Long wrote in the *Vieux Carré Courier*, June 27, 1969:

Legal records call 604 Esplanade a three story building, but actually it has five levels. The first floor height is enormous, taken up by a low storage level. An awesomely high entrance, framed with a Greek Key casing, opens onto a flight of stairs that lead to another Greek Revival doorway into the hall. This entrance is closed by a massive iron gate, richly decorated with a fret motif. It is said this gate is new here since the old school days, but it is a genuine antique and seems to compliment the doorway with distinction.

At the second floor level is a traditional narrow wrought-iron gallery in the cathedral arch pattern. Above French doors opening onto this gallery are splendidly detailed lintels. The shallower third floor windows have wooden panels extending to the floor and marking the attic is a deep cornice pierced with three horizontal windows and embellished with dentils and modillions.

At the rear elevation on the second and third floor are pairs of double hung windows, capped with arches filled with interweaving muntins. A wide, sheltered pavilion, supported on cast iron columns, connects the main house with the service wing across the rear of the lot. Jalousies line either side of this pavilion, and a great trap door in the floor opens to reveal a stair leading down to the courtyard.

The cuisine across the rear has finer details than are common in slave quarter structures. Its only balcony is across what is technically the rear. On the courtyard side are casement windows in the French manner, shielded with decorative iron screens. All stairways are internal, another unusual treatment. The old ground floor kitchen has a dumb waiter, still intact, leading to the premier étage which seems, judging from the plaster rosette in the ceiling and built-in china presses, to have been the family dining room. Above this were simple lodging rooms for servants.

Inside, the main house is replete with original details. The premier étage has a great hall leading to the rear where a good stair ascends to the attic. Flanking one side of this hall are twin rooms with fine black marble mantels, Greek Revival cornices, medallions, floor and window trim. These are the parlors, once filled with horsehair furniture, where the little Creoles paid their respects to the Mesdames Vatinel on le Jour de l'An.

Upstairs, in a pair of truly elegant parlors, are the same splendid mantels, with more sophisticated cornices, window trim and double door frames beween the rooms. Everywhere in this house can be seen facets of a former way of life: fine gas fixtures, interesting hardware, coke baskets, exquisite, once-gilded cornices of draperies, and all the comforts and accomodations of a century ago.

The third of Denis' townhouses, 606 Esplanade □ is documented as to changes made in 1859 which cause the once identical buildings to vary in façade and side elevation appearance. Denis sold the house to notary Felix de Armas at auction for $12,000 soon after construction; de Armas then sold it in 1835 to Michel Aime, brother of the famed Valcour Aime of St. James Parish. Aime turned the property over to Michel Doradou Bringier within two months. Bringier invested in various properties on the Esplanade and gave this house to his daughter and her husband Martin Gordon, Jr. Gordon sold it back to Bringier, and finally before J. Beck, January 29, 1850, a second notary, Edward Barnett, acquired the house.

The building contract between Barnett and Elijah Cox, architect and builder, is dated July 21, 1859, before S. Magner, "to alter and enlarge building on Esplanade between Chartres and Royal for $8,750. . . . The front and northwestern flank wall and all the present floors in the main building shall be taken down and removed also such other impediments now in the way of the new additions and alterations. The present main roof to be shored up and well supported. New walls of main building and wing and new walls of rear building. New mahogany stairs, elliptical arch between parlors, plaster cornices. Verandah over banquette on cast iron columns. Iron gate in front garden wall" (Mortgage Book 74/18). This contract included the addition of the great bay overlooking the side garden.

A watercolor drawing by A. Pueyo, July 24, 1844, plan book 22, folio 32 shows this house and its original appearance with the wooden lintels, fenestrations, and louvered blinds that remain on numbers 602 and 604. The barred entresol Gothic arches and the first levels of all three houses were dramatically changed. An imposing three-level cast-iron balcony on number 602 was added in the rose motif; it is repeated on the upper gallery of number 606.

The next house that now stands at number 612 is the third structure to occupy this lot. The Pueyo archival drawing of 1844, previously discussed, was executed for the auction sale of the double stuccoed creole cottage adjacent to number 606. The cottage, the first building on the site, had a tile, gabled roof with side chimneys, an abat-vent over the banquette, and six openings with batten shutters. A slant-roof stable in the rear side yard is indicated along the entire property line. Owned by Mr. and Mrs. Jean Longpré for many years, the property was auctioned in the Espinosa succession in 1844. This creole double house was demolished, probably in the mid–nineteenth century, for "a splendid two-story brick residence with iron verandah in front, containing two large parlors, sliding doors, dining room encased in glass doors, cabinet, large hall on side on ground floor, five bedrooms on second floor, hall, gas throughout, brick kitchen with three rooms, hydrant, cistern, etc., all slate and known as number 54 Esplanade Avenue." The house was so described on March 31, 1884, when Madame Louise Chapuis, widow of Alexander Mir, sold it to Pierre Bassony. The house now occupying this property, number 612, appears to be a late shotgun raised for apartments and enclosed behind a brick fence.

The first owner of the lots on which present 616 and 622 stand was Etienne Griffen, who bought them on October 24, 1810, before M. de Armas; he sold them fifteen years later to John Goldenbow, after putting some buildings and improvements on them. The Goldenbows held the property for twenty-five years. Later, owner Jules Cassard sold 616 to Edward R. Barnett in 1866, when the property was described "one-story frame house with brick front containing three rooms, stable and shed, waterworks." A late Victorian frame house occupies the Cassard site and is numbered 616.

The house now standing at 622 □ may well have replaced a creole cottage that, as indicated on the Sanborn map of 1876, existed there. This house is a late nineteenth-century stick-style version of the traditional New Orleans townhouses. The three-bay façade with recessed entrance leading to a side hall is traditional. The variable here is the wooden ballustrade leading around one side of the second-level balcony, and the third level, which has a deep front gable with shingles and jigsaw work associated with the late nineteenth-century stick-style of architecture. A portion of the two-story brick kitchen of the earlier house was possibly incorporated. The entrance transom contains the original etched glass, marking this house as number 58. An early photograph records it as the home of A. Xiques, a liquor importer.

Viliavaso-Maspero House

At number 628 a late Classic-style house dates from 1868 when Eugene Surgi, architect, contracted before O. de Armas on May 11 with Jean Ernest Villavaso, brother-in-law of James Gallier, Jr., to build a two-story master house with cast-iron verandah, entrance stair of granite, kitchen, and other rooms for $16,000. Just one year after the construction Villavaso sold the house to Pierre Maspero of the famous Chartres Street auction exchange. The Maspero succession sold the house on July 31, 1886, before notary E. Bouny, "elegant and enhancing two story family mansion situated on one of the most beautiful avenues and aristocratic neighborhoods in the city. The first floor contains a large hall, spacious arched parlors with white marble mantels, dining room, kitchen and some two rooms. The second story contains some six bedrooms, bath-room, cistern, etc. The yard in the rear is ornamented with a lovely garden, grape arbor, etc.'' At the auction, Henry Maspero acquired the property from the heirs via the Mutual National Bank of New Orleans, but he kept it only until 1890, when he sold to Albert Morlan. Whereas some of the above-described architectural elements are no longer in existence, the cut-glass sidelights and transoms are of the period, as are the graceful Greek Key entrance surrounds.

Zaeringer-Begué House

The first owner of the land on which the house at 632□ now stands was Jean Chabaud who purchased the lot with 62 feet front by 113 in 1810 before M. de Armas. The Barracks Street lot (631) which is directly behind 632 Esplanade is the first property associated with the Esplanade from the river to have a Spanish colonial provenance. Baron de Carondelet,

Spanish governor of Louisiana, sold the Barracks Street property which extended through to the future Esplanade to Francisco Garrel on August 14, 1793, ''with all the buildings thereon.'' Of this present pair of Second Empire houses identified as 632 and 634, the first was built in 1886 and the second a year earlier in 1885. Mrs. Mary Platz Zaeringer, at a cost of $5,000, hired Middlemiss and Murray to construct her home at 634, and Mrs. Ellen Donnelly Begué hired G. A. Thiesen as builder for 632; it cost $6,000. □

Madame Begué sold 632 in 1906 to Clementine Uter; in 1909 the Waldo Mills Pitkin family acquired the property, which continued through to Barracks Street, and they retained ownership until 1933. An investigation of the present interior double parlors reveals luxurious plaster molding and medallion details. The cornice moldings are of grape and leaf clusters and the elliptical arch-screen and consoles boldly set the room demarcation. The ceiling medallions repeat the ''horn-of-plenty'' motif, and the ebullience of the marble mantels in each parlor continues the theme.

Both houses were built to the banquette and have a second-level gallery of cast iron on 632 and a balcony with canopy at 634. There are fine paneled reveals at the entrance of number 632 and the façade of 634 is a plastered front set between wooden quoins. These two mansard-roofed dwellings represent a style fast disappearing from New Orleans. Demolitions along Jackson, St. Charles, and Esplanade avenues have caused the demise of one of New Orleans' most popular, imposing, and monumental residential house types. It is notable that while these two simple box houses reflect the Second Empire and Italianate style of decorative detail, the bay and floor plan continued the townhouse arrangement, which was popularized by the Americans in the city by 1830.

Robert-Gerard House

The corner masonry hip-roof creole cottage at 640 Esplanade was mentioned as early as February 22, 1822, when the owner Marie Elizabeth Gerard sold to François Marthe Galez ''a lot of ground designated by the number 10, making the corner of Esplanade

628, 632, 634

640

and Royal Streets, having sixty-two feet front on Esplanade by one hundred nineteen feet on Royal, together with the house and other buildings thereon." Madame Gerard had bought the lot in 1819 from the original owner, Pierre Robert. As the nine-year owner of a fine site on the new Esplanade, Robert probably built the present creole cottage, which would make it one of the earliest extant structures on the Esplanade.

The four-room cottage was restored in the late 1960s by Koch and Wilson, and no indication of the early building date was found in the fabric of the building when the firm investigated; there remained, then, evidence of a mid–nineteenth-century renovation date.

The lot, which Robert purchased from the City Corporation on October 24, 1810, before Michel de Armas, measured a full sixty-two feet and remained intact for seventy-four years although it had no less than eleven owners, including Florence Luling, builder of the Luling mansion at Leda and Esplanade. The original Robert purchase included the site of the present Second Empire-style house built in 1885 at 634 after Mrs. M. Zaeringer bought this corner cottage and garden from the widow of Henry Michel in 1884. Mrs. Zaeringer retained the corner creole cottage and had the adjacent large 2½-story residence built the next year by Middlemiss and Murray. Santo and Rosa Greco bought the Zaeringer corner cottage in 1913 and sold it twenty-five years later to Mrs. Matilda Geddings Gray. During the Greco and Gray ownership the cottage was rented to J. D. Junius, who established a tailor shop in the building in 1914 and remained there through the 1960s. It was probably he who installed the present bay display window on the Esplanade elevation. The present courtyard was planned by Richard Koch in 1939 at which time a shed not original to the house was demolished.

700 Block

Gauche-Stream House

The house at 704 Esplanade is the second complex to occupy the corner of Royal and Esplanade. As early as May 11, 1821, an ad in the *Louisiana Courier* indicates houses built by the first owner, Nicholas Rousseau who bought, from the municipality in 1810, lots 11, 12, and 13, according to the Tanesse survey: "For Sale—four houses built on two lots situated at the corner of Esplanade and Royal streets measuring one hundred twenty feet in front on Esplanade and one hundred feet front on Royal, opposite Dr. Heerman's house. The situation of those houses is the more advantageous, as by the demolition of Fort St. Charles there will be only a distance of two squares to the river. The owner only sells these houses because he intends leaving the country. . . . Apply on the premises to Mr. Nicholas Rousseau, the owner or in town to Ed. Meance."

Speculators James Ramsay and, later, Pierre Edmond Foucher bought the properties, owning them briefly, and on September 20, 1823, before notary H. Lavergne, Henry Raphael Denis, developer of 600–608 Esplanade, ac-

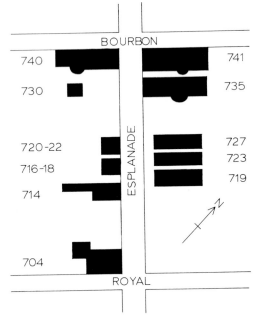

704

quired title to original lots 11, 12, and 13, "with the buildings thereon and especially the principal house, situated on lot 11 and facing Royal, with all other buildings." In 1837 the large piece of ground including sites of 704 and 714 were transferred by Denis to Armand Pitot in a sale that was annulled March 8, 1841, before C. V. Foulon, putting the four houses back into the hands of Denis. The sale to Pitot described "a portion of a square one hundred sixty-six feet front on Royal, by one hundred thirty-two feet, seven inches front on Esplanade, with the principal house fronting Royal Street and other buildings. The sale was made for $32,500 with the obligation of an annual and perpetual ground rent of $138 due the city corporation."

John Gauche purchased a corner portion of Henry R. Denis' property in 1856 in an act before Abel Dreyfous on March 26. He paid $7,500 for the property measuring 64 feet on Esplanade and 128 on Royal, indicative that at least the old house oriented toward Royal remained.

John Gauche was a prominent mid-nineteenth-century crockery merchant whose extensive business establishment once occupied buildings on Chartres between Conti and St. Louis. After the Civil War, Gauche employed architect James Freret to complete the notable Moresque cast-iron building on Lafayette Square (demolished), and his crockery business expanded there.

Soon after his 1856 purchase of the Esplanade site, Gauche tore down the old dwelling and built the present masonry mansion. The architect for the unusual and imposing residence is unknown, and the New Orleans *Daily Crescent* for October 21, 1856, reported among the building projects then underway the private residence of "John Gauche, corner of Royal and Esplanade streets . . . the finest residence downtown . . . built under his own superintendence . . . cost $20,000." John Gauche died in 1868, leaving the elegant Esplanade mansion to his widow and twelve children. An inventory notarized by W. J. Castell, April 9, 1868, enumerates the household furniture and the Gauche crockery factory inventory as well as his real estate holdings, valued at $577,954.93. Among his real estate holdings were three squares in the present midcity, which he had bought from Sheperd Brown on July 19, 1861, before A. Dreyfous. He owned a warehouse in Faubourg Marigny, comprising the square bounded by Levee (N. Peters), Victory (Decatur), Port, and Enghein (Franklin); the Moresque building valued at $150,000; and rental houses at 108 and 110 Chartres.

Although the widow continued to run the crockery business in the Moresque building and in the Chartres Street buildings, she moved from Esplanade, by 1877, to an uptown residence on St. Charles between Joseph and Arabella streets. In 1882 the Gauche family sold the house on Esplanade to Patrick R. O'Brien whose family owned it until 1911. O'Brien, a philanthropist and owner of the Columbus Cotton Press, financed, at a cost of $45,000, the Church of the Sacred Heart on Canal Street according to the 1900 *Times-Picayune Guide.*

A fire in 1893 destroyed the adjacent house, a twin building of present 714. In May of that year, O'Brien bought half of the lot from A. R. Brousseau, and both owners utilized the additional frontage as garden areas. From 1911 to 1936, 704 Esplanade was owned by Peter Spicuzza who sold it to John A. Freeman. One year later on March 1, 1937, Freeman sold it to Mrs. Matilda Geddings Gray, whose niece, Mrs. Harold Stream, is the present owner.

When Mrs. Gray purchased the house in 1937, she undertook an extensive restoration and renovation, Richard Koch being the architect. In 1969 the architectural firm of Koch and Wilson did further restoration, this time for Mrs. Stream. These are two well-documented twentieth-century renovations of an Esplanade Avenue residence. The recent one represents the analytical approach to restoration which is highly recommended as a prerequisite to ac-

tual drafting or construction. A comprehensive dossier was prepared in which title research property surveys, maps, plans, newspaper information, wills, and inventories were compiled along with old photographs. Descendants of the various owners of the house were interviewed and descriptions compiled and organized so that a successive record of the appearance of the house is recorded. By this method, previous alterations and redecoration can be peeled back to reveal the original fabric of the house.

The exterior has remained essentially as it appeared when built. The interior had lost its dry frescoes by the 1939 restoration, but the Greek Revival opening surrounds with anthemion motif remained. Such decorative details became popular here in the 1830s and continue to be seen through the 1850s. The original kitchen was located in the first room of the dependencies, and a modern kitchen replaces it there. The square masonry brick, block-style house has a center hall with the Greek Revival floor plan. Similar to the Gardère-Claiborne house (905 Esplanade), a stairway was situated in a side opening to the rear. Traditional to its building date, the two-story service wing extends from the rear of the house. There is also a detached back building.

Stylistically, however, the house is more unusual. The original dry frescoed walls of the interior reflected the finest standard of the Esplanade Ridge style of luxurious decorative effect. The simplicity of the exterior masonry surface and chaste granite portico is a stark contrast. Full-length casement openings are repeated at both levels, front and side elevations; repetition of fenestration proportion and spacing, the absence of moldings, surrounds, or cornices creates a clarity and evenness of surface that allocates great importance to the iron fence, the second-level balcony and the cast-iron overhang with double iron-bracket supports. Barely visible above the overhang is a restrained molding around the parapet.

Here, more than on most houses of the Esplanade, the site placement of the dwelling equidistant from front and side property lines, the height of the cast-iron fence in relation to the proportions of the first and second levels of the dwelling are all part of the total spatial concept. The cast-iron balcony is a unique pattern in New Orleans; its basic motif is that of a cherub dancing in a circle surrounded by a richly fretted square. A portico was seldom part of the design of any nineteenth-century New Orleans house types and styles and this Greek Revival example of granite gives dimension to a restrained façade here and at the Fisk house

(740), which is the exact design translated into wood.

Warner-Brousseau House

The three-bay townhouse in the Greek Revival style at 714 stands on the site of one of the four creole cottages that Nicholas Rousseau had built and sold in 1821. Henry Raphael Denis bought the lot and others to make up about one-fourth of the square in purchases from Jacques Larose and Pierre Edmond Foucher. Keeping the corner lot, the site of the Gauche-Stream house, Denis sold the lot where this house stands to Jonathan Lord Warner on April 7, 1843, before A. Mazureau, who retained the property just three years before selling it to Judah Touro in 1846. In those few years, however, the present house was probably built, since the act of A. Mazureau February 11, 1846, records a sale price of $8,000 including "a brick dwelling house and other buildings thereon" on a lot 30 by 120 feet. Judah Touro's estate sold the house in 1854 to André Brousseau whose family retained it until May 25, 1897, when it was sold by sheriff's sale to satisfy a suit initiated by the Canal Bank versus André Ringgold Brousseau. William G. Vincent made the successful bid at the auction, turning the property over immediately to another speculator. In 1899 Mrs. Marie Virginie Seixas Aldigé, widow of Jean Jules Aldigé, bought the house on March 6 before E. Grima, and the Aldigé family lived there for twenty years. Both the Seixas and Aldigé families are associated with other houses along the Esplanade.

The Gauche-Stream house and the Warner-Brousseau-Aldigé house at 714 are contemporary building types—the center-hall Greek Revival house and the three-bay, side-hall townhouse. Mrs. Harold Stream, the present owner of 714, also had this building restored by the architectural firm of Koch and Wilson. It was the second major renovation of the originally Greek Revival-style house; and an old photograph shows it with Italian Renaissance Revival exterior features applied to the house in the early twentieth century. At that renovation a circular portico was built which opened into the side garden.

The original townhouse, as seen in plan book 31, folio 27, had a full architrave applied in wood, the distinguishing and most imposing element on an otherwise restrained rusticated façade, also including a second-level, simple, wrought-iron balcony. From the rear of the house extended an attached two-story service wing, a style popularized by the Americans by the 1840s. The archival elevation was utilized

714

714

33

to return the house to its original 1840s appearance on the exterior. The interior, which had been the La Petite Ecole until 1969, was remodeled in the spirit of the early Classic period in New Orleans.

Fisk-Hopkins House

It is alleged that the Bourbon Street corner property of Esplanade, 740 and its neighbor at 730, were used during the Spanish colonial period as a small free burial place for military personnel. It is described in a story that appeared in the *Louisiana Gazette*, April 16, 1811, when that paper commented on the mayor's and City Council's voracious appetites for grasping everything public and private. "Near the 'glacis' of the work [fortification] on the northern extremity of the city, at or near the lower part of Bourbon Street . . . the [city] corporation under pretext of a grant from the United States, seized and tore down the wooden crucifixes, levelled, laid off in lots, sold and houses are now built over the tombs."

Indeed, the lots were laid off by Jacques Tanesse in 1810 and numbered 14, 15, 16, and were sold soon after to three different owners:

number 14, site of present 730, was first bought by Guillaume Plantey from the City Corporation, June 8, 1812, before Michel de Armas. Since Plantey owned the property for twelve years, it is quite possible that he built the four-room creole cottage depicted in the watercolor drawing by Henry Moellhausen at the tax dispute sale on May 5, 1845 plan book 57, folio 6. Magdeleine Mazes, alias Cece, free woman of color, was the second owner by 1824, reselling, however, a month later to Gabriel Henry Leaumont before Felix de Armas. Leaumont held the property for eleven years, relinquishing it in 1835 to another free woman of color, one Felicie Houssart, who sold a year later to James Ramsay, representing the firm of Ramsay and Parker. Miguel de Lizardi, a Cuban commission merchant, purchased from this company this sixty-one-foot lot, in 1838, indicating that the original lot number 14 was still intact. By the time Junius Beebe acquired it, in 1845, a partition into two lots had been made.

The spacious corner lot, number 15, had not been purchased until 1820 from the City Corporation, but the lot to its rear facing Bourbon Street, number 16, originally owned by Charles

Laveaux, was sold to Michel Lautrec Sterlin in 1812. It was he who built, at his own expense, certain buildings and dependencies which he sold with the land to Zoe Anne Plantey and Magdeleine Mazes, both free women of color. Zoe Anne Plantey bought out the Mazes interest and held the property a total of forty-three years, relinquishing it in 1855 by act of sale before Amadée Ducatel to Citye Rose Alvarez. This Bourbon Street lot sandwiched between lots facing Barracks and those facing Esplanade was, through several sales, to become incorporated into the rear sections of properties presently known as 730 and 740 Esplanade.

It is from this mid–nineteenth-century period that the Alvarez Fisk family became important owners of four properties, 730, 740, and the two rear lots. Kenneth Trist Urquhart, a descendant, wrote of his great-great-grandfather and great-great-granduncle:

Alvarez Fisk came to New Orleans from Massachusetts about 1812 and became a prominent cotton factor and planter. For many years he maintained his principal residence in Natchez, Mississippi, where he gave the

740

730 (Courtesy Kenneth Trist Urquhart)

property which was used to establish the Natchez Institute, thus laying the foundation for the public school system of Natchez. He named his antebellum mansion in Natchez "The Hall"; it is now known as "Choctaw." Alvarez's brother, Abijah Fisk, came to New Orleans about 1830 and remained here until he died unmarried in 1845. Abijah was a commission merchant who left his house on the corner of Customhouse and Bourbon Streets, to the City of New Orleans for the establishment of a free public library. After Abijah's death, Alvarez purchased several thousand volumes from Benjamin F. French and presented them to the City of New Orleans. This gift, combined with his brother's gift of his house, produced the Fisk Free Library, which in time, through other bequests, became the New Orleans Public Library. Alvarez Fisk married Eliza Wilkins in 1819 and had two sons and two daughters who survived him. He died on "Araby," his cotton plantation in Madison Parish in 1853.

At this time, according to the *Picayune*,

Alvarez Fisk, 72, who many years before donated the "Fisk Free Library," was dead at Araby Plantation, having previously consented that its six thousands or more volumes, many rare, be removed from Bourbon and Customhouse to a large, airy, well-lighted, quiet and very accessible room under name of "The Fisk Free Library of the New Orleans Mechanics' Institute," and under management of an Association committee. It contained full sets of reference works, including about one thousand volumes in French, and a small number in Spanish, Italian and German, formerly known as the Commercial Library.

Two years after the death of her husband, the widow Fisk bought the Esplanade corner lot and the rear Bourbon Street one, from Citye Rose Alvarez on May 11, 1855, before A. Ducatel; both had buildings and improvements at the time. The house that now stands at 740, the old number 84, was built by Mrs. Fisk as a home for herself, her three unmarried children, Stuart Wilkins, Edward, and Isabel, and her sister Martha Wilkins. In 1859 her daughter Alice, her son-in-law, Robert Dow Urquhart, and their three young daughters became part of the family living at 84 Esplanade. John P. Coleman gave his impression of the house when he saw it in 1922, long after the Fisk heirs had moved away:

A severely plain brick structure flush with the property line on the avenue, its remarkable beauty was not apparent until one had entered its spacious hallway and obtained through half-open doors a glimpse of the magnificence of the interior. There are twelve rooms in this building, six to each floor above and below—all commodious, well-ventilated and accessible from any part of the structure.

The fine, wide hallway on the lower floor extends through the center of the edifice to a beautifully constructed veranda in the rear. On the lake side, as one enters from Esplanade Avenue, are the double parlors, with handsome sliding doors between. Originally these rooms were a marvel of artistic embellishment, beautiful mouldings, lovely rosettes, marble mantels with a wainscoting of the finest wood, and above a panel made of some sort of composition resembling embossed leather rich in color and artistic looking. On the river side is the immense dining room, one of the loveliest apartments in the building, and, like the parlors on the opposite side, in the old days was decorated with exquisite taste. Projecting from the dining room is a very pretty portico with beautiful wrought-iron supports, facing what was once one of the most assiduously cultivated private gardens in New Orleans.

This garden land was added to the Fisk property in 1860 when Edward, Mrs. Fisk's younger son, bought original lot 14 at 730 Esplanade, from the heirs of Junius Beebe before notary T. Gueph on February 24. The rear part of the Bourbon Street property is included in its depth. Stuart Wilkins Fisk, the elder son, further enlarged the holdings when he bought a lot on Barracks thirty-one feet on the back line of 730 Esplanade.

An Allen D'Hemecourt plan clearly illustrates the Baroque garden with central axis in front and an additional one in the rear which occupied these areas, and they were further described by John P. Coleman: "In the center of the court yard was a fountain and surrounding it were flowers of singular brilliance and beauty rising from their beds like a veritable explosion of blossoms. Both court yard and garden extending back to Barracks street, were inclosed by a high brick wall, surmounting which was an iron railing of exquisite design, the whole literally covered with wisteria, tea roses, Malmaison, verbenas, etc."

A five-bay, one-level structure was built toward the rear of 730 probably soon after acquisition of this lot. Housed there were a library and billiard room for the gentlemen of the Fisk and Urquhart families who lived in the main house, then municipal number 84, now 740.

The Civil War and the capture of New Orleans by the Union forces in late April, 1862, disrupted the lives of those residing at 84 Esplanade. Early in April, 1862, Colonel Stuart Wilkins Fisk, C.S.A., left New Orleans in order to take command of his regiment, the Twenty-fifth Louisiana Volunteer Infantry, which had recently joined the Confederate Army of Tennessee at Corinth, Mississippi. Edward Fisk

730

joined his brother in Mississippi as an aide. Robert Dow Urquhart, a member of the Orleans Guards Regiment, was ordered out of New Orleans with his unit when Farragut's forces captured the city in late April, 1862. He eventually made his way to Jackson, Mississippi, and thence to Flat Rock in the mountains of North Carolina where he prepared a home for his family. Refusing to take the oath of allegiance to the United States, the ladies at 84 Esplanade petitioned General Butler, the Union commander of New Orleans, for permission to leave the city in order to go to North Carolina. Butler granted their request; they departed from their home in late June, 1862. They were accompanied by William Fogo, a Scottish commission merchant of New Orleans who had taken an interest in the ladies' welfare and a particular interest in attractive Isabel Fisk, whom he married in October, 1862, after the Fisks and Urquharts had established themselves as refugees in Flat Rock.

The family maintained its principal residence there until the end of the Civil War. During her absence, Mrs. Fisk's home on Esplanade and Bourbon was confiscated by the United States government for the use of the Federal officials in New Orleans. The three war years took a heavy toll on Eliza Wilkins Fisk's family. Colonel Stuart Wilkins Fisk was killed during the Battle of Murfreesboro, Tennessee, in December, 1862. Isabel Fisk and her husband William Fogo died in January, 1864, in Columbia, South Carolina, leaving an infant son, Stuart Wilkins Fogo. Alice Fisk (Mrs. Robert Dow Urquhart) died in July, 1865, while the family was preparing to return to New Orleans at the end of the Civil War. Mrs. Fisk, her sister Martha, her bachelor son Edward, her son-in-law Robert Dow Urquhart, her four Urquhart grandchildren, and one Fogo grandchild returned to New Orleans in the fall of 1865 and reopened the house at 740.

Six years after her return to her Esplanade Avenue home, Mrs. Fisk sold the garden site and library to Aristide Hopkins, agent of the Baroness Pontalba; the lot measured 55 feet, 1 inch on Esplanade and 141 feet, 9 inches, on the line of the Jules Tuyes property where two twentieth-century shotgun doubles now stand at 716–18 and 720–22. □ The Hopkinses resided in this building, adding a second level and cast-iron balcony supported by double braces of iron columns. Two years after Hopkins moved into 730 he had architect Benjamin M. Harrod design three 2-level frame houses across the avenue in the seven hundred block at 719, 723, and 727. □ The late Classic

structures were built by contractor Leonce N. Olivier for $5,000 each and were set off the banquette behind woven wire fences of the most attractive pattern. Only two of these three remain as they were; however, they are attractive with blended Greek orders and Victorian 1870s style. The Hopkinses sold their residence, 730, in 1925 to Mrs. Myrthe Celeste Stauffer Schwartz. Members of the Schwartz family continue to own and occupy the residence.

Mrs. Eliza Wilkins Fisk continued to reside at 84 Esplanade Street until her death in 1887. The house was inherited by her Urquhart and Fogo grandchildren who resided there until they sold it in 1889 to the McDonogh School Fund. It was used as a young ladies' school by the Société du 14 Juillet until it was purchased by the Home Missions Board of the Southern Baptist Convention in 1922. For forty years it served as the Baptist church mission, often furnishing a home and school for orphaned children. It was in 1963 that Imon Marshall Richardson bought the building at 740 from Edward Wood. The architectural firm of Parham and Labouisse was employed by Richardson to convert the Greek Revival-style single residence into twenty-four apartments; the cost was estimated at $500,000. The late 1850s Eliza Wilkins Fisk house entered a new phase with a modern patio and swimming pool.

Three of these Bourbon and Esplanade corners have existing 1850s two- and three-level brick houses which are not dissimilar in type to many Garden District residences. The Esplanade dwellings abutting the banquette create a dimensional effect which contributes to an overall avenue impression of massiveness. Two of these corner buildings (741 and 807), close to their neighbors, have three-level gable chimney ends, projecting three-level cast-iron balconies, octagonal bays, and are only slightly relieved by small side gardens. Number 741, □ directly across the avenue from the Fisk home, designed by William Freret for Adrien Barbey, soars above the property line on two elevations.

The placement and lot size therefore precipitated a building condition, now observed to be stylistically typical of the Esplanade. The magnificent twin to the Whann-Bohn house at 807, the Montgomery-Puech House, which stood on the corner of Bourbon and Esplanade at 806, was demolished. With its demise went a street-corner symmetry rare in the architectural evolution of nineteenth-century avenues.

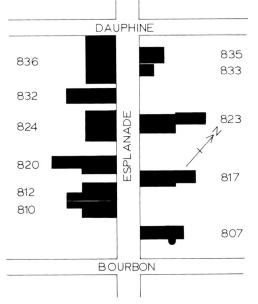

DAUPHINE

836   835
833

832

824   823

820

812   817

810

807

BOURBON

800 Block

Montgomery Houses

Jean Pierre Dufour, a physician, purchased from the City Corporation, October 24, 1810, before M. de Armas, a lot sixty feet from the corner of Bourbon along the Esplanade. The land was sold with an annual ground rent of $96. These sixty feet include the site of present-day 806, 810, and 812. Two years later Madame Suzanne Maurin bought the next sixty-one feet on this avenue; this land was acquired by act of donation from Madame Maurin and given to the three minor Dufour children on February 5, 1822, before R. Nuñez in Santiago, Cuba. Locally the act was filed with notary Marc Lafitte with the statement that the donation consisted of a house, covered with shingles, and the site on which said house was erected, also two other sites, without buildings, situated at the corner of Esplanade and Bourbon. In 1828 Louis Caire bought this property and one other lot from the Dufour heirs, and in 1832 Joseph Pilié drew a plan showing the original Dufour sixty-foot lot divided into three lots. Partially across the rear of these lots is what appeared to be a two-story kitchen or service building.

810 and 812

When William W. Montgomery bought this property from Caire in 1832, the lot became a larger portion and measured seventy-six feet along Esplanade. This owner erected, possibly as rental properties, the two Greek Revival common-wall townhouses which remain at 810 and 812. The *Daily Crescent* of September 9, 1859, reported "Dwelling of William Montgomery, Esplanade between Casacalvo [Royal] and Bagatelle [Bourbon], F. Wing & Bro., builders, for $20,000." It is most likely the paper meant to say Bagatelle and Greatmen [Dauphine].

These gable-sided, plastered brick houses have an attic frieze with triple string courses in brick. There are identical second-level wrought-iron balconies. The pilaster-style recessed entrances are adjacent, and the simple granite lintels, sills, and entrance steps complete the typical American Greek Revival ensemble popular in New Orleans in the 1830s. Unusual octagonal sidelights around the front door of 812 are seen in a similar row house at 1316 Carondelet Street. A two-story kitchen wing still extends from the rear of 810.

On the Bourbon and Esplanade corner Montgomery built a large three-level masonry building with a garden (formerly 806); it was identical to the Whann-Bohn residence directly across the Esplanade at 807. □ (This latter house, built in 1859, still stands, but the Montgomery house was demolished after 1900.) The Montgomery property was purchased in 1870 by Ernest Puech of Paris and New Orleans, one-time president of the Cotton Exchange, who lived there with his family, which included four granddaughters, until it was sold in 1889 to Supreme Court Justice Edward D. White. Major Puech had been a Confederate in the Orleans Guards, and had served under General Beauregard at Shiloh. In 1875 his daughter Althée married James Monroe Winfield, from New York state who had, ironically, fought against his father-in-law, Major Puech, during the Battle of Shiloh.

An undated watercolor of the house by C. M. Lurio is in the possession of Mrs. J. C. Rathbone, who is a granddaughter of Mr. Puech. Presently a totally inappropriate Vieux Carré and Esplanade Avenue house occupies the 806 site; only the elegant brick garden wall along Bourbon Street remains.

Dufour House

The next property at 820 is a 3½-story masonry townhouse in the Italianate tradition and stands on land which belonged to the Dufour family for ninety-eight years. Jean Pierre Dufour purchased it in 1816 from Jean-

Baptiste Guerin, and his granddaughter, Mrs. Louise Dufour, widow of Boyd Goodrich, sold the house to Jules S. Dreyfous in 1914. The Dufour family had retained only this lot of all they once owned to the corner of Bourbon, although they also held a family home facing Barracks at Bourbon. It is quite possible that the Dufours built this townhouse with the traditional floor plan of side hall, double parlors, etc., in the 1860s. Interior moldings, medallions, and cornices reflect the mid–nineteenth-century grand Esplanade style. The three-bay façade features have segmental arch openings with dripstones or labels terminating along the sides with consoles, reminiscent of some Gothic Revival buildings. This property has the unusual depth of 151 feet.

The rear property remained open and connected with the property of 819 Barracks, owned in 1859 by Cyprien Dufour. Dufour had purchased this space with buildings from the city, which had acquired it from the John McDonogh estate. These Dufours remained in the Barracks Street house until 1884 when it was sold by Howard Louis Dufour.

Guerin House

The history of the present house at 824 Esplanade goes back to 1813 when Jean-Baptiste Guerin purchased two lots from the city through Mayor Augustin Macarty as registered by M. de Armas, November 18, 1816. They were numbered 20 and 21 according to Tanesse's survey of 1810. Guerin built a house on his new property sometime before 1833, at which time he sold to Sylvain Peyroux, Rivarde, and Company "with buildings with which the buyer is familiar." The building referred to in the act of sale was probably the present house of 824 Esplanade because the act refers to Mr. Guerin "who lived on rue Esplanade between Bourbon and Dauphine." Peyroux, Rivarde and Company dissolved their partnership in 1835 leaving Peyroux and another partner, Louis Arcueil, with this house. They sold the house and outbuildings to P. A. Schreiber and Leon Chabert before L. T. Caire, February 16, 1837. Two years later Emile Sainet purchased the property in three separate transactions from William Frederick Vigers, to whom Schreiber and Chabert had sold it. Sainet, a commission merchant who lived in Paris, kept the house until his death, at which time his son, who also lived in Paris, acquired the property in 1843.

Sainet, Jr., had the house remodeled, raised, and enlarged in 1853, adding a ten-foot-wide double cabinet gallery. The building contract of June 9, 1853, between Armand Soubie,

824

proxy for Jean François Emile Sainet, and Jean Olivier is translated as follows:

The roof ridge to be rebuilt fully, reusing the good wood. Roof to be covered in slate with laths placed in the ceiling of good wood. House to be raised eighteen inches [note the present oval ventilators from this 1853 renovation]. All the ceiling will be lathed and plastered with three coats of good mortar made half of yellow sand and half of river sand for the first two coats and the third will be of white mortar with plaster. The two side walls [outside] will be lengthened [roof raised] by five feet, the rooms will be divided according to the plan with a gallery of ten-foot width having a cabinet at each end according to plan. The gallery as well as the cabinets will be built of wood and with double floors of good wood millworked and nailed and all the inside will be lathed and plastered.

The [wine] cellar will be made into a room with flooring and an opening according to the plan. The kitchens will be covered with slate. Also the floors and principal chimney and the hall will be renewed. All the rooms in the house will be put in good condition, the kitchens will be yellow or white on the outside and inside. The doors, which are in too bad a condition, as well as the locks will be changed. The pavement of the yard will be redone according to plan. The inside walls of the house will be scraped and put in a condition to be papered. The outside walls will be

whitewashed. The two doors of the room which connect the front room will be raised by a foot, renewed and single-fold. The door opening on the dining room to be enlarged and made single fold with three hinges. The door of the west side room will be rebuilt; the dining room will have two doors according to plan. The Esplanade Street front will have four openings according to plan with lintels of wood [this fenestration is verified by a 1939 photograph showing the four identical openings] and the stairs will be renewed.

The fence gates facing said street will be remade like the yard entrance door. The north fence gate will be rebuilt of good planks. The gutters will be of white iron and the overhang rebuilt. All new wood three coats good paint; that already painted two. Façade painted to taste of owner. Floors raised all over house and underneath of house banked so as not to collect rainwater, as before. Front room floor entirely new.

These alterations were made and the house continued as a revenue investment for the family living in France until 1858 when William Montgomery bought this house and the land going to Dauphine, measuring altogether by this time 163 feet on Esplanade and 166 feet on Dauphine.

Jules Alfred Montgomery, an heir of William, acquired this house "a one story brick house" on February 1, 1865, before A. Boudousquié.

He and his sister, the wife of Leon Maximilien, Count de Bethune, sold it in 1866, at which time Pilié and DePouilly made a survey of the property extending to Dauphine which shows the six-room and cabinet-gallery house. One of many subsequent owners has altered the one-story brick house further. The casement openings have been replaced by double-hung windows, and the original transoms have had muntin, mullions, and glazing removed and replaced. The 1939 photograph shows four identical façade openings with no front entrance. The left side entrance with raised stair and iron railing was certainly utilized as the main entrance for a number of years.

Charbonnet House

Sharing an early nineteenth-century land ownership history with number 824 is the double-galleried, side-hall house which stands at 832. □ The original owners were the same Guerin, Peyroux, Montgomery investors. Even though the present house is a late nineteenth-century one, it is the first to stand on this lot. The land was vacant with the exception of some cabins on the rear of the property from the time New Orleans was settled. By 1893, Dr. J. N. Charbonnet had Fourchey and Fourchey, architects, build the present Victorian frame house at 832. The house remains a fine example of the double-level four-column three-bay structures of this period being reproduced on many of the streets of New Orleans, continuing an Anglo-American building type tradition begun in the 1830s.

The corner property presently occupied by 836–42 □ Esplanade is included in the original Guerin early history and the Montgomery mid-nineteenth-century ownership. In 1812 Guerin had purchased the Dauphine-Esplanade corner from Jacques Rouly, one of New Orleans' most active nineteenth-century blacksmiths. Rouly had an $800 building on this corner and sold this and the lot for his purchase price of $1,350 with a payable ground rent of $81 per annum. Guerin agreed to place a picket fence around this entire property within six days of purchase. It is quite possible that some of the very earliest brick service buildings of the creole cottages along Dauphine Street date from the Guerin development of this property. From the titles it is obvious that the Montgomery family had through many sales been the largest landowner in the square. These corner buildings, as illustrated in the 1866 Pilié and DePouilly survey, were demolished in the early twentieth century, and the present building erected. Number 836 was once Jack's Grocery Store and residence and could, with a minimum amount of exterior maintenance, be a picturesque complement to the block. □

The Guillot Institute at 1308 Dauphine formed the rear property line of 824, 832, and 836, to the Dauphine Street corner. The Guillot Institute with Mademoiselle Marie Guillot as principal was first listed in the *New Orleans City Directory* in 1892, with its address as old number 316 Dauphine Street. In 1898 Miss Valsina is listed as the music teacher in the girls school which continued at this location, according to the directories, until 1927.

Across, on the downriver 800 and 900 blocks of Esplanade there are a wide range of unusual dwellings: the earliest extant house, two architectural types unique to the avenue, a fine example of the late nineteenth century, and a poor example of the twentieth.

Whereas number 833 Esplanade, □ the Claiborne-Perrilliat house, is undoubtedly one of the oldest houses remaining on the entire Esplanade from the River to the Bayou, its constant alterations belie its construction date of 1810. Sections remain of its original form, and its dormers have their original placement. This house has not been restored; it has been modernized and renovated.

The unusual two-level brick house standing next to the Claiborne-Perrilliat home is the François Girod residence, built in 1833 by Charles Thompson; it is now municipal number 835–37. □ There are no other central passageway houses of this type along the avenue. To return its exterior finish to a painted red surface penciled with white joints would be appropriate.

According to the 1866 archival drawing of the house in plan book 78, folio 36, which still stands at 817, a scored plaster façade and tasteful side garden would renew its exterior grandeur. The house could be inexpensively restored in the absolutely correct manner of the drawing. Such nineteenth-century documentation is available to any owner whose house was auctioned; the watercolors were made available to advertise the sale and are now preserved for the public at the Notarial Archives.

900 Block

Gardère-Claiborne House

Built by François Gardère in 1833, the Gardère-Claiborne house at the corner of Dauphine at 905 is a rare type to the Esplanade. Many raised, columned houses were constructed in the Lower Garden District and the Garden District in the 1830s when this house was built, yet no other example of this raised Louisiana plantation type exists along the avenue. Its interior was changed, however, to reflect all the exuberant Victorian scrolls, screens, and bronze oil lamps so popular in most of the homes built along the street during the 1850s and 1860s. The François Mugnier photograph □ records the original Greek Revival cornice and column caps and the entrance before the late Victorian renovation during the Claiborne ownership. The vertical board fence seen in the photograph did not heighten the beauty of this gracious residence, which has remained for over eighty years in the Claiborne family, descendants of Louisiana's first American governor, William C. C. Claiborne.

François Gardère also built the creole townhouse at 917. □ Constructed in 1831, just two years before he had the corner mansion built, the property was held by him until 1836. The title seesawed among the equity holdings of the members of the Gardère family for a period of ten years and now is owned as rental property by architect Leon Impastato.

The brick walls of 917 and 919 □ touch, although they do not share a common wall. The two townhouses, though they vary stylistically, have compatibility. The history of 917 adds further glamour to the avenue by having been

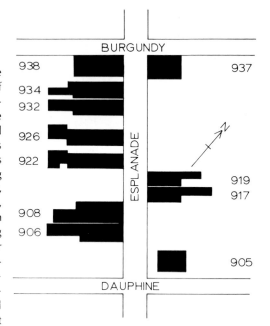

owned by a nephew of Napoleon Bonaparte, Achille Murat, and his wife, Armantine Mercier. They held the three-story masonry house for two years and relinquished it to creditors for $16,000 in 1837.

The intrusion of the present-day house at 935 was made possible by the demolition of number 921, seen in plan book 79, folio 16, which did have a common wall to above-mentioned 919; both were constructed for the Architect's Company, in 1833, by Edouard Grastour. The New Orleans College was operated in a two-level frame building next to the demolished 921, and was another mid-nineteenth-century institution to have its beginning on the Esplanade. The house at 935, which was approximately the site of the New Orleans College, would accommodate itself well to the Carrollton-uptown area where a spacious front and side garden would provide an important feature necessary to the raised twentieth-century basement houses. It is inappropriate on the banquette of this historic street surrounded by vintage masonry and frame dwellings that were designed with consideration for their lot placement and relationship to the street. A tradition, ironically, is being continued by the existence within the house of the Vieux Carré Day Nursery School.

An important surviving specimen of the Second Empire style, 937 Esplanade, □ has a gallery with segmental keystoned arches and a jaunty angle to its square side tower. If the

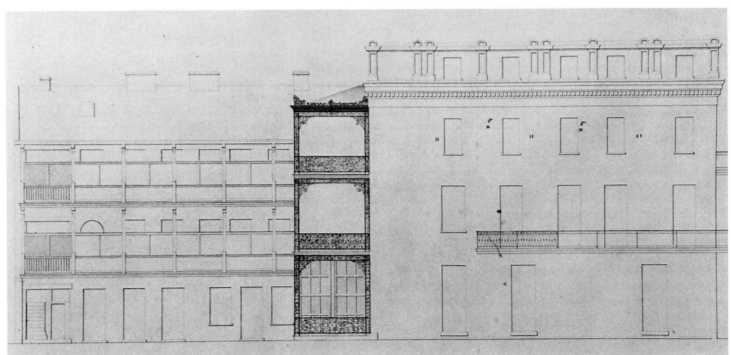

906 and 908 (James Gallier, Jr., side elevation, courtesy Historic New Orleans Collection)

upper gallery were opened, windows raised to full height, and awnings removed, this would be an excellent New Orleans example of stylistic architectural blends, utilizing a bit of Victorian Gothic, Victorian Italianate, along with a suggestion of the Baroque and the Classic in the upper-level Corinthian capitals. Built by G. A. Lanaux in 1884, the dwelling is well maintained and could be outstanding.

LeBreton-Madame Marigny Houses

Crossing Esplanade and Dauphine to the "uptown, lake corner" of the 900 block, one finds through research, that the first lot was owned from 1810 to 1830 by four owners: Joseph Castel, Charles Bonifay, Carlile Pollock, and Felix de Armas; the latter two were well-known notaries who professionally and personally were involved in many nineteenth-century real estate transactions. It is most likely that a modest revenue-producing building occupied the sixty-by-one-hundred-foot lot, for it was sold "with improvements" October 20, 1830, before A. Mazureau, by F. de Armas, to Charles Derbigny. When Derbigny sold the same lot to Noel Barthelemy LeBreton on January 20, 1835, before F. Grima for $10,188, there was a brick building thereon measuring forty-three feet long, by fifteen feet wide. LeBreton also bought from Louis Cornie, free man of color, an adjacent property assembled from the original owner Jacques Zino's holdings on Dauphine and Quartier (Barracks). The Dauphine Street lot had "a brick house with a terraced roof, a kitchen of scantlings [small beams] and other buildings." LeBreton undoubtedly had the present three-bay, side-hall townhouse at 906 constructed immediately after this 1835 purchase, for when his neighbor Madame Celeste Destrehan, widow of Prosper Marigny, signed a contract for 908 with the building company of John G. Boyd in 1836, it was for a "three-storied brick house and kitchens, and other buildings like those of Mr. LeBreton." The contract is housed in the notarial records of H. B. Cenas, July 25, 1836, and registered the building cost at $14,500. This contract clearly requests "dormant [sic] windows, in the garret like those in the adjoining house [906]." This is documentary proof that 906 did not have in 1836 the fourth story it now has.

Edward Simon bought 906 from LeBreton in 1842 for $20,000. It was probably during the Simon proprietorship that the fanciful fourth story was added to this main building and to the service wing. An undated drawing attributed to James Gallier, Jr., beautifully depicts this masterful addition and the delicate three-

level cast-iron gallery which provided a rear and side elevation of distinguished beauty. Julien Meffre-Rouzan purchased the land from Simon in 1858 for $22,500. Nearly a hundred years were to pass before monetary appreciation would be continued on this house, for in 1922 its value dropped to $9,500 when the Edward Ludwig family became owners. In 1948 its price had risen to $48,000 when purchased by Mrs. Janet Dumesville Conrad Caballero from Mr. Irma Brechtel and her husband, Michael Mellaney, before notary H. Midlo.

Today eleven large apartment units fill the building at 906, which is advertised along with the corner property and 1309 Dauphine in a package sale for $630,000. The Dauphine Street corner, formerly the garden area, is overbuilt with a 1960s modern building, □ containing six one-bedroom apartments, which totally destroys the symmetry of the two fine homes.

Like its neighbor, 908 had a large side garden area, which it alone retains. Madame Celeste Marigny, who had legally separated from Prosper, son of Bernard Marigny, and who, after his death, had married Alexander Grailhe, sold 908 to Joseph Oscar Robelot for $20,000 in 1839. The Robelot family owned the house until 1910, leasing it to the Board of Directors of the public schools of New Orleans in 1908. For six years in the 1920s the house was owned by the Louisiana Society of Prevention of Cruelty to Children. Since 1927 the house has had nine owners including Clay Shaw who sold this property and the corner 906, to Rex Moad.

Olivier House

Cesaire Olivier bought the next lot, measuring 63 by 107, from Jonathan Lord Warner, on April 21, 1855, before A. Ducatel. Prior to this transaction it was part of a larger lot acquired from Charles Edouard Forstall in 1847. This larger property was bought in 1819 by Eugene Macarty from the Louisiana Corporation. Cesaire Olivier hired August Roy in 1856 to build this late Classic-style house, now numbered 922. □ It was briefly described by notary A. Ducatel in the contract as a wood house, with attic, five-foot balcony having bathrooms and gas . . . $9,500. Eight years later in the Olivier inventory the house was valued at $25,185.49. When widow Giraud, who had purchased the house in 1871, sold in 1882, a press clipping attached to the act of M. T. Ducros described the house: "The improvements comprise a splendid two-story frame residence with two, two-story frame buildings attached to

926

922, 926, 932, 936, 938

main building, having on the ground floor two large fine parlors, arched, a wide side and rear hall, large dining room and side galleries, pantry, kitchen with cooking-range, store room, privies, two bedrooms, two cabinets, side and rear hall, balcony, four bedrooms with side gallery, two other bedrooms, flagged yard, cisterns, flowers, shrubs, etc. This property subject to lease in favor of John B. Lafitte, expiring September 30, 1882, valued at $11,600." The relatively blocklike or squared appearance of this house front, emphasized by the wide pilastered Classic entrance, is typical of a number of late Classic houses along the Esplanade and in Faubourgs Marigny and Tremé. Such proportions are seldom seen elsewhere on townhouses, most of which are taller and narrower in effect.

Schinkel House

The two-and-one-half-story plastered brick Greek Revival townhouse with stepped gable sides at number 926 was built soon after a contract was signed between Achille B. Courcelle, builder, and Edward Schinkel on August 21, 1856, before notary E. Ġ. Gottschalk. Schinkel had purchased the lot in 1853 from Jonathan

Lord Warner, former owner also of the land on which neighboring 922 stands. The house was copied from the Schinkel home next door which had been built four years earlier. The building contract for 926 was for "two story brick house with attic adjoining his property on Esplanade between Dauphine and Burgundy as per specifications for his own house built for him [at 932] by J. Sewell. Cost $9,100." Just two months later there appeared in the *Daily Crescent* of October 21, 1856, the following: "Built during the past year: Residence of Mr. Schinkel on Esplanade, near Burgundy. Cost about $12,000." This house was described for an auction sale in July, 1871, to settle the succession of Edward Schinkel:

Upon lot #1 and a portion of the strip of ground 15 feet wide(total measure of 40' 6" by 107') there is a superior and elegant two story and attic brick, slate roof dwelling #112 Esplanade Street occupied by Mrs. Chalaron containing on the first floor one large parlor with sliding doors, cornices, centerpieces, marble mantels, a large hall and dining room and on the second floor, large hall, three bedrooms, each with closets, the whole elegantly finished and well fitted, with gas

throughout and requiring only the usual repairs; also two story brick, slate roof, back buildings, containing kitchens, ironing room, store room and privy, the yard is flagged in which there is a hydrant and cistern; the side walk in front of the house is also flagged.

A 1939 photograph of the left side elevation shows no side iron balcony, although one presently exists. The first owner of these lots, which comprise the sites of 926 and 932 and which were designated as one lot by Tanesse in 1810, was Richard Owen Pritchard, who purchased it in 1819. Pritchard became a well-to-do American merchant and had James Gallier, Sr., design and build several commercial buildings for him in the American sector. The next lot that Edward Schinkel bought from Jacques Dupré of St. Landry Parish before A. Chiapella was the site of 932, and the following year Schinkel had his builder John Sewell design a two-story attic house with a cast-iron balcony. In the Schinkel succession sale of 1871 it is described as being an elegant dwelling house (old number 114) occupied by Mr. de Lizardi and in every respect the counterpart of the one described above, meaning

932, 936, 938

Plan Book 28/17

938

old number 112 or present 926. The side-hall residence at 932 is today a finely proportioned example of the townhouse style with handsome Greek Revival entrance featuring fluted Ionic columns. This projection and the shallow cast-iron gallery at the second level lend texture and depth to the severe front.

Both houses vary only slightly in grillwork design. The front of 926 is plastered and scored; 932 has a façade treated for paint and penciling. Either treatment is correct for the period. The Classic-style door treatment has narrow sidelights and transoms. Number 932 has a handsome two-story service wing extending from the rear and a rear gallery added in wood; 926 has a three-story service wing extending from the rear.

Dupré House

The archival drawing by Allen D'Hemecourt, April 25, 1848, depicts the house at 938 when the owner Jacques Dupré, who was a major Esplanade Avenue promoter, was offering it for sale at auction. It appeared then as a two-level, hip-roof creole townhouse with small arched attic dormers. The front elevation included three bays with a wrought-iron, cathedral-patterned balcony which extended around the side. A rear, detached, two-level brick service wing appears along the Burgundy property line. The arched entrance in this drawing has a fanlight over a paneled door which is flush with the façade. The fenced garden contained large shade trees and more than likely a parterred section. The drawing, then, indicates a fine federal or creole-style residence in the manner of the 1820s, perhaps built for tailor Etienne Cordeviolla, free man of color, between 1816 and 1831 when he sold this lot with buildings to Edward Soniat.

The floor plan indicates the creole interpretation of a side-hall house; the main and second floors have two rooms of equal size, and a narrow hall leads to a rear stairway and cabinet. Keeping the house less than a month, Soniat sold it in 1831 to George Legendre, who held this property until 1839 when he sold to Jacques Dupré. At that time, the original sixty-foot lot was divided into two and bore the numbers 3 and 4, with 4 indicating thirty-five feet on Esplanade according to D'Hemecourt's plan. The Joseph Domingo Bosque family had purchased both lots in 1848 from Jacques Dupré and sold them to Madame Adèle Villeré Lavergne in 1850. Members of the Lavergne family retained interest in this corner property and adjacent property for the next thirty-nine years, when the final family transaction was settled as a result of a law suit, *William F. Goldwaithe* vs. *Jules Lavergne*. As a result of this legal action this house on its present thirty-five feet was sold to Lietaud, Carron and Goldwaithe for $6,000 in 1879.

It was completely renovated to suggest an Italianate townhouse in 1882 by C. De Puppé, builder for Victor Edouard Sarrazin, for $1,700.

The present paneled frieze with heavy parapeted cornice was added, as were window cornices on both levels, Greek Key entrance surround and cast-iron balcony supports. However, the Federal-style dormer and early hip-roof were untouched, as was the wrought-iron balcony. A press clipping attached to the Grima sale of 1887, when Sarrazin sold to Adrien Cassard, noted, "The splendid two story brick and attic residence, having iron balcony on both streets, and on the lower floor large double parlors with sliding doors, with large side hall and dining room, privies on both stories, water works, cistern of 2,500 gallons, etc., and some four rooms in the first story, two story brick building, having three rooms on upper floor, bath room, coal room, kitchen on lower floor, etc."

This building has housed a veterinarian office since 1939 and is still used for that purpose. Terrazo floors and plywood paneled walls completely desecrate the original interior of the house. If a proper restoration were attempted on this, one of the earliest remaining houses along the Esplanade, the inventory of the house annexed to the 1858 succession of Madame Lavergne, found in A. Ducatel 77/453, could prove very helpful.

The late Victorian frame house at 934–36 Esplanade occupies the portion of the original corner lot that was once the early garden of its neighbor 938. The frame two-story double house had been recently constructed when it appeared on the 1897 Sanborn map. It has shallow upper-level side galleries.

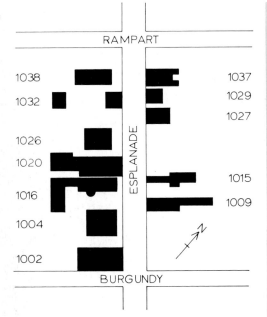

RAMPART

1038   1037
1032   1029
        1027
ESPLANADE
1026
1020   1015
1016   1009
1004
1002

BURGUNDY

1002

1000 Block

The Esplanade along this square in the 1000 block was part of the revetment of Fort St. Jean, the second fort to guard one of the corners of the Vieux Carré. Since the Esplanade was not part of the original Adrien de Pauger plan of 1721, the lines of the fortifications from Fort St. Charles on the river to Fort St. John at Rampart ran obliquely through the depth of the block separating Barracks from Esplanade. Title research revealed that this square began its development after 1819 with the Burgundy-Esplanade corner improvement begun as late as 1830.

The three-level residential brick building that occupies this corner, 1002, was once "a two-story brick building and other buildings [dependencies]" erected by the New Orleans Improvement Company when they acquired the site from Gabriel Montamat on April 19, 1834 before Felix Grima. Joseph Dusuau had

acquired the Greek Revival townhouse by 1839 and contracted with Henri Gobet, a builder, to "repair and add one story to the house at Burgundy and Esplanade at a cost of $1,830 (L. T. Caire, June 22, 1843)." The third-level cast-iron balcony and side gallery were added at this time, but the plain merchant rod, wrought-iron balcony on the second level was a part of the original two-story structure. A subsequent addition of a two-bay extension on Burgundy is in the style of the 1843 renovation; it adds considerable space to what was once a single-family dwelling. The present window frames and lights at the lower level date from the late nineteenth century, replacing a three-over-three light arrangement necessary to preserve the architectural and period integrity.

Two common-wall two-story brick townhouses once stood next to this building. They were described as having "five or six rooms, a kitchen of brick of two stories, hydrant, water closet, etc.," having been built either by the New Orleans Improvement Company at the

same time as 1002 Esplanade or by the 1835 owner, James Madison Zacharie. These houses appear on the Sanborn map of 1876 but presently are replaced by an 1897 shingle-style frame house at 1004. □ Approximately eight feet of the original corner property were sold and are now incorporated into the side yard of 1016 Esplanade. These lots and buildings were owned by no fewer than twenty-nine investors between 1821 and 1858.

Freeman Annable House

The land from which the lot at 1016 emanated was purchased by land speculators and changed ownership, probably as a bare lot, from 1819 to 1827. When Pierre Roup, free man of color, sold in 1835 to Pierre Montamot on February 16 before H. Pedesclaux, it was for a forty-foot front Esplanade lot "with the edifices which had been constructed after the acquisition of the lot by Pierre Roup" in 1827, and the kitchen of the Roup complex is illustrated in plan book 85, folio 20. Roup would have been continuing the tradition along the Esplanade of early proprietorship of land and development by free persons of color. This Esplanade property backed into other land owned by free persons of color on Barracks Street. Rosalie Chesneau, free woman of color, purchased a sixty-foot front lot on Barracks in 1819 and sold it to the Reverend August Jean-Jean in 1822 before M. Lafitte, December 20. The Barracks Street lot also contained "edifices" as accounted for in the 1833 act of sale between Madame Marthe Fortiere and François Girod, "buildings . . . having been constructed since the acquisition by Mme Fortiere."

Roup sold his cottage and kitchen in 1835 to Pierre B. Montamot who held the property until 1839 selling to Juan Ignacio Laborde. Laborde's sale in 1845 to Madame Pascual Mendoza indicated "buildings and improvements" which would still have been the Roup creole cottage complex. Madame Mendoza sold the property to Freeman Annable in 1847. It is likely that Freeman Annable built the present three-bay, side-hall townhouse with pillars running through a two-level gallery seen in plan book 21A, folio 40, drawn by Adolphe Knell for the Annable estate sale of 1851. The Annable house had seven owners between 1851 and 1886, any one of whom may have made the alteration to the 1847 house, enlarging it and redecorating it to its present appearance. The Sanborn Insurance map of 1874, however, retains the early Roup kitchen building which would indicate that the house was enlarged and remodeled after Charles Perrier bought the house in 1874, selling it as it appears today in 1886. The remodeling included adding a room behind the double parlors, demolition of the original back gallery and kitchen, and the addition of service wings to extend from the right and a side bay. The house today retains Greek Key opening surrounds and the cast-iron railing seen on the archival drawing. Most notable façade alterations appear in the cornice treatment, now Italianate with brackets interspersed with modillions and a heavy parapet. Eight fluted columns with Corinthian capitals replace the simple, two-level box columns seen in the 1851 elevation. Late nineteenth-century alteration of the original double-hung windows also makes stylistic interpretation difficult. The high vertical-board fence that crossed the property in 1851 was replaced with a handsome iron fence affording a view to the garden and rear building.

In 1840, this present garden area was part of a larger lot and held a house which was at that time described as "a new two-story brick

1016

1020

house, a two-story brick kitchen including servants' rooms, washing rooms, and a stable, privies and a good well; which house is rented until August next at the rate of one hundred dollars per month." That house had been built by Sampson Glossman in 1838 and was demolished between 1874 and 1896. It was not until 1893 that the three lots comprising the present garden of 1016, the site of the house, and the sixty-foot lot adjoining the house in the rear on Barracks Street came under single ownership. That is when Cassius J. Meyer purchased the property from several owners. The Sanborn map of 1897 indicates that the property extended back and included the Barracks Street land by that time. This rear portion has been separated again. The house and garden were recently sold by Mr. and Mrs. Theodore V. Deagano to Samuel Miceli, Jr., for $275,000.

Nott House-Italian Hall

The building presently at 1020 Esplanade is a composite structure, the first portion of which dated from 1835. It was described by Edith Long in the *Vieux Carré Courier,* September 30, 1966:

The Rampart side is the remains of a building of major historic and architectural importance; the Burgundy side was built as a dance hall in 1920. The original Esplanade front building has suffered . . . modification. . . . The original rear building fronting on Barracks, designed to be a carriage house, has been somewhat modified, but its original nature is retained. . . . The great and the famous have lived and loved here. And much of the history of New Orleans and the South has centered on this large plot of ground. . . .

The property at 1020 Esplanade was composed of two . . . lots [in 1819], each measuring 60 by 100 French feet, one fronting on Esplanade and one fronting on Barracks. For 16 years these lots passed through the hands of [speculators]. . . . The records indicate no buildings here; if any existed they would have been little more than squatters' cabins. The present dwelling was [probably] the first and only one to occupy this site.

In 1835 both lots were acquired by the prominent business man William Nott, who had also been the first consular agent of the Netherlands in New Orleans. It was Nott who built on these two lots as a single unit; they have remained in this state ever since. William Nott, in 1835, engaged the great Greek Revival architect, James Gallier, Sr., to design an elegant home for him on this spacious site. The contract for the building is an extensive document, ten pages long, in the Notarial Acts of H. B. Cenas, Vol. 5, folio 173. Written in English, it goes into the most specific details of the masonry, carpentry work, ironwork, and millwork.

This was a splendid three-story [masonry] building of the richest detail, with a white marble entrance, and a wrought iron balcony railing with cast iron ornaments in the panels. There were many fine Greek Revival interior trimmings. The Ionic fluted columns, for instance, on either side of the sliding doors between the parlors, were patterned after the Temple of Erectheus at Athens. The cost of the building was $33,500—an appreciable sum for that day. It was one of the great ornaments of New Orleans in its time.

Nott died in 1837 and there was a flurry to reaffirm contracts and payments, and so a spate of further documents exist with his inventory. The ground plans are to be found among Gallier's papers in the Labrot Collection at Howard-Tilton Library of Tulane University. At Nott's succession sale a prominent Creole lady, who was related to him, purchased the property; then it was picked up by Rezin Davis Shepherd, business partner of John McDonogh, to hold briefly. In 1851 the Hon. John Slidell acquired this establishment as a home for his family.

Slidell, a brilliant lawyer, was also one of the distinguished statesmen of the South. It is said he was political boss of New Orleans for three decades. A romantic figure, Slidell served in local, state, and national posts, with particular renown in the United States Senate. Passionate in the cause of the Confederacy, he resigned his Senate seat after Secession, and in 1861 Jefferson Davis appointed him Commissioner to France to seek recognition of the Confederacy. Effective diplomatically, Slidell was defeated by economics and history; his fortunes declined. He remained abroad after the war, in exile, and died in France.

In 1835, while his star was still rising, John Slidell married the beautiful young Creole Mathilde Deslonde. Mme Slidell had a younger sister, the frail, but lovely, Caroline. This splendid mansion on Esplanade was given to Caroline Deslonde as a wedding present in 1855 when she married the great creole confederate general, Pierre Gustave Toutant Beauregard. In her novel, *Mme Castel's Lodger,* Frances Parkinson Keyes describes this house on Esplanade at the time Beauregard was courting Caroline. It was here, on Esplanade, that the Beauregards lived until Mme Beauregard's death [during the Civil War].

The property was sold again in 1866. A newspaper description of the establishment, attached to Mme Beauregard's inventory reads: '. . . That elegant, well finished and commodious three story brick dwelling, together with the lot of ground on which it stands, situated on Esplanade. . . . The house is in all respects one of the most desirable residences in the city, from its size, location and distribution. It contains two parlors and one dining room, all elegantly finished and communicating with each other by folding doors, eight large bedrooms, with closets attached; hall on each floor eleven feet wide. The back buildings—two story and of brick—contain store rooms, kitchens, washing and ironing rooms, five servants rooms, bath rooms, etc. In the rear, and attached to the back buildings, there is a large carriage house and stables containing five stalls, with hay and grain loft above. Connected with the yard, which is spacious, there is a handsome flower garden, highly improved and filled with shrubbery and ornamental trees. . . .'

Other contemporary accounts describe the life of the Slidells and Beauregards in this dwelling, and mourn the passing of the old aristocracy that once occupied this home. But other prominent families continued to live here; from 1884 to 1912 it was known as the Baldwin mansion.

In 1912 the property was purchased by the Italian Hall Association, in whose hands it has remained until recently. About 1920 the building was remodeled extensively by the Italian Chamber of Commerce. The building fronting on Esplanade was drastically altered at this time. Originally this was a three-story house with a side garden. Two two-story service wings extended back into the depth of the lot; and at the rear, fronting on Barracks, was a large two-story carriage house. The Unione Italiana removed the second and third floors of the dwelling, filled in the side garden with a dance hall, and built a second story auditorium over the entire structure. The front façade was then completely redesigned in the Italianate manner.

The two double-story service wings seem to have remained basically as they were. The carriage entrance on Barracks was filled in with another plain new building, but the old carriage house appears to be virtually intact. Openings have been altered somewhat, but the original 1835 building is still there.

The site of the frame two-story Edwardian-style house which is 1026□ Esplanade also was owned after William Nott by Rezin Davis Shepherd and John Slidell. When Caroline Deslonde, wife of Pierre G. T. Beauregard, was given this property by her brother-in-law, Slidell, in 1855, it was just half of the original lot or thirty-one feet, eleven inches. A small galleried cottage set back from the banquette was probably constructed soon after 1855 and survived until Edward J. Zeidler, one of the many subsequent owners, bought the house and property from Joseph Bauer, April 1, 1898. Zeidler replaced the Beauregard cottage with the present twentieth-century frame house, after financing it through the Firemen's Building Association in 1902, and sold the house in 1915 to Hugh C. Davidson.

Pinson-Pizetta Property

All the land from the Nott residence to Rampart was first owned by Albin Eusebe Michel, then Jean Felix Pinson and Maurice Pizetta. It

1032

measured 120 feet along Esplanade. Today this ground is divided into four lots, but was originally lots 40 and 41 on Joseph Pilié's plan of 1820. Pinson and Pizetta bought lots 40 and 41 from Michel on October 20, 1820, before Michel de Armas, and it is thought that these men, who were both Spanish colonials and architects, built the cottage that now stands at 1032 Esplanade.

If the architectural firm Pinson and Pizetta did indeed construct this house in the 1820s, it joins number 833 Esplanade as being one of the oldest on the avenue. It was remodeled, probably, in the late 1850s, at which time four Corinthian columns were added to the gallery and an iron balustrade in the "widow's mite pattern." Above was installed a bracketed, denticulated cornice with a heavy parapet. These features are seen on a twentieth-century photograph made before a second, more recent renovation, in which the house was restructured to appear as it does today. Box columns have replaced the Corinthian ones, and the gallery floor has been raised to the new level. A detached two-story service and stable building, dating from the original construction period, remains across the rear of the lot. The rear elevation of the main house features a federal-style arched opening, reflective perhaps of the Pinson period of the 1820s.

Demourelle-Villeré House

Insurance maps indicate that there was a wood and coalyard on the corner of Rampart and Esplanade as late as 1876, and that between that time and 1897 a large galleried Italianate house occupied the corner site. In 1897 this two-level frame residence, set back from Esplanade, had a large side garden between it and the present cottage at 1032. A two-level octagonal bay extended into this

garden area and probably had doors connecting it in the front and rear to the side galleries which continued from the front to the farthest point of the service wing. It is not known whether this house was standing when James Demourelle bought the property on December 8, 1883, before C. G. Andry from Madame Victoria Marie Lawrence, who was the wife of Francis Dalley Fisher of London, England, and her sister Marie Alice Lawrence, wife, of Herman Adolph Hertz of Paris, France. The present house which stands at 1038 Esplanade□ was known as the Demourelle house until it was sold by Fernand J. Demourelle to René L. Villeré on September 8, 1926. The act was recorded by notary F. T. Doyle. Villeré first had a pharmacy at 1225 Royal in 1901 and moved to 1001 Esplanade in 1906, according to the city directory.

In November of 1967, Adèle Forstall Villeré announced that the pharmacy which had become a familiar landmark was going out of business. The building is presently being renovated and is attractive although it is adjacent to a used-car lot which occupies the tiny corner section at Rampart. Fernand J. Demourelle had sold this corner piece of the original lot 41 to the Standard Oil Company in December of 1924.

Shortsighted sale of these corner properties for commercial use damages not only the immediate intersection, but seriously affects in a rippling action surrounding properties many blocks away. Every intercepting street with a major city artery introduces into four squares an atmosphere which either aids or detracts. The responsibility is even greater where intersections of two primary streets force many people to stop and there, consciously or subconsciously, suffer the ugliness and brutality of commercial expediencies.

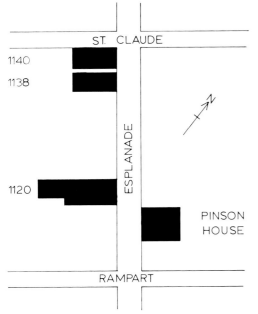

ST. CLAUDE

1140

1138

1120

ESPLANADE

PINSON HOUSE

RAMPART

1100 Block

The Tanesse plan of New Orleans in 1816 shows the new Esplanade intersecting Rampart Street continuing for two blocks beyond Rampart as a narrow street called St. Julie. At this Rampart intersection Esplanade was to enter lands established as the French colonial plantation of Charles de Morand who had come to the colony as an employee of the Company of the Indies. Morand had established a brickyard and faïencerie for the company on the left side of Bayou Road beyond the city boundaries. In 1738, when the Company of the Indies properties reverted to the French crown, Morand purchased the brickyard. Today the land is bound roughly by Rampart, Claiborne, Dumaine, and Bayou Road, as outlined on the Zimpel plan. He added to this plantation two contiguous concessions on the right side of Bayou Road which he acquired from the French government in 1756. These two new tracts comprised the area surrounded today by Bayou Road, Rampart, St. Bernard, and Galvez. These two concessions and the previous purchase were known as the Morand habitation, operated by him, then his wife and four children and their executor until 1775.

After a partition of the Morand estate the plantation was sold intact to Pablo Moro and his wife Julie Prevot (Juliana Prevotier). Madame Moro eventually sold and gave the first two Morand tracts to her granddaughter Julie Moro Tremé and her husband Claude. This was accomplished in a series of transactions between 1795 and 1800 with Estevan Quinones acting as notary. Monsieur and Madame Tremé also received title to the third tract excepting a portion ten arpents by three along Bayou Road which Madame Moro had sold in 1780 to Andrés Almonester y Roxas, royal notary. Tremé sold this large tract of land behind the city to the municipality in 1810 for $40,000, excluding the lots which he had sold privately between 1795 and 1810. In an act of sale before Michel de Armas he accounted for these previous sales.

Just as the Sigur and St. Maxent heirs had sued the city claiming a portion of the city's purchase, so did the Morand heirs. They claimed that a portion of the original Morand tract was not acquired by the Pablo Moro purchase in 1775 from Charles Morand, Jr. This suit also involved definition of measurement and even the relative significance of Spanish words *finca y habitación* and the French word *habitation*. The Morand heirs lost the case to recover a triangular section of land along Rampart to Fort Ferdinand before the Louisiana

Supreme Court on June 4, 1832. The court also defined the French word *habitation* as follows:

For it is to be admitted that the latter [*habitation*] alone would not convey the idea which in English is attached to the word plantation. Yet when united they certainly mean something more than a mere house for dwelling in. The term *habitation* in the French language seems to have been used in some of the colonies of that Government to convey the idea of what is called in English a plantation or farm. And it is shown by many examples cited by the Counsel for the defendants that the same word *habitación* in Spanish has been frequently used by the officers of the Government after the acquisition of Louisiana from the French King in the same manner as it had been previously used in the Colony by the first proprietor . . . [therefore] being of opinion that Charles Morand just required title to the land in dispute by the adjudication of 1772 and that the title thus acquired has been regularly transferred to the defendants [through Moro and Tremé], it is unnecessary to examine any other question in the cause.

It is on the basis of this court definition of the word *habitation*, for purposes of describing the lands through which the Esplanade would cross, that the term is used interchangeably with *plantation* and *farm*. It is synonymous with any tract of land no matter how small·or large on which there are dwelling house, outbuildings, and cultivated land.

In 1836, Rampart Street and the Esplanade formed right angles before continuing on as one-lane streets. Rampart was Love Street in its downriver, easterly direction. Esplanade ran but two blocks to the Estevan Plauché plantation and was called Julie, St. Julie, or Julia for Claude Tremé's wife and was even known for a short period in 1814 as rue Thérèse. It paralleled Bayou Road, then the primary artery between the old city and Bayou St. John.

By 1822 a double row of trees on the neutral ground (median) enhanced the Esplanade from the Levee to Rampart, and the city envisioned continuing the avenue at the boundary of Faubourg Tremé all the way to Bayou St. John. A "plan to serve for the prolongement projected of the street of the Esplanade to Bayou St. Jean, New Orleans the 26th of April, 1822, signed Joseph Pilié, voyer de la ville," is to be found at the city's engineers' office. This plan was approved by a city council resolution and signed, "Nouvelle Orléans, le 6 Mai, 1822, Mayor J. Roffignac." A watercolor of 1834 by John H. B. Latrobe in the Historic New Orleans Collection illustrates the intersection of Esplanade at Rampart, looking toward the river.

The city's concept for the extension of Esplanade was triggered by the purchase of the

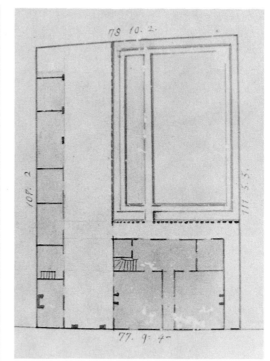

Plan Book 65/32

city from Claude Tremé of his three parcels of land to the rear of the city, on March 17, 1810, before Michel de Armas. This sale mentioned a transaction for two streets, each of forty feet width, to be known as St. Claude from Bayou Road to the northeast to join Faubourg Marigny and St. Julie beginning at the limits of the plantation (Rampart) and running to the northwest to join the habitation (of the Plauché). St. Claude and St. Julie had been laid out by Carlos Trudeau, principal arpenteur, on May 10, 1799, as a private development of a portion of the Tremé plantation.

While Julie Tremé and her husband lived in the family home on Bayou Road (site of grounds of St. Augustine's Church on Governor Nicholls Street), they sold lots along each side of Bayou Road and St. Claude and St. Julie. Tremé sold what is presently the 1100 block of Esplanade, odd side, to one Nicolas Jean Pierre, as seen in January 7, 1807, act of Philippe P. Pedesclaux. The 1100 upriver side he sold to Chalinette Duval, free woman of color, in 1810. Most of the two 1200 blocks on this even side were sold by Tremé to Demahy Demontil, free person of color, who sold the property to Pierre Lavergne in 1807. The remaining section of the 1200 block property was sold or bequeathed by Tremé to François Boisdoré and Joseph Dolliole, both free men of color.

Pierre-Pollack House

Nicolas Jean Pierre, immediately after his 1807 purchase of the 1100 block downriver side from Tremé, divided it into large lots. The corner lot, Esplanade (rue Thérèse) and St. Claude, he developed for Pierre Boivin as notarized by Philippe Pedesclaux on March 5, 1808. He had already begun a building there, and he agreed to complete it for Boivin in two and a half months for a total sum of $5,100. An 1814 drawing by Tanesse of this brick creole cottage with a tiled and hip-roof illustrates the four rooms as "deux chambres" on the left and the "salle de compagnie" and "salle à manger" on the right with "deux cabinets" having "caves" underneath. The galleried servants' building included four "chambre à negroes," a large kitchen, and an attached stable and coachroom. An enormous kitchen garden separated the principal house from its dependencies. The property of the Masonic Étoile Polaire was adjacent; its building would soon be built and face St. Claude; then another, the present one, would in 1840 front on Rampart Street.

Boivin then acquired all the front lots along rue Julie, including one he bought at auction from the city at the corner of Rampart and Julie, as registered in Michel de Armas, November, 1809. He held them until 1811, when he sold to Pierre Philibert. Two and one-half years la-

ter, Philibert was bankrupt, and François Meffre Rouzan controlled auction proceedings that placed five lots for sale, including the above-described tile-roofed cottage on the corner. Joseph Pavie bought three of these lots, and by 1818 his heirs had sold them to notary Carlile Pollock on April 28 before M. Lafitte. Pollock may have occupied the corner cottage, but he later utilized the house as rental property. Pollock further subdivided the land behind the cottage into lots, two of which he sold to Felix Pinson by transaction in the office of Philippe Pedesclaux, May 27, 1826.

Pinson Houses

Pinson built two fine houses illustrated in the plan books 65/32 and 61/39 on these lots in 1826. His design concepts incorporate interpretative Classic elements which mark him as an architect and builder of distinction and sophistication. Pinson's floor plan for the house, illustrated by Pietro Gualdi in 1855 (65/32), was basically a two-story version of a creole cottage, with the downstairs space square in dimensions but divided into two large rooms rather than four, and having the introduction of a narrow central hall leading to the creole-style cabinet gallery and rear cabinets. Exterior detail suggests the delicacy of the Federal style. End pilasters and an arched transom on the front are reminiscent of the

Boutin-Flettrich house at 1445 Pauger.

Pinson lived in the house on Esplanade and rented the one he built next door (plan book 61/39). There Pinson set a principal house and kitchen of almost identical sizes facing one another, both with side-street elevations. A large garden of parterres with flowers and fruit trees was paved with bricks "du Bassin." Near the house and kitchen were smaller service buildings, one of brick used for washing and ironing and servants' rooms, a wooden stable and coach house, and several small frame wood and coal houses. The result was a self-contained unit facing a central courtyard. All were insulated from the street by the front garden enclosed behind a high brick wall. His own house next door was linked by a high brick wall to its kitchen, the side of which was set along the banquette.

Both of Pinson's main houses had wallpapered (tapissiés) main rooms with marble mantels. His front yard was flagstoned, while the rear area "for the use of carriages and horses" was shelled. Pinson did not wait for the city to put in improvements, but built and paid for his own banquettes.

In 1836 Pinson sold both houses to René Salaün. In the act of sale before T. Seghers, March 8, he observed that "the depth of the lots is less than that stated in his acquisition" because he had ceded land to the city for the widening of Esplanade. He also mentioned that he had built the buildings on the properties, had constructed the sidewalks, and planned to "have the enjoyment of the house he occupies until next May 1 with no rent." Salaün paid $30,000 for the two properties.

In 1836 René Salaün had bought, in addition to the Pinson properties, the early creole cottage at St. Claude and Esplanade owned in this same square by Carlile Pollock since 1818. Salaün paid $18,000 for Pollock's property on May 18, 1836, before T. Seghers. At that time the property still included 210 feet on St. Claude, indicative that the Esplanade widening had not yet eliminated the Pollock house. Three months later, August 5, 1836, a Mazureau act specified that Salaün had sub-divided the property, orienting it toward Esplanade, and sold lots fronting thirty-six feet on Esplanade by only 140 feet depth on St. Claude. These he sold to Louis Schmidt and Frederick Furst with no mention of buildings. He apparently ceded the necessary footage to the city to widen Esplanade whereupon the Jean Pierre-Pollock house was demolished.

The following year, 1837, Rene Salaün went bankrupt. It was three years before all of his holdings were liquidated, but in the interim, surveyor Volquin was commissioned to make elevations of the two Esplanade Pinson complexes, which he did on February 11, 1837, and on March 2, 1838. The 1837 plan and elevation in plan book 61, folio 39, survives today to furnish the precious evidence of the second of Pinson's constructions, the one used as rental property. The other elevation, that of 1838, has not been found. Fortunately, however, the same house was drawn for an auction two decades later by Pietro Gualdi in 1855, plan book 65, folio 32.

Prior to this 1836 period, activity at the

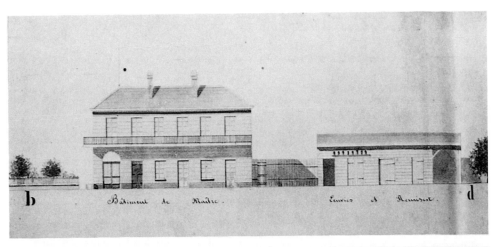

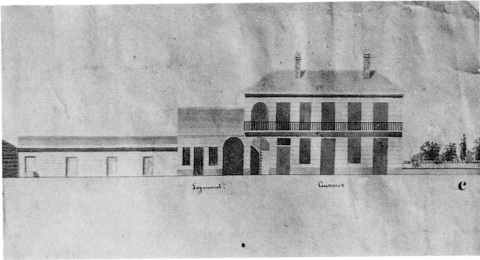

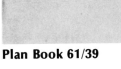

Plan Book 61/39

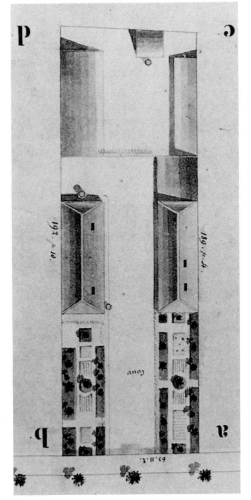

corner of Esplanade and Rampart had continued. Anne Zizine Dazema, free person of color, bought the Esplanade-Rampart corner property in 1813. In 1823, by an act of private signature she sold the property to "Antoine Delpuech, alias Cadet or Antoine Lavergne." The act stated, "I sell to Antoine Lavergne a house 30 feet long by 22 feet wide composed of two rooms and two cabinets, in Faubourg Tremé, 'masonnée entre poteaux' (masonry between posts)." The house was built on a lot 47 by 140 feet deep, with a 6 percent city ground rent because this land had once been part of the City Commons. The sale included a Negro slave named Crispin, "aged about 40 years, creole of St. Dominique, belonging to me for having purchased him from Mr. Lacroix, $1200 cash." The lot was described as the same that Anne Zizine Dazema had purchased from the syndic of the creditors of Pierre Philibert, situated on the Promenade Publique and rue d'Amour, at the entrance of Faubourg Marigny and Tremé, near the Fort St. Jean.

On July 26, 1830, Felix de Armas recorded that Antoine, alias Cadet Lavergne, made an agreement with the city to cede forty-one feet of his lot to the corporation "in order to regularize the extremity of Esplanade and Rampart at their junction." The sale was made for $500 and cancellation of the annual 6 percent ground rent owed on the lot. In 1846 Antoine Delpuech, alias Cadet Lavergne, died, and Antoine Delpuech, Jr., inherited the lot. Felix Pinson was the testamentary executor. The heir sold to François Castaing of Agen, France, on August 18, 1846 before A. Chiapella. Castaing retained this Rampart corner lot until his death in 1863. After the auction of his estate notary J. Cuvillier on February 27, 1864, described the house as "a lot 49 feet [American measure] on Esplanade by 106.6 feet deep with a one-story wooden house, having a large store of two rooms, privies; also on said lot a frame building in the yard, belonging to the party to whom the property is rented, who is ready to remove same if required, or rent from purchaser. The "locatoire" or tenant was Jean Philippe Simon, who operated a large grocery there, as seen in the archival drawing in plan book 76, folio 14. Hubert Rolling bought the corner property in 1871 and resold it the same year to the Ursuline nuns.

The Pinson houses lost by René Salaün to his creditors were sold to Nicholas Bertoli for $14,900 and then to Joaquin Viosca in 1840; L. T. Caire recorded the act, May 21. Pinson's home apparently survived into the 1890s after it was sold through two intervening family ownerships to the Ursuline nuns. The nuns retained it until 1892 when they sold the entire corner of Esplanade from Rampart extending 127 feet on Esplanade to the Sacred Heart brothers.

Pinson's building next to his home fared less happily. In 1847 it was sold by Joaquin Viosca to Charles Moore before F. Percy, November 13, 1848 for $7,500. Charles Moore sold it four days later to Gaston Bruslé, who resold within four years to Mrs. Glendy Burke, wife of a prominent attorney. Mrs. Burke sold, in 1854, to Felix Labatut, who resold in 1859 to Pierre O. Lauve. In 1865 Henry Clement Story, Benjamin Saxon Story, and Norman Story came into ownership. Henry Clement bought out his family, and by the time of his death in 1880, the Pinson rental house had long been replaced by an Italianate two-story brick house outlined on a plan of Arthur de Armas, July 20, 1880. This house was purchased by Antoine Lanata in 1885 and was listed in his 1894 estate. It too was demolished for St. Aloysius school.

Next to this house Antoine Lanata built, about 1885, a large mansard-roofed house in the Second Empire style, 1137 Esplanade, □ the contents of which were inventoried by James Fahey on March 20, 1894, after Lanata's death. This fine house was demolished in the early 1970s.

Two late-nineteenth-century houses that stood on the early creole cottage site (Pierre-Pollock houses) of St. Claude and Esplanade were numbered 1141 and 1145. These too were demolished along with the school building that filled the remaining lots.

The odd side of the 1100 block of Esplanade, once the site of some of the finest expressions of one of New Orleans' leading early nineteenth-century architects, awaits a new development. It is to be hoped that a new late-twentieth-century development will complement the neighborhood in scale and will advance architectural credibility by blending styles compatible with the centuries.

The twentieth-century fate of the 1100 block, even or upriver side, of the Esplanade has been equally grim. A corner gas station replaces a luxurious garden, and two townhouses of architectural consequence were demolished in the late 1960s. The first houses built here were hip-roof creole cottages, probably for Chalinette Duval shortly after her purchase of the land from Claude Tremé in 1810. Two years later, Chalinette's daughter, Mercelite Hazeur, had acquired the St. Claude and Julie property, 120 feet on St. Claude and 145 feet on Julie. Mademoiselle Hazeur, who lived in Paris, retained the property forty-five years until she sold it to Elie Choisey before O. de Armas, July 25, 1857.

The property included two, 30-foot hip-roof cottages facing St. Claude with two other hip-roof cottages on Julia (then Esplanade). One had a two-story kitchen of wood and the other a two-story brick kitchen. A 45-foot frontage along Esplanade and Rampart is shown on a T. Guyol plan of 1857 as having belonged to Felix Pinson, who by this time had moved from his home across rue St. Julie. Pinson previously had sold a narrow 30 by 180-foot strip of this land to the First Municipality for 4,000 piastres in 1836 so that Esplanade could be widened at this point. The act of this sale was recorded June 3, 1836, before notary Michel de Armas.

Avet-DeLaup House

The house that stood on a portion of the above land became number 1120 Esplanade; it survived a hundred years before being ripped away, the land to remain a weed-infested open space. It is possible that the above-mentioned Hazeur cottages on this property existed until they were purchased by J. F. Avet in 1868. At that time a garden and plot plan seen in plan book 26, folio 36, were drawn and placed with notary E. G. Gottschalk. There are strong indications that Avet engaged Jacques DePouilly, New Orleans' leading French architect, to design a new residence on the site. DePouilly had by this time built St. Augustine Church on Governor Nicholls, which is one of his few remaining buildings. The St. Louis cemeteries I and II retain more examples of this prolific architect's work than do the streets of New Orleans.

The Avet mansion, as it became known, was a jewel of French Baroque design and reminiscent of chateau architecture popular in the nineteenth-century Loire Valley. The front elevation was segmented into a series of horizontal and vertical panels perforated by two windows and a double recessed door. Four decorative bull's-eye relieved the regimentation and prepared the viewer for the slightly projecting denticulated cornice. Three dormers with graceful curving details ornamented the slate roof. Extraordinarily precise, paneled step gables were interrupted by a series of side elevation windows closed with exterior louvered shutters. A side cast-iron gallery in a lyre motif was supported by three tall iron columns. The Esplanade garden was enclosed behind a brick and cast-iron fence and, like the parterred garden of 1868, extended to Rampart Street.

A newspaper ad described the house, when auctioned in 1897, as a "charming one story with attic brick building, having parlor, library,

1120 (Demolished)

1120 (Courtesy Louis Sporl)

1120 (Courtesy Louis Sporl)

closed up hall, dining room, four rooms, gas throughout, cistern water works and garden." In the succession will and inventory of Mrs. Louise Athenais Malot Letellier, widow first of Joseph François Avet, then wife of Jean Dominique Bruno Amand, Baron Chaurand, the property was bequeathed to the Ursuline nuns, the Society of the Little Sisters of the Poor, and St. Mary's Catholic Orphan Boy's Asylum. The Ursuline nuns, represented by G. W. Nott, bought out the other two religious agencies for $6,200 and seem to have sold for a loss in 1912, when Gabrielle E. Roux, wife of Dr. Sidney Philip DeLaup purchased the land for $3,650.

The DeLaup family was an illustrious one, established in New Orleans in 1809, when François DeLaup arrived from Santo Domingo after the slave insurrection there. He founded the newspaper *L'Abeille* in 1827 and continued to publish it until his death in 1878. Gilbert and Kelly surveyed this establishment in 1942 when Mrs. Lulu Hodge, wife of Mark Curtis, bought it from Mrs. DeLaup. James O'Conner and Malroy E. Mayley were the recorded owners in 1967 when there was a loan registered to them of $38,500. The house was

demolished soon after, and New Orleans lost an incredibly fine example of interpretive European architecture.

The house immediately adjacent was a mid-nineteenth-century two-story side-hall townhouse with an elaborate, two-level, cast-iron gallery covering the banquette, as seen in plan book 85, folio 20, dated 1865. The façade was plaster, the sides weatherboard, the cornice similar to those of the 1860s. It too was demolished. Next to it and extending to the St. Claude corner, three once identical frame, three-bay townhouses stood in a row. Two remain at 1138 and 1140 Esplanade and represent the style of the 1870s with heavy decorated box cornices. The entries feature Greek Key architraves capped by dentiled cornices. The twin oval-light doors are original although partially covered as seen in the photograph. The houses, set at the banquette, have traditional second-level overhanging balconies and galleries. One has a balcony with turned balusters and piers. At 1138 (left) box columns with elongated neckings perform a more pronounced but similar structural function to the applied jigsaw brackets at 1140. These buildings are now threatened by the amount of vacant nearby land.

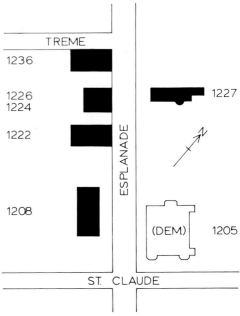

1200 Block

It was a simple task for Joseph Pilié, the surveyor, to project the prolongment of the Esplanade from Rampart to the Bayou in 1822, but it proved an extremely difficult task to execute. A tripartite municipal government, established in 1836 because of political and economic differences between the Creoles and Americans, did not aid in speedy solutions to mutual problems. There was a mayor with veto powers over each of the city councils, but the complexities of communications reduced the city government to limited control, and each municipality operated with utmost autonomy. A lack of funds was perhaps the only point of unity. The even side or upriver Esplanade from the river to Bayou St. John was included in the First Municipality, and the odd side or downriver Esplanade was placed in the Third Municipality.

It was necessary for several mayors, over a period of many years, to appoint a joint committee of improvements from the two municipalities to continue the Esplanade Avenue project. Instances of caustic relations appear in the committee reports. On December 21, 1836, Mr. Duvigneaud, committee spokesman, reported that:

The committee of improvements, charged with being aware of everything which could embellish and assure the prosperity of the Third Municipality . . . admits that the responsibility is great but agreeable; the committee is convinced that there is a poor layout of Esplanade Street into three narrow

1138 and 1140

walks, without intersections, and equally convinced that the planting of the trees is tasteless and unflattering to the houses which they shade, interfering with the sun and air which is so necessary during the winter in an area as humid as ours. Therefore the committee resolved that Esplanade Street, from Rampart Street to Bayou St. John, be of sixty feet in width, and the Banquettes be of twenty feet. Resolved, that a walk of laurel trees, said to have large leaves, be planted on each side of the street from Ramparts to Bayou St. John. Resolved, that it is the duty of the surveyor to procure by the end of next year the quantity of trees necessary to effect the planting mentioned above. Resolved that the secretary of this council is required to transmit to the council of the First Municipality an official copy of this report . . . for its sanction.

A few days later, on January 4, 1837, the mayor of New Orleans, Denis Prieur, responded to the members of the council of the Third Municipality with great vehemence:

Whatever it costs me to thwart some of the views that you express for the improvement of the section of the City that you are called to administer, I must fulfill . . . the duties imposed upon me by the law. . . . These thoughts are suggested to me by the feeling that I must return for your further consideration a series of resolutions passed in your last sitting, one of which tends to prescribe that the part of Esplanade Street that is included within the 3rd Municipality shall be *sixty feet wide*. The street in question being in the whole one hundred feet wide in the part that is opened and the axis of this street serving as boundary to the 1st and 3rd Municipalities as far as Bayou St. John; it ensues that the part included in the Section that you represent can be only fifty feet wide; or if you wish to give it sixty feet, this increase of ten feet in the width can be obtained only by cutting through all the properties located on the prolongation of the present line of the street.

And see what shall be the consequence of this latter operation, if it is done? The prolongation of Esplanade Street as far as Bayou St. John is not a new project; it is for over fourteen years that the City Council is working on it; and the faith of the public for a long time, that this project shall be realized, has induced owners of ground to gratuitously cede the passage of the street on their ground, and speculators to purchase lots facing the contemplated prolongations and we have even seen several persons build on the line already known of this prolongation, commodious and elegant continuing the present line of the Esplanade, this new street, scarcely cut through, would be embellished, with several houses which would speed the erection of other buildings and give rise to speculations, every one favorable to the development of this district. Whereas if you widen the street ten feet more, these same houses must be destroyed, and then not only would you greatly increase the expenses occasioned by the execution of

1208

the project that is occupying you, but you shall have the unpleasantness of having a long deserted avenue on which there would remain only the ruins of the buildings across which you have opened it. These reasons which I request you to ponder upon, appear to me to sufficiently justify the return of the resolution in question, and I am pleased to believe that you will recognize that they are in the interest of the 3rd Municipality and to be sure in the interest of the contemplated improvement.

Mayor Prieur expressed a genuine concern and gave vent to actual social and economic conditions, but in reality he completely misunderstood the intent of the council. Therefore, they persisted in their resolutions, overriding his veto with the following explanation: The council did not intend to widen the Esplanade, but only make the street sixty feet instead of eighty feet, and reserved the center for the trees thereby redistributing the existing space.

It is evident that these resolutions were not placed into immediate effect, for legal notification through newspaper advertisements was necessary, as were negotiations with the landowners through which these improvements would be made. In the *Louisiana Courier* of January 27, 1837, the following advertisement was placed:

Agreeably to the foregoing resolution, and by virtue of the first and second sections of the act approved the 3d April, 1832, concerning the opening and improvement of the streets and public places in the city of New Orleans, Notice is hereby given, that it is the intention of the Council of the 3d Municipality to have Esplanade street extended in a straight line from Rampart street to the Bayou St. John, as soon as the formalities presented by the said act should have been duly attended to; this projected prolongation of Esplanade street to be effected across the properties hereafter described: In suburb Tremé across the properties belonging to J. Mager; F. Boisdoré f.c.m.; Jh Dolliol, f.c.m; E. Plauché; Marie Louise Dauphin, f.c.w.

Jean Mager House

Prior to the Tremé plantation sale to the city, Tremé and his wife sold many lots immediately around the plantation house on Bayou Road. These diverse segments along St. Julie were reassembled by Jean Mager in 1814 with the exception of the Boisdoré and Dolliole strip, which would today apply to numbers 1244 through 1262. Mager purchased from Pierre Barran, a native New Orleanian and leading merchant, and the landholders to whom Barran had sold on January 12, 1801, before notary Broutin. Among these were Charles Gayarré, Sr., father of the noted New Orleans historian, and also Richard O. Pritchard, a

prominent real estate investor who owned property on Esplanade at the site of 932. Mager, a commission merchant, was also a land speculator and owned at the time of his death many properties, previously discussed, among which were on Decatur and Esplanade.

In 1834 the city of New Orleans was negotiating with him for purchase of his property to widen St. Julie into an extension of Esplanade, a projection which would bisect his own house and garden. The council proposed to purchase only that portion of the house and gardens actually needed for the widening of Esplanade. Indignant, Mager replied in a letter to the city council dated July 24, 1835:

In the council meeting of July 17, it was inferred that I was opposed to the prolongment of Esplanade across my property. Permit me to correct his error. I have indeed not offered any resistance since this road was represented to me as indispensable to the public good. I had consistently reported that this property cost me a considerable sum and that it would be painful to me to abandon my residence which I built and embellished in the hope of always occupying. But that as for its disposition, this property was not divisible. I was not able to sell it except as a totality and not in part, since the proposal acts to cut a third of my house and the most important and productive part of my gardens. The usefulness and agreeability of this residence would be destroyed if this portion were removed for Esplanade, and the residence would have to be abandoned. The city had previously requested to prolong Quartier [Barracks] Street across my property on the left; today it asks the passage of Esplanade Street at right, then projected the continuation of Tremé across, until finally there will soon be nothing left but irregular pieces, narrow and isolated. After these considerations, observe that this property cannot be cut without causing its ruin, I then propose to the city to sell it entirely, with the exception of the plants, for the sum of $35,000.

Considering that Claude Tremé had sold a vast amount of land for $40,000, it is evident that Mager's sale was a profitable one for him. Surveyor Bourgerol drew a plan for the city in December of 1836, and the city purchased the total Mager property on February 22, 1838, before notary de Armas. The sale included the site of the 1400 block of Treme Street, not yet cut through. Necessary land sections were used for the widening of Esplanade, and on January 15 of the following year, surveyor A. Bourgerol divided the remainder of Mager's former property into lots for sale at auction. The auction was held on February 2, 1839, and "the house formerly belonging to Jean Mager" with five lots was sold to Donatien Augustin.

Two years previously, Donatien Augustin had married seventeen-year-old Eliza Melassis

Hermogen LaBranche of St. Charles Parish, whose mother was a Trepagnier. Eliza came into the marriage well dowried, bringing $2,000 in trousseau and jewels, three female slaves, and $20,000 in cash. Augustin, a native of Port-au-Prince, Santo Domingo, was of no mean circumstances. He owned a $6,000 house on Conti between Burgundy and Rampart, $5,000 in notes and movables, two slaves, and nine hundred acres in Avoyelles Parish. They bought the Mager house and gardens for a family home. Hidden beneath layers of nineteenth-century additions at 1208 Esplanade □ are the original Mager foundations of 1815. Although documentary proof does not exist, evidence strongly suggests that the Augustins rebuilt the Mager house in the style of the 1840s. They retained it for seventy-eight years. It was extensively remodeled in the style of the succeeding generations, when Victorian alterations and a large Italianate wing and front "tower" were added, obscuring the French-style roof lines. The cast-iron gallery was probably added during the 1850s. Today the early house could easily be overlooked, but documentary research spurred close observation of the high hip-roof, and raised basement with its lowered French arches, old casement doors, and fireplace in the basement. The present front entrance is in the style of the 1840s, perhaps dating from the Donatien Augustin remodeling.

Occupying the side garden of this Mager-Augustin house at 1212–14 □ is an early twentieth-century two-story frame double. Its cornice is decorated with a bow-and-garland frieze; modest brackets support its parapet. An iron fence with the maker's mark *Ironworks* joins it to the one surrounding the former Mager house. The first level is unattractively filled in, but the house, with paint and minor changes, could be greatly improved.

Ducros-Crozat House

Next to 1214, the property now numbered 1222 was also part of the original Jean Mager estate. This property, to the corner of Treme, was sold in the succession of Martin Broderick in 1855, and R. J. Ker recorded it on April 7. At that time, the site of 1222 Esplanade contained an old shed which was about eleven feet wide and extended the depth of the lot. Gustave Ducros purchased the present property from Broderick along with an adjacent bare lot for $1,425 and had the present house built soon after 1855. Two years later, Ducros sold to Mrs. Celine Douce Beverly, and Mrs. Beverly resold in 1859 to the Washington Henry McLean family before F. Percy, on January 21. The complex remained in the McLean family fifty-nine years,

1222

after which it was sold to George Bernard Crozat, whose family owns it today.

The simple Classic-style frame townhouse at 1222 □ reflects the continued use of the floor plan and decoration popularized twenty years earlier. The shape of the entire house is boxlike with an almost square façade, and the three openings are widely spaced. As with its counterparts at 1236 and 1240, the decorative effect is achieved by the use of a cast-iron balcony and canopy. The recessed doorway has sidelights and transoms behind a Greek Key entrance. Moldings and cornice treatment are absent.

At the same time that Ducros built this townhouse, he also built a detached kitchen the side of which bordered on Esplanade. This is now a separate dwelling numbered 1224. □ This kitchen shares a common wall with 1226, which was also a kitchen, built in 1848 for the building on the other side, 1236. They were located beside, rather than behind, the main buildings. Such structures housed not only the kitchens, but storerooms or pantries, ironing rooms and bedrooms for domestic help and for

the older boys of the family. The central wall these two dependencies share has a fire extension visible at the roof ridge and is pierced by chimneys serving back-to-back fireplaces. Partial enclosures of the upper galleries and new doors and walls alter the original appearance of the pair.

Broderick House

A house that appears to have always been a two-story residence but was constructed as a store-house is on the corner of this block. Like 1222 Esplanade, 1236 was part of the original Mager estate that Martin Broderick bought from the city before J. Cuvillier, August 4, 1848. On the bare lot, Broderick built this structure as a Classic-style store-house with its entrance on Treme Street just prior to 1850. An archival drawing (46/2) for the Broderick succession sale shows this building as it appeared in 1855. The exterior was of exposed unpainted brick and had four full-length, shuttered openings across the Esplanade Street front. There was a simple dentiled cornice rather than the present cast-iron canopy, but the balcony and railing are original. The

ground floor was one large room used as a commercial space with five exterior openings on the Treme Street side, the rearmost being a Classic-style entry, having a transom with octagon lights.

The building was probably converted to full residential use soon after the 1855 sale, perhaps by purchaser Albin Soulié. By 1879 Auguste Graugnard sold to Claude Maurin "a house composed of rez-de-chaussée and premier étage" before notary J. Fahey who was also an Esplanade resident at 1415. There was no mention of a store; the building was "#176 Esplanade." Claude Maurin sold to Aristide Delaville in 1880. Subsequent owners were Henri Gelpi, George Villeré, and Dr. Joseph Numa Charbonnet, whose residence was at 832 Esplanade. Few original interior walls and moldings remain, but there are remnants of the old rear stairhall, and recent renovation by H. Koppel and J. Musser has stabilized the building.

The land between Treme and Plauché (Marais) streets continued to be held by François Boisdoré and Joseph Dolliole, original purchasers from Claude Tremé around 1800, until as late as 1841, when they were still negotiating with the city for the municipal right-of-way of Esplanade. Where other property owners along this block had given the required land in return for banquettes, these two free men of color insisted on full compensation. Undoubtedly the land held simple creole cottages, probably rental units. Dolliole was a builder, and his family had developed many Faubourg Treme and Marigny properties. By January of 1841, the joint First and Third Municipality committee delivered the following statement:

Esplanade Street is opened from the Levee up to Mrs. Castanedo's property on the Bayou Road with the exception of the space between Plauché and Tremé Streets, where the said street is intercepted by the properties of Dolliole and Boisdoré. The opening of this street through its other parts was affected at great expense which would remain without advantageous results if these properties were permitted to remain.

Therefore, your committee, imbued with the necessity of removing the obstacles which up to this time have prevented the complete opening of this street, has come to an arrangement with the owners Dolliole and Boisdoré and submits the arrangement made with them, to pay them for the ground needed for the opening of this street at the rate of twenty-five cents a foot, payable at six, twelve, and eighteen months. 10,833 feet of ground is necessary. The portion within the First Municipality is of about 8242 feet, and in the Third, 2591 feet; which brings the quota of each of the two municipalities to about

1236

Plan Book 46/2

$2,060.50 for the First Municipality and about $647.75 for the Third Municipality. . . . (signed) M. Cruzat, Chairman of the Committee of the First Municipality, and François Coquet, Chairman of the Committee of the Third Municipality.

The city took eighteen months to pay and a considerable length of time to survey the land before the last connective link from the Esplanade to Johnson Street could be completed.

Tiblier-Aubert House

Continuing on the even side at the corner of Treme and Esplanade is number 1240, occupying the last edge of the property which Mager sold to the city. This plastered brick American townhouse was the first built on the land and was designed in the Greek Revival style. Alexander Hypolite Sampson drew the plans, according to a building contract filed with notary Amedée Ducatel, August 31, 1854, and constructed the house for owner Claude Tiblier. The three-bay house measures twenty-eight by fifty-three feet. It has a recessed entrance, Greek Key architrave, and its original door. Short double-hung windows beside the entrance have persiennes, or louvered shutters, as stipulated in the contract. At the second level a balcony with cast-iron railing serves full-length double-hung windows and is shaded by a handsome canopy of cast iron supported by a series of double iron brackets. Cap-molded lintels and a simple molded cornice with dentils at the roofline keynote the restrained elegance of the building, which is a handsome contrast to the row of two-level, galleried frame houses sharing the block.

Inside, double parlors flanking the hall were originally separated by sliding doors on a track called *portes à coulisses*. Greek Key exterior door surrounds remain. The ceiling cornices project by one foot, and the original center rosettes, or ceiling medallions, are three feet in diameter. They were "of a $15.00 value" when installed, and the smaller two-foot rosette in the "vestibule" was of "a ten dollar value." The front door was originally "painted in imitation," and the balcony iron-rail pattern was not specifically designated but was to be "modèle de la forte" to be chosen by the owner. The house was once illuminated by a whale oil system, the pump for which is still in the attic. Three detached buildings originally served the main building; these have been connected into a rear wing.

In 1865 the house was purchased by Leon Godchaux, who may have executed the changes. The full impact of this sophisticated residence is appreciated when viewed from the Treme Street side. The dentiled cornice returns around the corner, the full depth of the main

1240

1240

house. Beyond a cast-iron fence set on a very high broad base is the handsome two-story service wing extending from the Marais Street side of the property. This wing has cast-iron galleries of grape motif, which match those of the rear gallery of the main house. The wing is in fact larger than the main building, and it houses the dining room, which is ornamented by a black slate mantel with iron centerpiece. The rooms beyond, originally the "rooms for domestics," contain metal mantels.

Boisdoré-Dolliole Habitations

When Boisdoré and Dolliole finally sold, François Escoffier bought their land to the corner of Plauché (Marais). Adolphe Pluche purchased a lot 50 feet wide by 204 feet deep from Escoffier on July 27, 1846, before J. Agaisse and built the next house at 1244 the following year. When the complex of the main house, outbuildings, and enormous garden-orchard was complete, Pluche had them surveyed and illustrated for auction sale by Eugene Surgi. Surgi's 1848 drawings in plan book 65A, folio 63, depict the house as it appeared before its restyling in the 1870 .

A hip-roof originally extended above a double-level gallery supported by box columns rising the full height of the front. The gallery extended across the entire front and down both sides of the house, a circumstance that reduced the available interior space. The gallery served as a corridor to reach the curving stairway situated in a partially enclosed loggia. The house had no hall. There were double parlors below, bedrooms above, and one cabinet at each level, a floor plan reflecting creole usage. The kitchen and a service building were detached.

Pierre Paul Jules Tuyes purchased the house from Pluche at the auction sale for $6,000 and held it only four years before he sold, in 1852, to Belle Elizabeth Aubert, a free woman of color. Fifteen years later, Belle Aubert died, leaving a notarized will which bequeathed the house and furnishings to her grandson, William LaRue. The inventory of her succession taken before notary Joseph Cohn on February 18, 1867, described the house as "#184 Esplanade with furnishings in front parlor, back parlor, front [bed] room, second [bed] room, hall, pantry, kitchen . . . gold watch, thirty oz., old silverware, etc." The grandson, William LaRue, sold the house in 1870 to Mrs. I. D. Maignan, who was probably responsible for altering the house to its present late Classic style. □

The principal change was a deemphasis of the high hip-roof by the superimposition of a parapet, wide entablature with a projecting cornice, dentils, and scroll brackets. The two-

1252

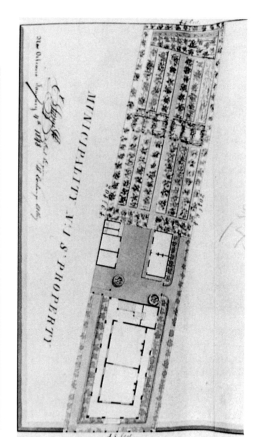

Plan Book 65A/63

1244

1252

first parlor and fluted pilaster ones in the second parlor. The second-level interior has been renovated in a contemporary style. The design is one of "façade architecture," consisting of a double-level gallery appended to a rectangular or box house. A doorway with splayed footings and a cresting with anthemion motifs in the Greek Revival style adds sophistication to the plastered façade of the frame house. The deep, well-landscaped lot extends in the rear to Barracks Street.

The property at 1260 Esplanade □ at the corner of Marais, which consists of four lots, was owned after François Boisdoré's 1844 sale by a succession of free men of color. A building stood on the lot facing Barracks during Boisdoré's ownership, prior to the widening of Esplanade. Cesaire Olivier acquired the property by 1855, when he bought his partner E. A. Desandre's shares at a sheriff's sale. Olivier sold within two weeks the property facing Barracks to Achille Tardie; it extended to Esplanade. The price for the larger area was $4,700 and included Boisdoré's early cottages. When Tardie sold this complex to Valerien Chopin in 1860 at auction before C. E. Forstall for $8,000, there was on "four lots (from) Barracks to Esplanade . . . fronting on Barracks . . . a large frame building covered with slates."

The present late Classic-style, double-galleried townhouse was built on the lot facing Esplanade sometime in the 1860s. Valerien Chopin sold four lots, with this or the earlier building, to Alfred Lemore for $6,500 on February 23, 1866, before F. Grima. Within one year, Lemore sold the property to Emile Legendre for $8,500. The Legendre family kept the property from 1867 to 1901. They probably built the house which the widow Anais Armant Legendre sold together with the four lots to Dr. A. P. Rocquet for $7,500 in 1901.

Tower-of-the-wind columns, cornice with brackets and dentils, the parapet, and scored or rusticated wood façade are reminders of architectural fashions of the late 1860s. Cast-iron canopies, a side bay, and the extended service wing are impressive features. The house remains basically intact including mantels and chandeliers. It is presently undergoing renovation by architect Ronald Katz.

Across the avenue on the downriver side, the extra long 1200 block of Esplanade remained the property of Jean Mager until his death in 1848. His only heir was a widowed sister, Agathe Alexandrine Mager Collard, who resided in Paris. The landowners who purchased from this estate within these two blocks constructed most of the 1850 and 1860 houses that survive today.

story box columns were replaced with superimposed single-level ones, and the open gallery was partially enclosed. An octagonal bay was added, as was a side entrance. Through successive generations of renovation, the diamond-pattern wood gallery railing has remained. The original two-bay façade, as indicated in the drawing, had formerly been plastered; the present narrow weatherboard is a twentieth-century change. The original wood fence design, with pickets on a paneled base and enclosed with piers, was exchanged for a simple iron fence with decorative adjunctive ornaments.

Number 1252 Esplanade □ is a house built in the late 1850s on the property which François Boisdoré sold, in 1844, at a sheriff's sale to François Escoffier as a result of a suit between Boisdoré and Eulalie Mandeville. François Escoffier sold this lot to Myrtille Courcelle in 1849. Eight years later William La Rue bought it from Courcelle for $4,200 indicating property improvement and the existence of this house. La Rue sold, in 1869, for $9,500 to Louis Cabiro; when Cabiro sold it thirty years later to St. Anna's Chapel, the house was valued at $6,500. It remained the property of the Episcopal church until recently purchased by architect Ronald Katz.

This double-galleried American townhouse has a relatively simple decoration, with a front entrance modeled on the Greek Temple of Erectheum. Greek Key architraves are used throughout the interior, cornices are molded coves, and ceiling medallions are foliated. There are black marble pilaster mantels in the

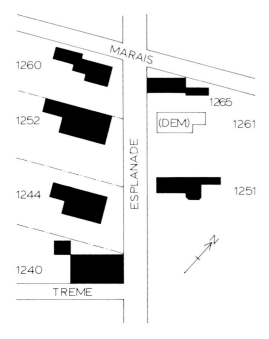

Wright-Slocomb House

A bare lot at the corner of Esplanade and St. Claude interrupts the street symmetry. Here, just six years ago, at 1205, stood one of the city's most monumental and sophisticated residences, known as the Wright-Slocomb house. Built in 1856 in the grand manner of Italian Renaissance architecture, it occupied four lots at the fashionable intersection from which it was designed to be viewed from all sides. Its original owner was Hamilton Mercer Wright, an enterprising cotton factor of the firm Wright, Allen, and Company, and it was built at a cost of $90,000, making it one of the most expensive nineteenth-century homes in the city.

This two-level plastered brick mansion, like the Florence A. Luling house at Esplanade and Leda by James Gallier, Jr., was designed with emphasis on a surface sculptural effect. Heavy exterior wall rustication alternated with three projections of smooth plaster. The tripartite window openings had paired arches and interior louvered blinds. All upper-level windows included triangular pediments supported by scroll brackets. The entrance was a one-story Corinthian portico having paired fluted columns supporting a balustraded balcony. Two polygonal bays flanked an arcaded portico on the St. Claude elevation. The roofline was defined by a Baroque cornice, supported by multiple brackets and having a central pediment over both entrances. Additional moldings form stringcourses between the stories, outlining recessed panels at the attic level and at the chimneys.

Hamilton Mercer Wright, for whom the house was constructed, remained a British citizen and was forced to flee to London with his family during the Union occupation of New Orleans. An agent was charged with the management of his property, and a sheriff's sale was required in 1866. Henry Hope Stanley, who lived on Carondelet Street and later Annunciation Square at the corner of Orange and Pecaniers (Chippewa), bought the magnificent deserted residence. Stanley was the adoptive father of the English boy John Rowlands who became the renowned African explorer, Sir Henry Morton Stanley. Stanley sold the house in 1869 for $45,000 to Mr. and Mrs. Cuthbert

1205 (Demolished)

H. Slocomb; the act was passed by notary P. C. Cuvellier on February 25, at which time it was described: "Four lots adjoin and are now one piece . . . with elegant two story brick mansion, garden, outhouses." Cuthbert Slocomb was a successful American attorney who continued a hardware business founded by his father. Four years later in an act deposited in the office of T. Guyol, February 14, 1873, the widow of C. H. Slocomb registered the sale of the house and three lots to her mother-in-law, widow of Samuel B. Slocomb, and kept one for herself.

By 1886 Joseph Potts Horner had acquired the house, and his wife and six children inherited it when he died in 1899, according to an act by notary Charles T. Soniat. These heirs sold immediately for $18,000 through an auction sale to Placide Louis Chapelle, archbishop of New Orleans. Bishop Chapelle, one year before his death from yellow fever in 1904, sold the property to the Archdiocese of New Orleans for the purchase price. The house was rented to several New Orleans families including the Pierre Verloin De Gruys, according to legend. It was the residence for a religious order, and although designated for many years as an official church residence, the authorities ordered its demolition in 1970. A historic house of such excellent architectural detail and monumental scale should have been recognized by its ecclesiastical owners as a valuable asset to the public. As guardians of tradition and promoters of education, churches and universities should lead the community in efforts that preserve and profitably reuse the past.

Still standing is a much simpler but characteristic mid-nineteenth-century Esplanade-style residence at 1227 Esplanade. ☐ The frame two-and-one-half-story house had a double-level gallery and side-hall, double-parlor floor plan. The upper gallery has been filled in with a makeshift twentieth-century device that annihilates architectural integrity. This too is typical of the fate of many avenue homes. Nevertheless, this galleried townhouse, built for the G. W. Houghtons soon after they acquired the lots in 1852, continues to have an imposing iron fence, unusual double-level iron side galleries, and well-proportioned, fluted Ionic columns on the front lower level; the enclosed upper section probably was enhanced with Corinthian columns. The bare lots, which

emanated from Jean Mager, were purchased by Jean Crusiers from the widow Collard succession in 1851 and sold immediately on December 29, 1852, to Madame M. A. V. Bordugat, wife of G. W. Houghton, before notary H. B. Cenas.

The Houghtons had been recently married, as indicated by their marriage contract, dated February 18, 1852, and they had the galleried Classic-style frame house built on the lots. By 1858 the Houghtons sold the house with six lots to Henry Rathbone for $13,000 before Theodore Guyol on June 26. Rathbone, a bank president, and his family occupied the house for ten years when the property was valued for the purpose of the family meeting, at $18,000. The subsequent owners, the Lalande family, occupied the house for fifty years until they sold in 1923 to Joseph Schwartz. In 1942 a Mr. Cortinas mortgaged the house through Fidelity Homestead for $6,000.

Interrupting the luxurious grandeur evinced by the Esplanade homes is the pseudo-redwood mansard apartment building at 1229. ☐ No attempt to understand the street architectural development is apparent. When tasteless expediencies invade a neighborhood they are worse than the bare, unproductive lots which also negatively punctuate the street scene.

Continuing down the Esplanade at 1251, also Mager land until 1848, there remains a Classic-style townhouse with galleries built by Jules LeBlanc in 1850 and sold by his widow Felicité Labutut in 1862. The entire façade is of rusticated wood while the lower side elevations are brick. The Ionic columns below and the Corinthian above gracefully support the denticulated, bracketed cornice and parapet. The house was described in the 1862 sale as "a two-story house, with kitchen and service rooms, having a first story built of brick and upper story of frame." Gas fixtures were specified in the main house, and it was sold then for $7,005. The house was twice auctioned, once in 1865 and again in 1868; it was then described as a "jolie maison haute" and identified as number 183. The property contained a front parterred garden with fruit trees, a paved court, waterworks, and a stable. The fruit trees are gone, but four crape myrtles shade this small area behind a spiked iron fence which has a tendril ironwork gate similar to that in

front of 1227. The Charles Schmidt family sold the house in 1905, and the Eugene May family continued ownership until 1943.

Castera House (demolished)

It took Louis Castera eleven years, from 1848 to 1859, to assemble his lots from the Mager-Collard heirs. The house at 1261 Esplanade ☐ was built for Castera on the first of the lots purchased on September 15 and March 16, 1848, before A. Mazureau. The fine two-story, double-level galleried townhouse was documented by a building contract between Castera and the builder, James Stephenson, on February 6, 1849, before notary A. Mazureau, and was estimated to cost $4,800.

The contract indicates that the house plans were designed by a professional and used by Stephenson. Unfortunately, neither architect nor plans have been discovered. The specifications contain small drawings illustrating doors, moldings, fillets. Many of the descriptions enumerated such as those pertaining to baseboard and architraves, continued in use until the 1880s and would be suitable for most nineteenth-century houses. This house, 1261, one of the earlier Greek Revival houses along Esplanade, was demolished in 1973 while this book was in the research stage. Residents and preservationists failed in their efforts to convince the Episcopal Church not to destroy it. One wonders what could replace it for the $50,000 remodeling estimate they received. The lot remains vacant.

The house at 1265 Esplanade ☐ was built for Aribert Desjardin, who purchased the land in 1848 from Agathe Mager Collard. Mager had purchased this lot from Charles Etienne Gayarré, Sr., father of the historian, in 1826 in an act before H. Lavergne, June 19. Gayarré had purchased from Pierre Barran, who had bought from Claude Tremé. In 1857 Desjardin sold the house to Aristide Bienvenu. A subsequent owner was J. H. Augustin, who held the property from 1887 to 1917. Like several others in the 1200 block, this two-story Classic-style frame house with side hall was built in the late 1840s. It has a simple two-level gallery supported by molded box columns. Its hip-roof in later years was obscured by a heavy entablature and parapet. The cast-iron railing and paneled piers at the second level were undoubtedly replacements.

1251

1300 Block

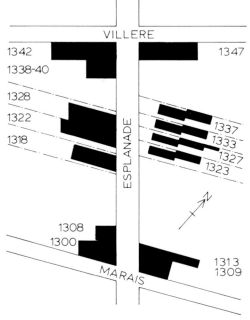

Having acquired the right of way to the limits of the Plauché habitation by 1838, the city had A. Bourgerol make a plan showing the subdivision of the next three small habitations in 1836. Tremé had sold one arpent along Bayou Road by six arpents on the right side to Cristobal de Armas, a lieutenant in the infantry, by act before notary Pierre Pedesclaux on September 25, 1798. Michel Reynolds acquired de Armas' strip fronting Chemin de Bayou through marriage to Catherine Couperthwaite. He sold it in 1811 to Pierre Amboise Cuvillier, an attorney, who the following year sold it to Michel Zeringue for 3,800 piastres. Zeringue, a builder and investor and resident of the Chapitoulas, in turn disposed of the property to J. L. Isnard, April 28, 1813, before Pierre Pedesclaux. The property was then described as follows:

a lot of ground on the bayou St. John Road, on the right while leaving the city, together with the buildings and other constructions which are upon it; having one hundred-eighty feet on the said road by about two and a half arpents in depth, such that is bound by the barrier that actually exists beyond the fish pond, bound on one side by Mr. Hulin and the other by Louis Dolhiole [Dolliole], and behind by Sieur Nicolas Jean Pierre; another lot of ground on the said Bayou St. John Road, on the same side as the first, together with the buildings which are upon it, having thirteen feet in front by about two hundred-fifty in depth, bound on one side by Agathe Montreuil and the other by Sieur P. A. Cuvillier.

Isnard died, and his widow Marie Ann Euphrosine Marchand became the wife of J. B. Plauché. Madame Plauché, who lived on Bayou Road in the house probably built for Michel Zeringue, purchased a second piece of property on April 13, 1816, from François Balthazar Languille, which her husband Isnard

Plan Book 21/25

had previously owned. It was described in the act of sale before C. de Armas partially as above, yet included the names of many surrounding neighbors, "another piece to rear of this one one-hundred-seventy-nine feet by seven-hundred-eleven feet deep . . . bounded by property of Monsieur Bernard Marigny and bounded on the St. Claude Street side by properties of Mr. Lavergne [later this was Jean Mager's property], Jacques Martin, Prosper Foy [later property of the widow Guerlain] and Thérèse Street [later the Esplanade]."

Most of the Plauché plantation at this corner was absorbed into the continuation of Marais Street. When A. Bourgerol made his survey in 1836 for the bisection of Esplanade, the 1300 block immediately above the Plauché habitation was to cross the properties of widow Dupuy, Dauphin, and a partnership holding of J. Saul and S. Jaudon, all of which emanated from Cristobal de Armas' purchase from Claude Treme in 1800. These properties are illustrated on the Zimpel map of 1834, and the Dupuy land acquired from Mr. Hulin, a real estate speculator, was so noted on the Pilié map of 1822. Pilié attributed the Dauphin property to a free woman of color, Françoise Ducoudreaux, and the Saul and Jaudon quarter-arpent stretch to Philip Pijeaux. Pijeaux had been active in the area since 1807, according to an act before notary P. Pedesclaux, on July 6.

A survey of the Dauphin property by L. Bringier dated 1843 in plan book 98, folio 34, shows that the Dauphin house survived the extension of Esplanade but would be removed when Villere street was extended. A small portion of the Plauché plantation included the upriver corner of the Esplanade and Marais, which when it was developed in the early

1840s contained a row of creole cottages. One of these occupied the site of the Marais corner where a late Victorian store-house now stands at 1302. The L. Surgi archival drawing dated May 11, 1844, in plan book 21, folio 25, of the floor plans and elevations of these four creole cottages reveals that the corner property narrowed to twenty-three feet on the back boundary and necessitated a slender two-story kitchen with an attached stable rather than a square four-apartment service building as shown behind the other three cottages.

Passebon Row

The 1843 owners of this creole cottage row were Pierre Passebon, Henry Legendre, and Carl Kohn. They shared the costs of land and construction according to the terms of a private signature agreement executed in December, 1843. Each house was to be sold as soon as completed; exclusive of lot expense the building costs were projected at about $800 each. The investors realized an average sale price of $2,100 each including land in an 1844 auction. Passebon owned other properties which he developed in Faubourg Tremé, whereas Carl Kohn was a developer in the Lower Garden District.

Number 1308 Esplanade, □ the only remaining creole cottage of the four, was sold by its developers upon its completion to Athalie Drouillard, free woman of color, and shortly thereafter resold to the Phillips family where it remained until 1881. Later it was owned by the De George family, and early in the twentieth century it became one of several Esplanade investment properties of G. W. Nott. One of the demolished cottages was the home of Eugenie Glesseau, free woman of color, and her nine children fathered by Jean Baptiste Azereto,

whose family history is told in the pages of *New Orleans Architecture, Volume IV: The Creole Faubourgs* in an essay entitled "Free Men of Color" (see also plan book 21, folio 25, for elevation and floor plan). The Azereto children occupied the fourth of the cottages until the mid-1860s.

Number 1318 Esplanade is a late Classic-style house which replaces the fourth creole cottage of the Passebon Row. Francisco Cheti, who was agent for entrepreneur Jean Baptiste Azereto, presented the early house to Eugenie Glesseau by intervivos donation before F. Percy, July 27, 1844. The children kept the cottage until 1869 when Clothilde Azereto sold it to A. P. Archinard for $3,300. It is difficult to determine the actual building date of the present house at 1318 since Archinard sold the property at a loss for $3,000 to Joachim Parra in 1872 before A. Ducatel on May 4. Ten years later Parra sold it to Robert Madison Flaute for $3,850.

The simplicity of the pilastered entrance, box columns, and bracketed cornice would suggest that Archinard built the house around 1869; it is presently remodeled into apartments. A ceiling medallion of floral pattern and a simple marble mantel in the front fireplace remain. These and the screen between parlors recall the Esplanade style. A wood mantel in the second parlor is fashioned in the style of the more expensive marble one in the front parlor.

The next house at 1322 Esplanade was purchased from Passebon by Mrs. H. Delery Labarre in 1845 and recorded by F. Percy, April 11; Domingo Bachino then acquired the property in 1855 from the Delery succession and retained the property until 1884. The present house could have been built by Emile Vergnes, whose wife acquired the property in

1885. Although dating from the late Victorian period, the house continues the American townhouse floor plan with certain modest Italianate decorative devices on the traditional box-columned façade. The hip-roof is not hidden by a projecting cornice, but there is a box panel frieze articulated with paired brackets. Quoins and drop siding reflect the 1880s building date. The piers supporting the first-level box columns are twentieth-century replacements.

Number 1328 Esplanade dates from the early 1870s, and the façade exemplifies a local variation of the Italianate style. Wooden segmental arches between the box columns have champfered edges. Modillions rather than dentils add interest between the jigsaw brackets on the cornice beneath a hip-roof. Interior decoration continued the Esplanade Ridge tradition. Although no original fireplaces remain, there are two ceiling medallions and a plaster screen between parlors that incorporate female heads and floral motifs alternating with Greek designs. The wide opening between parlor and dining room is a trabiated, or simple Greek Key, design with segmental openings.

The lot on which 1328 stands was purchased from Claude Tremé in 1902 by François Roche Blave, "a resident of Gentilly, actually in this city, parish of St. Louis." Roche Blave sold to F. A. A. Hulin, whose widow sold to widow Asemia Doricourt Genois. The land faced Bayou Road and ran through to the property of the widow Guerlain or the future Col-

umbus Street; Zimpel records this plantation as that belonging to "Wdw. Dupuy." Asemia Doricourt, after marrying S. Dupuy, donated the property in 1854 to her daughter Blanche Dupuy, wife of D. Labédoyère Kernion, whose heirs sold in 1880 to Alphonse Labarthe "with a frame house, #202 Esplanade, having four rooms and a frame kitchen of three rooms." This was obviously a creole cottage. The present house was probably built for Labarthe, who mortgaged the property in 1883 "together with a two-story frame dwelling house #202." in 1883 as described that year by C. G. Andry, August 9. In 1934 the house was purchased from the Harding Realty Company by the administrators of the will of Thomy Lafon.

Healy-Howard House

The brick creole cottage at 1338–40 Esplanade stands on the nineteenth-century Dauphin habitation property and occupies a lot formerly numbered 11 in notarial plan book 98, folio 34. John Healy bought this still bare lot for $800 in 1850 from Leopole Dearuth at a sheriff's sale. Healy entered into a contract with John McVittie, builder, on April 18, 1852, to erect a double house according to plans of architect Henry Howard and with Howard's supervision of the construction. The price to be paid McVittie was $3,000 according to notary A. A. Baudouin.

The contract stipulated that the bricks were to be painted red, with the joints penciled in white. The Greek Key façade door casings

1318, 1322, 1328

1338–40

were referred to as "six and one-half inch band moulded architraves." All other frames had four-inch casings. The raised brick fire extensions along the gable sides were pierced by chimneys. Paneled doors are original, although steps and railing are new and incorrect.

Interior mantels, which cost $10 each, were wood and of the plain pilaster design. Those in the parlor were to be painted in imitation of marble, while others were to be painted black and varnished, as specified in the building contract. Biloxi firebricks lined the hearths. Floors were yellow pine with edges "secret nailed." The baseboards, or plinths, were one foot high and had a band of molding in the parlor and bedrooms. In the finished attic or half story, and in the detached kitchen, these beaded "skirtings" were eight inches high. The rear gallery was supported by box columns eight by eight inches and divided by a board partition. The kitchen, also brick, is two stories and was originally detached. The roof was covered with Welsh slate, finished with English ridge tiles. The yard was paved with brick, and two 2,000-gallon cisterns had wood covers and

brass locks. The yard was bisected by an eight-foot whitewashed cedar fence to accommodate the division between two families.

Within six years of the construction date, John Healy lost the cottage at a sheriff's auction when the house and lot sold for $2,525 to John C. Norcross. Healy's wife, however, repurchased the property in 1862 and retained it until 1877 when she sold to Mrs. Ophelia Porrier, wife of Bienvenu Breaud. Subsequent owners were Mrs. Horatio J. Lange, Mrs. Victor Roux, and Mrs. John R. McMahon. The first homestead company to hold a mortgage on the property was the Excelsior in 1909.

The adjacent lot at 1342, □ once part of the J. Saul and S. Jaudon holdings, was purchased by speculators, and the present corner townhouse dates from the 1850s as observed from stylistic analysis. Here is a relatively chaste and simple frame townhouse following the American, three-bay plan, but there are remnants of creole influence evident on the façade. The frame building has gable ends and a single pilastered and pedimented dormer on front and rear elevations. The entrance is quite narrow,

in the creole fashion, although the embellishment here is the Greek Key surround with wide facia board and molding which serves as a cornice. The second-level gallery is suspended above the banquette at front and side elevations. This wide and imposing cast-iron gallery obscures the primary decorative feature of the structure—the early Classic-style entablature with dentils and molded cornice.

Lieutaud-Wagner House

Across the avenue at the downriver corner of Marais, the property included a small section of Faubourg Plauché as indicated by title research. This parcel was purchased by the Gueno daughters through their father Matthew Gueno. Maria Gueno, widow of David Soumâstre, bought out the other Gueno heirs' interest in 1838, with the adjoining lots that contained "buildings and improvements." She sold this and the adjacent property through a sheriff's sale to Paul Lieutaud, June 10, 1846, for $1,410. Paul Lieutaud probably built the house which occupies the corner lot at number 1313. □

When Lieutaud sold to Mrs. Thomas Blois, née Emilie Demourelle, in 1859, it was with buildings and improvements for the price of $3,500. Mrs. Blois owned the property from 1859 until 1866, when she sold to Cora Prieur, daughter of Mayor Denis Prieur, and wife of notary Edward G. Gottschalk. The sale to the Gottschalks, it was specified, included the "gas chandeliers and gas fixtures" in the house for a total of $10,750. Later, after a divorce from Edward Gottschalk, Cora Prieur married Eturbial Fortier, and in 1870 she sold the house, which had been her separate property, as specified by the her marriage contract to Gottschalk. For the next ten years the owner was William Cruzat.

Architectural details, with the exception of the narrow twentieth-century weatherboards, indicate that the present house at 1313 was constructed in the 1850s. Segmental openings, or paneled architraves, are complemented by an ornate iron canopy and a denticulated cornice with paired brackets. Neither the present millwork nor the wood-turned balcony is original. A Mugnier photograph as late as 1895 shows this house with its original hip-roof and cast-iron second-level gallery. The cast-iron canopy with skirting and anthemion cresting, presently a distinguishing exterior feature, is a remnant of this gallery. A fine door with sidelights and transoms remains, as does a two-story service wing that extends from the left rear side.

Notable interior details include an elaborate Della Robbia-style mantel and ornate ceiling cornices in the ten-foot-wide hall beside the stairway. The interior spaces have been rearranged, some ceilings lowered, and certain mantels removed. These changes may have occurred during the twentieth-century ownership by Joseph M. Wagner, who owned the residence until 1927, along with the drugstore which stood on the corner. The 1895 Mugnier photograph marked the pharmacy's position with a large wooden mortar and pestle poised on a painted pole.

The house was acquired by St. Anna's Episcopal Church in 1960, and it retains the ownership along with the next property. St. Anna's, the adjacent high-pitched one-story marble-faced building, dates from 1956. □ It replaces a frame church that occupied the site. The needle steeple of this former church was visible above rooftops and trees, a familiar landmark for nearly a hundred years.

Next to St. Anna's Church is a frame two-level residence at 1323 □ built directly on the sidewalk, a positioning that forced a bowing of the double gallery. The lots angle considerably here; and the next three houses face

Esplanade on a diagonal line, following the old habitation lines. Like its three neighbors, the house at 1323 □ dates from the late nineteenth century; all four are indicated on the Robinson map of 1883. These houses continue the Esplanade Ridge tradition, being galleried box structures, with simple yet eclectic selection of architectural details. The basic side-hall floor plans afford partitioning into apartments without difficulty.

The Lazaro Roca family owned the next property at 1327 from 1859 to 1920. A single owner, Anatole J. Forstall, owned the following two lots, having purchased them from Octave Victor Fernandez, as recorded by O. Drouet, February 20, 1877. These three houses, 1327, 1333, and 1337, were perhaps identical with slight cornice and side bay variations and were erected at the time of the Forstall purchase in 1877. The Forstall lots extended then 320 feet in depth to Kerlerec Street and were subdivided as separate Esplanade and Kerlerec lots. The three buildings appeared on the 1883 Robinson atlas, a year after Forstall had sold 1337 to Leon Joubert de Villemarest while retaining the center house in his wife's name until 1920. Villemarest sold 1337, then known as 207 Esplanade, in 1893 to Raoul Dupré. The municipal numbers changed in 1905, when the widow Dupré sold to Mrs. T. Hugh Jones.

Of the three, only 1337 has not experienced exterior alterations. The upper galleries of 1327 and 1333 once had Corinthian columns with turned wooden balusters. These galleries have been filled in and are now braced by cast iron, which produces a temporary scaffolding effect. The small increase in interior space in no way compensates for the loss in architectural detail. The balance and uniformity created by the row of double-level, galleried houses with fluted Ionic and Corinthian columns and modified Italianate cornices have been destroyed.

The stage was set for the intrusion of the white brick three-story apartment building surrounded by concrete parking areas erected at number 1341. □ A mansion with a side bay and enormous garden filled this space back to Kerlerec Street in 1883. When new structures are thrust into abandoned spaces on a historic street, bona fide residential areas can be ravaged. The individual structures lose; the neighboring structures lose; the community loses.

Withstanding the assault by its neighbor at 1341 is a corner side-hall raised four-bay cottage at 1347, □ dating from the 1880s. In the early nineteenth century, the land on which it stands was an edge of Alexander Milne's Bayou Road holdings. This was originally part of the upper Charles de Morand eighteenth-century tract sold to Pablo Moro and Claude

1337

Tremé. The Jean Paul Viala family bought the property in the 1850s and built a narrow three-room, two-story house, which the Vialas occupied until the 1860s. This house was demolished in the 1880s by a French woman, Ursule Marie Danae Texier duPaty Soyé, widow of Martin Soyé. Widow Soyé replaced in 1881 the Viala house with the present one, which stands at 1347 Esplanade, corner of Villeré, and she lived in the house for the next decade. The *Daily Picayune* of April 11, 1891, carried the auction notice for the impending sale and described the house as "a charming one story and attic frame slated cottage, raised about nine feet from the banquette, having front and side galleried, large hall on the side, double parlors with marble mantels, six bedrooms and several cabinets, stationary washstands in the principal bedrooms, dining room and pantry; also, a two-story frame kitchen with four rooms, paved yard, and privies; gas throughout; the whole in good order." A wealthy investor, Edward J. Bermudez, purchased the raised cottage and added it to his collection of real estate investments along the Esplanade, in Marigny, Tremé, and Bayou St. John. The house at 1347 remains, well detailed, with slender, fluted Corinthian columns, a segmentally arched dormer window, and triangular cornice. The brick raised-basement cottage is unusual to the Esplanade; however, this one has been a well-maintained example since the Bermudez sale to the Emile Lefebre family in 1893, and has provided a commodious dwelling for many owners for ninety-four years.

ROBERTSON

1433

1423

1418

ESPLANADE

1415

1407

VILLERE

1400 Block

The 1400 and 1500 blocks of Esplanade traverse the rear fields of philanthropist Alexander Milne's habitation on Bayou Road. The Milne house which survived into the twentieth century, was described as a Scottish castle constructed by Milne to recall his birthplace, Fochabers, Scotland. Milne came to New Orleans in 1790 and amassed a great fortune through diverse businesses and renowned thrift. He died a bachelor in 1838 at the age of ninety-four, owning vast stretches of lake-front land as well as real estate in every part of the city. He donated his entire estate to charities in New Orleans and in Scotland. Milne had purchased his Bayou Road property from present Villere to Claiborne from Claude Tremé in two parcels. The first sale, before Pierre Pedesclaux, September 24, 1798, was land measuring 70 by 270 feet, fronting on Bayou Road bound by lands of Mariane Bodaille, free woman of color, and on the other side by more lands of Claude Tremé. Milne then bought to the rear of this first parcel, extending to the boundary of Bernard Marigny's land, from Tremé on March 20, 1800, before Pierre Pedesclaux. This land appears on the Pintado Papers in the Louisiana State Museum library

1400 Block

as 1,723 superficial arpents bound above by José de Lisa in front and by lands of Don Juan Lugar (Lucas) in the rear. The gardens and Esplanade holdings were not subdivided by Milne's estate executors until 1844, at which time auction proceedings were recorded in the files of Carlile Pollock on June 5.

The first lots offered by the estate are in the square bounded by Esplanade, Kerlerec, Villeré, and Robertson streets, and were numbered 2, 3, 4, 5, 6, and 7, each having a 30-foot front on Esplanade by a 120-foot depth according to a plan of L. Bringier, surveyor general, dated September 27, 1836, also deposited with Carlile Pollock. Lot number 7 forms the corner of Esplanade and Robertson, and on lot number 5 there were improvements, viz: "a House bricked between posts, a Kitchen etc."

Also offered were lots forming the corner of Esplanade and Claiborne, extending across the projected continuation of Barracks Street, indicating that although Esplanade was cut through at this point in 1844, Barracks did not yet reach Claiborne. Among the many properties offered were those recorded in a building contract with Carlile Pollock on November 17, 1840. Feuillas Dorville, testamentary executor for Alexander Milne, contracted with Claude Gurlie, builder and architect, for "buildings and improvements" of a lot belonging to the succession of Milne in Suburb Tremé in the rear of the late residence of Milne.

The plan for this house was attached, and the cost was reported at $10,000. Also attached was the original contract between the two parties done under private signature with specifications for four houses.

Two other houses were described as having fifty-six feet on Esplanade by a depth of forty-two feet. Each had a twelve-foot-high rez-de-chaussée and included eight rooms, rear galleries, and double cabinets. The houses were of brick painted gray or red and penciled with white joints. Each gabled roof had four dormers, two on the front and two on the rear elevation. Wooden abat-vents extended from the roofs supported by iron bars and were painted white. The doors and windows were closed by shutters. These buildings were included in the Robinson 1883 map in the 1500 block.

There remain along the Esplanade in the 1400 and 1500 blocks some homes that were built soon after the subdivision and the 1844 sale of the Milne property here. They include 1433 Esplanade, built in 1846 (altered); the corner creole cottage at 1500 Esplanade, corner of Robertson, dating from 1844; and 1518 and 1519 Esplanade, both built soon after 1845. A brick-between-posts creole cottage

1400 Block

1407

1415

with dependencies offered at the 1844 sale on lot number 5 may be the one illustrated in plan book 7, folio 7, as it appeared for an 1862 sheriff's sale; a twentieth-century brick-basement house now occupies this site at 1430. The corner house set far back from the banquette at 1432 □ was a simple two-story frame, three-bay residence with double-level box columns, possessing at the time of its construction, probably in the late 1850s, a modest elegance. By bricking the first level, shortening and adding aluminum windows, this erstwhile uncomplicated building has been mutilated. The Robertson Street banquettes on both sides and for some distance across Esplanade are brick laid in a herringbone pattern; these sidewalks prevailed in the nineteenth-century street scene.

An early photograph from *Art Work of New Orleans* illustrates Esplanade Avenue in the Milne tract, 1400 and 1500 blocks, at the turn of the century. Young live oaks line the neutral grounds and the granite-block street. Wooden planks in the center of the double line of trolley tracks retarded the growth of grass and provided walkways on the "neutral grounds." Wide sidewalks were paved, deep granite gutters were spanned by iron panels, and the street scene imparted a sense of order and tranquility. Villere Street contained a double row of tracks

in order to accomodate the Villere electric car line (later named the Gentilly Terrace line), which opened October 15, 1895, and ran all the way from Canal and St. Charles, down North Villere to Lafayette Avenue (later called Almonaster Avenue and presently Franklin Avenue). This line continued in use until 1948.

On the downriver Esplanade side of the 1400 block, a row of Italianate galleried houses were set back behind heavy iron picket fences with tall corbelled pier gateposts. These four houses, seen in the right foreground of the photograph, remain today, although alterations diminish their aesthetic effectiveness. 1407 (far right) has lost its champfered box columns and paneled pier bases. These have been replaced by cast-iron supports, which modify the original appearance. The side balcony with railing, once identical to those of the front, is gone. A clumsy addition protrudes at the first level and eliminates the visual impact of the Italianate two-story rear bay. An unusual hanging bay on the left side at the second level is supported by consoles decorated with panels and bosses. Heavy but graceful louvered shutters were discarded and replaced by metal awnings. Remaining features include a large transom with original paneled storm doors. This house was built soon after 1877 for Louis Amedée

Coutourié, who purchased the lot that year from the widow of John Eaton. He resold the property with this building in 1883 to Mrs. James Fahey for $13,000 before M. V. Déjan, May 17.

Number 1415 Esplanade, second from right, has survived for almost a century with fewer exterior alterations, but a fire in March of 1976 may have caused yet unforeseen changes. The greatest exterior loss, prior to the fire, was that of its lower cast-iron gallery rail and the iron picket fence, which it shared with both its neighbors. Visual damage was done when the fluted columns were cut and set on brick piers. The garden and lawn that surrounded the house have been paved over so that exterior unity of house and land was eliminated.

When J. A. Blanc purchased the land on which 1415 stands at the Milne auction sale, he had two earlier buildings constructed that were undoubtedly creole cottages. These were purchased as investments by François Gardère in 1851, and they remained in his family until 1880. It was probably then that these cottages were demolished and the present 1415 Esplanade constructed for Mrs. Nelson Peychaud. The house is about the age of its neighbors at 1407, 1333, 1327, 1337; its galleried exterior, with bracketed cornice and

1433

segmental openings, is typical of the late 1870s. The attic level is ornamented by paneled openings with applied jigsaw work. A side balcony and rear polygonal bay are similar to those at 1407 Esplanade. The interior, however, has been completely stripped except for a beveled glass transom, a stair post and railing, and a section of decorative plaster screen in the entrance hall. Across the rear of the lot is an extensive two-story service building with a hip-roof. This structure has a second-story gallery with box columns and square wood railing. Alexander Brewster, a yacht club commodore, purchased the house in a 1904 auction sale and retained the property until 1938.

Aldigé House

The third house in the late nineteenth-century photograph is 1423 Esplanade. □ It is a slightly modified Victorian-Italianate structure built about 1882 as the home of Jean Jules Aldigé. Jules Aldigé and his wife, Françoise Leprêtre, with their five daughters and two sons occupied the house many years. Jules Aldigé died in 1893. His wife, one married daughter, and grandchild were fatalities when the steamship *Le Bourgoyne* sank after a collision on July 4, 1898. An extensive inventory attesting to the elegance of this residence and the opulence of its contents was taken in 1899 by Felix Puig. In 1918 the estate was partitioned among the five remaining heirs.

Although a concrete and plank porch mars the lower story of this frame house, much of the exterior is intact and still reflects the florid style of an era that delighted in animated, sculptural detail. The extravagant decoration was well integrated by dark green full-length shutters, front garden beds, and an iron fence. Symmetrically placed two-level side additions widen the house and are excellent modern annexations. The design includes a second-level Corinthian portico projection with segmentally arched architrave and decorative keystone. Emphasis upward continues at the roofline to multiple scroll brackets that support a cornice crested by ornate cast iron. The sculptural exterior surface is devised by quoining, drop siding, fluting, jigsaw work, and projection.

Gasté-Lange House

The oldest remaining structure in this block is the charming cottage at 1433 Esplanade. Almost 130 years old, its own history is hidden by late Victorian modernization. The house was built in 1846 for Leonor Gasté by a builder

1418

hitherto unknown, Marc Mornier. Gasté bought the bare lot in 1844 from the succession of Alexander Milne when notary Pollock recorded it on June 6; it is therefore the first building on the site. A building contract was executed on July 23, 1846, between Gasté and Mornier before Herman Lucas, a notary; this notarial record has been lost. Fortunately, an extract of the accompanying mortgage is still preserved, documenting the origin of this house. Leonor Gasté sold the house two years after its erection to Ferdinand Nerestan Geringer at a price of $3,150. Charles Choisy and George Montgomery were subsequent pre-Civil War owners. When Michel Ovid Andry purchased the house and resold it in 1862 to Mrs. Charles G. Durle, New Orleans was under Union occupation commanded by General Benjamin Franklin Butler. An interesting document attached to the act of sale indicated that both vendor and purchaser had to declare their oath of allegiance to the United States or the sale would not be recognized.

The house was originally a large, four-bay, full hip-roof creole cottage with canted eaves incorporating a simple overhang. No gallery would have existed, or front entrance projection with its triangular gable, applied jigsaw work, and elongated brackets. Turned spindle colonnettes and balusters and the apron covering are also additions. Of paramount interest are the remaining hip-roofline and fine dormers with rounded lights divided by angular muntins.

Another dormer with identical configuration faces Robertson Street.

After the Civil War, Louis W. Perkins owned and occupied this house for many years. He sold the property about 1890 to his next door neighbor, Jean Jules Aldigé, and moved to Washington, D.C. Jean Jules Aldigé, Jr., acquired the house in 1892 from his father and sold it to Mrs. Horatio J. Lange in 1899.

Jumonville-Gambino House

The only architecturally significant structure on the upriver Esplanade side of the 1400 block is an American center-hall cottage at 1418. The 1½-story residence built for the Jumonville family during their ownership between 1854 and 1861 was designed without the Italianate embellishments that presently predominate. These late nineteenth-century modernizations include carved double brackets, drop siding, and champfered box columns.

This cottage was originally the home of Louis Chevalier Jumonville de Villiers, the son of Charles Jumonville de Villiers and Aimée Beaumont Livaudais. Mrs. Louis Jumonville was the former Marie N. Commagère of Jefferson Parish. The Jumonvilles had been married ten years when they purchased from Robert Murphy the three lots comprising this site in an act before T. Guyol, June 2, 1854. They occupied the house until 1862, when they sold to John Eaton for $17,000. Notary E. Barnett on March 21, 1862, stated that the act was passed at the domicile on Esplanade and the residence sold because of Mrs. de Villiers' illness.

Eaton resold in 1864 to Coralie Bernard, wife of Charles Davenport, and the house remained in the Davenport family until 1878. During that time it was leased to Alexander Bonneval. The auction notice in 1878, attached to notary E. Bouny's act, was for "a splendid family residence, #220 Esplanade, containing wide hall in the centre, with three rooms on each side of hall, large dining room in the rear, two very large rooms in the attic, kitchen with three rooms above and three rooms below, the whole slate covered, gas throughout main house, garden, etc." The buyers were Mr. and Mrs. Étienne Ducros, who retained the house until 1920, when Giovanni Gambino purchased it. The house remains in the Gambino family today.

As the Esplanade experiences a renaissance and revival, so this cottage might again become a "splendid family residence." The unusually large 96-by-128-foot lot is intact, the excellent iron picket fence with arched gateway remains, and a turned wooden or heavy iron railings might replace the present gallery railing. Paint might be applied to the exterior and the remaining full-length shutters, and suddenly the resemblance of this structure to many Garden District homes and to 2023 and 2033 Esplanade would become immediately apparent.

1500 Block

The land formed by the intersection of Robertson and the upper Esplanade side was subdivided by L. Bringier in April, 1837, for Alexander Milne before his death. George Jackson Morgan bought this corner site, now 1500, measuring 30 by 120 feet, and paid Milne only $300 in 1837. At the time, lots of the same size along the more developed Vieux Carré and Marigny sections of the Esplanade were commanding prices five times that figure. A creole cottage, one of the rare remaining ones along the avenue, was constructed for Morgan. His succession sold the house and outbuildings in 1844 to William Cuthbert Budd for $5,500. Originally a two-story brick kitchen was part of the property; it was referred to in two transactions of the 1840s, when Budd sold to Robert Murphy "together with a new brick house containing six rooms, cabinet, and two story brick kitchen"; the note is included in T. Guyol's act of May 31, 1848.

In 1849 a similar description was made for a deed of sale to Mark Thomas. The house remained in the Mark Thomas family forty-three years; it was sold in 1892 to Lazaro Roca as "the double one-story and attic cottage #228 Esplanade." Roca and his family continue to own 1327 at this time. The design honesty of these creole cottages withstands the onslaught of twentieth-century disfigurement. The gable ends extended by fire walls readily identify the structure, which probably had four façade openings, two dormer windows, and chimneys penetrating the slate roof. With a minimum of exterior renovation this 139-year-old building could remain commercial yet provide a spirit of simple authenticity to the Esplanade.

Milne-Wagner

The galleried, creole cottage with dormers at 1518 Esplanade □ is an 1840s-style building which probably was relocated to this site. The Robinson map of 1883 indicates that two common-wall creole cottages filled the front of this lot. A building contract for several houses was registered in the office of Carlile Pollock, November 17, 1840, and signed by architect-builder Claude Gurlie and Feuillas Dorville, testamentary executor for Alexander Milne. Sections of these buildings and improvements could be included in 1518. Joseph François Valentine purchased through an intermediate owner, from the Milne succession before A. Chiapella, April 17, 1845, a portion of this property. Valentine married Madelena Bathilde Narcisse Alva, widow of T. Leon, and the property remained in their possession forty-seven years; it was inherited in 1892 by her daughter, Angela Leon. The property was sold

1500

1518

in 1892, either with this house or as a bare lot, by Angela Leon to J. M. Wagner for $3,250. The Sanborn insurance map of 1896 shows this space as a bare lot.

The original location of the present cottage is unknown; there is the possibility that one of the original Milne cottages was moved, raised, and incorporated into the present house. The well-proportioned dormers, the central chimneys, and the sweep of the front gable are fine details which have been preserved through the moving or alterations; addition of an attached service wing, re-siding, and mutilation of the gallery are objectionable changes. Four well-proportioned box columns should support the gallery, and archival examples could be employed to facilitate proper restoration.

In 1883, as seen on the Robinson atlas, a large frame mansion occupied the corner site neighboring to 1518. This the J. Waldo Pitkin residence had a bay on the left and a service wing across the rear to the Claiborne Street property line. This structure was replaced by a

filling station, and another elegant Esplanade building was lost.

Marsoudet-Caruso House

At the hectic intersection of Claiborne and Esplanade avenues is an elegant American center-hall house which predates the nationally acclaimed Pontalba buildings flanking Jackson Square in the heart of the Vieux Carré. This house, 1519 Esplanade, built in 1846, stands alone now between a corner filling station, vacant lots, and corner concrete-block food store which began two years ago as a small tent operation. Everything around, about and above threatens the present and future existence of 1519. An elevated expressway crowds the intersection, overshadowing, diminishing everything far, near, or below. There is an atmosphere of urgent clamoring, intimidating din.

Once inside the house, the menacing environmental features disappear. The brick exterior walls of one and one-half brick and all

1519

1519

interior walls, of one-brick thickness form an effective sound barrier. The brick foundations, which support not only the exterior walls but run in chain fashion beneath the interior ones, cushion the vibration rumbles emanating from the streets and elevated highway. It is an early nineteenth-century oasis.

A nine-page building contract written in French describes the structure as it existed before the many present additions and late-nineteenth-century increments. When Mrs. Eliza Ducros Marsoudet, in 1846, entered into the contract with builders Nicholas Duru and Jacques Michel St. Martin, she was acting in a separate capacity from her marital community, although it is stated that her husband assisted her. Originally the house stood in the center of ninety-five-foot Esplanade frontage; it measured fifty-four by sixty feet deep. The contract stipulates:

[There will be] seven rooms, also a hall in the middle, the gallery will be closed and separated from the hall by a door of eleven feet width which will be two folding doors. . . . The height will be fourteen feet from floor to ceiling . . . entrance door will be four feet, four inches width, by nine feet high . . . (entrance) stairway will have seven steps, part inside part outside [indicating a recessed entrance]. . . . The glassed door leading to the courtyard will be of the same shape as (builder's house on Dauphine) . . . and will have a transom to match the entrance door. There will be twelve windows [with sashes] . . . four doors leading from rooms to the hall, connecting door from the two bedrooms will have three feet, eight inches width . . . . The two cabinets [petites pièces] will each have a door and a stairway. All openings will have outside framed and panelled shutters. The sliding door, the entire width of the 'appartemens,' will be without transoms and have at least eleven and a half feet height not counting the surrounds . . . . Each of the seven rooms will have a fireplace, those of two parlors and the two big rooms will be at least five feet four inches wide. All will be calculated to burn coal and in a way to forestall all smoke and odor of coal. . . .

The Entrepreneur [builder] . . . to furnish the wainscoting of the fireplace for four rooms only, they should be of an elegant shape and of good work. A trapdoor will be employed in one of the cabinets for the use of the attic with a convenient and portable stairway. The floors of all the house will be tongue and groove . . . the attic, all one foot wide planks, not tongue and groove. . . . The house will be gable-ended; [in each gable] there will be two window-doors, four feet two inches width by nine height, closed by square shutters. . . . The roof will be no less than nineteen feet height of the best slate. . . . The "abat-vent" will overhang at least five feet without counting the overhang and prolongment of the slate; and also opening on the courtyard another overhang of at least two feet without counting the overhang of the slate. Four dormers, two in front, two behind, and of a dimension proportioned to the building. They will each have two paned sashes. The gutter of tin-plate well painted will be placed behind only, to divert equally the waters in two cisterns which will be placed on each of the corners of the said house. Each of the two cisterns will measure 1500 gallons of water, they will be of well painted wood, they will each have a wood cover to keep out the dust and the effects of the sun. . . .

The whole interior of the house will have a black coating well prepared in a way to receive the paper, the ceiling only in white, well finished. The owner reserves the right to provide the cornices and rosettes; [they are] outside of the stipulated price. There will be three fireplaces in marble furnished by the owner. . . . The façade will be painted in red with white lines, designating the bricks, the three other façades will be of one color. The owner reserves the right to determine later the imitation of wood she wishes for the openings. . . . A kitchen of timber, everywhere lathed, which will have forty-six feet length by twelve feet depth, divided in eight rooms, and in the middle a stairway of six feet to reach the first floor. There will be two double fireplaces which will thus give one fireplace in each room, all the rooms below will each have two doors and a window at each side wall, one of the windows only will be glasses. . . . The doors will each be square, the laths will be whitewashed only on the façade and the side wall in front. All of the kitchen will be painted outside in three coats, as well as all the openings. The outside shutters as well as all those of the house will be a beautiful green.

Mrs. Marsoudet signed the agreement to pay $5,800 to Duru and St. Martin, and they constructed the large and still solid residence for her. Very few items from the specifications are missing from this 130-year-old residence: five marble mantels, two foliated plaster rosettes, one magnificent bronze whale oil chandelier, room configurations, all remain. Moldings are intact, although three strange fluted, wooden Corinthian columns have been placed without visible structural significance into the center hall walls, and one in the far corner of the main parlor replacing the original sliding doors. At least four extensions and additions have been connected to this main house through the years; however, the structure's original integrity survives. Mrs. Marsoudet retained this property until 1875 when it was sold along with other property to Miss Julia Riley, wife of Edmundy De Hart, for $9,000 before F. Grima on November 2. The Urbin Laroussini family bought it in 1880 for $7,250, held it until 1911, at which time the V. E. Michel family acquired it and occupied the home until 1926. The Caruso family has owned the house since that time.

A photograph in *Art Work of New Orleans* indicates that a hip-roof cottage once stood at the Robertson corner where the makeshift grocery now stands. When the picture was made the cottage had been adapted into a store, perhaps the Van Houten emporium. It later became an early movie house, and a talkie could be viewed in the afternoon for a nickel. Next to the corner property, presently a vacant lot, a two-story masonry residence was still a viable part of the photograph's street scene, as was the house immediately next to it.

It is known that W. de Mahy built for Mrs. W. Soulé, widow of Henry Darcantel, a two-story house for $5,000 in this square. The plans and specifications are recorded in A. D. Doricourt's records of June 16, 1868. There was a total of five houses filling the front of this square in 1883. The open lots on both sides of the 1500 block of Esplanade are excellent sites on which to relocate endangered nineteenth-century houses or to design well-proportioned new buildings compatible with Esplanade styles.

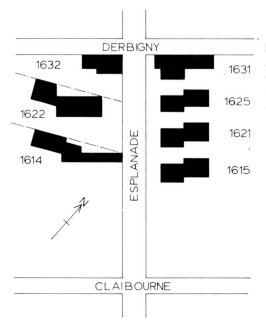

1600 Block

Beyond Alexander Milne's land, at Claiborne, between Claiborne and Galvez, was another series of small habitations through which the Esplanade had to cross, properties that had been carved out of the original French colonial plantation of Charles de Morand by the widow of Pablo Moro, Juliana Prevot. Her husband Pablo Moro had bought the entire plantation in 1775 from the heirs of Morand. This purchase included the third tract, one which Morand also acquired by concession in 1756. This third section of land roughly ran from Claiborne to Galvez, from Bayou Road back to the Marigny plantation boundaries near St. Bernard Avenue. The widow Moro disposed of a part of this Morand-Moro property September 7, 1780 before L. Mazange, when she sold ten arpents along the right side of Bayou Road by three arpents deep, from Claiborne to Galvez, to Andrés Almonester y Roxas.

Estimating two arpents per block, this is equal to five blocks. This sale was the first division of the various properties carefully collected by Morand between 1731 and 1756 and held by his heirs until 1775. Widow Moro's sale read, "I, Dona Juliana Provotier [Prevot], widow of Don Pablo Moro, sell to Don Andrés Almonester y Roxas ten arpents of land facing the Bayou Road on the side of the Cuerpo de Guardia, which is at the gate to this Road, by three arpents depth which is to the cypress swamp bound on one side by lands of the seller and on the other with lands of Don Gabriel Perault [Peyroux] Boticiara in the units of which in the olden days the King reserved one arpent. . . . These ten arpents came to me from my deceased husband and Carlos Morand before him," from whom it was bought April 25, 1775, before J. B. Garic for 700 pesos. The lower boundary began near the present Claiborne and was sold in 1800 to Milne.

Almonester sold this same land the next year, and it was registered by L. Mazange, January, 1781, to Joseph Chalon and his wife Marie Elizabeth Desruisseaux. The description was the same as the previous sale. Chalon did not subdivide but sold it intact to Carlos Chesse (Charles de la Chaise) before the same notary on April 22, 1782. Chesse sold the same land to Joseph Cultia before Perdomo on March 14, 1785, and it was from Cultia's sale of the ten-by-three-arpent tract that numerous small habitations fronting Bayou Road were formed.

After 1785, Antonio Ramis, a Spanish colonial from the island of Majorca, became a prominent speculator in this ten-by-three-arpent tract behind the city. Ramis acquired portions of this ancient land by purchase from Joseph Cultia and by inheritance of approximately four arpents from his father-in-law, Juan M. Rodriguez, comprising the present 1600 and 1700 blocks of Esplanade.

He turned all of the property over to different owners by 1800. The first tract above Claiborne, as seen on the De Woiserie plan of 1803, had gone to José Ignacia de Lisa. De Lisa was Antonio Ramis' stepson, for Ramis' wife Maria Ignacia Rodriguez was first married to Cristobal de Lisa, who died in 1774, leaving four sons to inherit, according to notary Almonester in January 1772 and 1774. By 1822 the same strip belonged to one "Dumford." In 1834, when the property was being purchased for the Esplanade cut through, Curval and Company were the owners as seen on the Zimpel survey. A plan housed in the Louisiana State Museum library, dating from after 1834, shows the projected cut-through of Claiborne Street to Esplanade, including this intersection then belonging to Anthony Fernandez, Emile Barthe, and the city-owned land acquired from "Laurant."

Behind this land, part of which became Claiborne Avenue, were two arpents fronting Bayou Road which had passed from Cultia through Ramis and were owned in 1822 by a free woman of color, Josephine Tasse, and then in 1834 by the Perault brothers. The land was subdivided and sold by the succession sale of François Perault, as illustrated in "a plan of eighteen lots" dated March 26, 1835, notarial plan book 14, folio 32. Esplanade Avenue had not reached this point, and the Perault plan showed the habitations of François and Philippe Perault facing Bayou Road, with lots divided off on each side of the proposed new Esplanade Avenue, formerly their rear field. François Perault's house is in the way of the projected Derbigny Street and was therefore to be moved or demolished. His house was French colonial in style with an "L" shaped gallery, having a cabinet at each end. Philippe Perault had a galleried hip-roof creole cottage with two large outbuildings; it was not offered for sale. These houses, of the two Peraults and the one belonging to Curval, seen on the edge of the plan near Claiborne, must have been built some time after the subdivision of the larger tract by Cultia, who had purchased it in 1785. Toward Claiborne is seen the Curval house in the French colonial style with front gallery and rear cabinet gallery.

On March 5, 1793, before Pedesclaux, Ramis sold property measuring one by three arpents to Joseph Suarez (who also in the late eighteenth century owned a concession near

1622

present Broad on the upper side of Bayou Road). This land is described as bound above by more Ramis property and on one side by land of the widow Moro (toward Marigny). Suarez sold it January 11, 1796, in the office of Pedesclaux to Joseph Cabaret, free man of color, and Cabaret's land is shown on the 1803 de Woiserie map at the present Roman Street (1700 block Esplanade). Cabaret held this property until 1819, at which time he sold it to the Cousin-Rouquette family in an act registered by M. de Armas on April 14. The Cousin-Rouquette family sold it to Terence Carrière on July 1, 1828, before L. T. Caire. Carrière sold it to Auguste Reynal and his wife Suzanne Hazeur, both free Negroes.

On June 29, 1836, the council of the Third Municipality accepted the proposals of Dupuy, B. Coquet, Veuve Mathé and Chalinette Duval to give to the municipality the ground needed for Esplanade Street, "requiring only for compensation the building of banquettes in Curb-Stones and the repair of the fences." The council rejected Auguste Raynal's [Reynal] proposal, making the same offer but requiring also one hundred piastres. Three months later, the council agreed to pay Reynal fifty piastres "for the damage occasioned to his property by the opening of Esplanade." Antoinette Hazeur, Suzanne's daughter, married Basile Raphael Crokin, who acquired a portion of the Reynal

land through an act registered by G. Le Gardeur, on February 5, 1835. Both names appear on the Zimpel map.

The houses on both sides of the 1600 and half of the 1700 block of Esplanade occupy the old Cultia-Ramis properties. The existing houses date from the mid-nineteenth century. The first architectural development here was a group of small habitations dating from soon after 1785. These hip-roof colonial-style homes were replaced soon after the 1835 subdivision of the habitations with creole cottages, similar to the ones seen in plan book 16, folio 27, on the former Curval property. These in turn were replaced by the mid–nineteenth-century homes which remain today.

Aleix House

The galleried raised-basement house at 1614 Esplanade□ was built between 1868 and 1872 for Mrs. Emma Goldenbow, wife of Joseph Aleix. Joseph Aleix was a partner in the "commercial house" of Generelly and Aleix along with Theotine Generelly. The Aleixes purchased the bare lot at auction in the spring of 1868 from Marie Aline Samory, who also owned the house next door at 1622 Esplanade. The site of 1614 was recorded in a newspaper clipping on March 30, 1868, as being in "a high state of cultivation as a garden, planted with vegetables and a great variety of fruit and

ornamental trees." The Aleix family retained the property only until 1876, when they sold it for $6,000 "including the chandeliers, brackets and gas fixtures" to Auguste Rauxet. Eugene Ecuyer and Nunzio Acosta have been subsequent owners. The Robinson map of 1883 indicates that this house with its bay and rear section was not at the banquette but set on a plane with 1622.

Deep wood rustication, end pilasters, and four fluted Corinthian columns are complemented here by the paneled gallery ceiling. The curved door and window cornices with dentils are remaining architectural features. These details and the projecting bay to the right are Italianate devices which are combined with a Classic-style dentiled cornice. By filling between the plastered brick piers, the raised basement has been truncated. If these areas are original, they were intended for ventilation, service area, storage, and sometimes dining. Carefully remodeled, this basement could provide an attractive space. Proportions would be reestablished by lengthening the fluted Corinthian columns to gallery floor level. Below the columns a molded facia should be reinstalled across the façade. The extant pilasters should have caps, and the space between the pilasters should be scored plaster. Doors should not be placed in this basement level.

Samory House

Archival research has provided an unusual amount of documentation for the 120-year-old house at 1622 Esplanade. Two building contracts, one for its erection in 1858, another for "repairs and addition" in 1863, have been used for analysis. Auction descriptions from 1868, 1872, and 1902 completely record the appearance of this cottage. The house was designed and built by A. H. Sampson for Mrs. Henry Samory, whose husband was a prominent investor in the firm of E. Roger and Company. According to terms of a building contract executed July 30, 1858, before notary A. E. Bienvenu, the cost was to be $2,575. This provided for a "frame house twenty-seven feet wide by seventy-two feet deep, set on brick piers four feet apart and three feet, nine inches above the ground. Two double chimneys, a front balustrade [now missing], two other galleries with turned balusters, a left side balcony eight feet long, a right side balcony four feet square, and stairs with wooden balusters" were among the specifications mentioned. The rooms were to be thirteen feet square, and the roof was to be slate.

By 1863 Mrs. Samory contracted with builder Henry Stewart "for repairs and addition of a room and hall" before A. Barnett, March 24, 1863. The work totaled almost as much as the original building. Mrs. Samory realized a return on her investment just five years later when she sold the house at auction for $8,800. The newspaper article attached to O. de Armas, March 30, 1868, described the sale: "splendidly built raised one-story frame cottage, retired from the street; front and side galleries; parlor, three bedrooms, dining room, wide rear gallery, two-story frame building in rear used as a kitchen, having four bedrooms, wine cellar, wash and ironing rooms, cistern, wells and stabling. Yard paved, front and side beautifully shaded with a vigorous growth of ornamental and shade trees."

Henry Tête purchased the property from Mrs. Samory and resold within five months to Jean Baptiste Bertin, also before O. de Armas. Bertin held the house four years; his estate sold to Jules A. Massicot in 1872. Two years later Eliza Beauregard purchased the property for $7,000. In subsequent years Oliver Carrière and George Lanaux, Jr., became owners. This galleried Classic-style cottage would regain its original character by installing full-length columns and replacing the entablature section of the gallery cornice. Proper weatherboarding should replace the asbestos siding.

At the corner of Esplanade and Derbigny on part of the former A. Perault early nineteenth-century plantation, Leon Joubert de Villemarest sold a fifty-five-foot lot to Antoine Carrière. At the time of purchase, June 25, 1874, before James Fahey, Carrière immediately had built a two-story frame residence, now 1632 Esplanade. □ The main house included a hall, double parlors, dining room, sliding doors, vestibule, back gallery, and upstairs a hall, four bedrooms, bathroom with closet and back gallery, and front and side balconies. In the yard adjacent to the main house, there was a two-story frame building with three rooms on the first floor and three above. The yard also contained a water closet, cistern, wash and coal shed, a brickyard, and garden. In 1885 J. L. Robichaux purchased it for $6,500 and immediately sold to J. G. Schriver. The house, which is presently owned by Mrs. Joan Marie LeFevre Mullet, is divided into apartments.

Crossing the Esplanade and returning to the Claiborne intersection, one is painfully aware of the encroachment of filling stations, and the detrimental effect which proliferates to adjacent properties. The once proud double-level frame houses which face Claiborne Avenue in this downriver Esplanade square are partially burned and ravaged by neglect. The Cenas school, now demolished, filled the corner site, Esplanade and Claiborne, from 1875 to 1910. It once shared the graciousness of a fine residential section. The structure at 1605 Esplanade □ is but another which has been abused and gutted for commercial misuse; this time an unsightly barroom fills the lower half.

Next to 1605, three one-time identical townhouses of the 1870s struggle to maintain their identity. Only number 1615 has the original appearance; its heavy projecting box cornice with segmented parapet is supported by deep scroll brackets and overhangs a wood balcony with wood spindle railing at the second level. The first level has a gallery with Corinthian columns. Victorian, Italianate, and late Classic elements blend to produce a pleasing façade style. Similar to these are the Harrod-designed 719, 721, and 723 Esplanade built for Aristide Hopkins. The original owner of the three houses 1615, 1621, 1625, was Charles Couteux, who collected, in early 1869, the 101-foot frontage forming the three lots. By 1873 he had auctioned the properties with the new buildings. Julius Socha purchased what amounted to a part ownership of the three properties in October of 1873. Unfortunate remodeling has resulted in disfigurement of the galleries at 1621 and 1625. Slender Corinthian columns were replaced by badly proportioned tapered posts on brick piers. The turned balusters between piers at balcony level could be replaced. Façade restoration for these two houses would be simple and effective.

1631

1625, 1621, 1615

Beugnot-Beauregard House

At 1631 Esplanade, the upper gallery reflects the former beauty of a once gracious dwelling. Slender, fluted Ionic columns "in antis" between box columns support an elegant and tastefully ornamented cornice. An original railing of cast iron, drop siding, quoins, and window cornices are presently spoiled by an enclosure. The first-level millwork has been replaced with unsightly brick piers.

Number 1631 was the last home of General Pierre Gustave Toutant Beauregard, who died there in 1895. Beauregard purchased the house through an intermediary from its original owner, Dr. J. F. Beugnot, who collected four lots for the site in 1881. Dr. and Mrs. Beugnot occupied the home for six years, and it was sold at auction following the doctor's death. An advertisement for the sale attached to the E. Grima act of January 26, 1889, described the house as the "elegant residence and grounds #225 Esplanade . . . attractive and complete, being modern in construction, with wide hall and galleries, spacious parlors, dining room, library, pantry, numerous large bedrooms in the main and rear buildings. The property was constructed less than six years ago of the very best materials and is in excellent condition . . . [also] grounds . . . handsomely laid out." In a second auction sale the house was purchased by Alfred E. Lionnet in February of 1895. Six years later, Lionnet died, and a third auction of the nineteen-year-old home was held in 1901. It sold at this time for $8,000 to Mrs. A. S. White.

Prior to the construction of the Beugnot-Beauregard house in 1869, the American Missionary Association had purchased the ground to establish a university for the higher education of Negroes. A building was erected by the United States government and dedicated in February, 1870, receiving its name in honor of the Honorable Seymour Straight, who was a liberal donor to the institution. A newspaper article in the *Weekly Pelican* on January 29, 1887, describes the opening and closing:

Great numbers flocked to its doors and though, in the confused state of affairs at the South in those early days, little could be done in the way of collegiate or normal training; still it was a great boon to the people from the first, and to-day thousands are reading the blessed Bible as a result of the education received at the 'Straights' and hundreds are teaching all over the South, who were at least aided there. In 1877 the building was destroyed by fire and almost immediately ground in a far more desirable situation for the purpose was purchased, and the present University building erected on Canal street. It was ready for occupancy October 1, 1878, the school meanwhile being held in Central Church on Liberty street.

In 1935, Straight University became a part of Dillard University on Gentilly Boulevard.

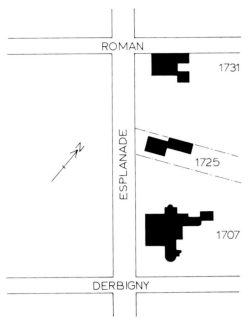

1700 Block

Dufour-Baldwin House

Because of its architectural value and its historical associations, the Dufour-Baldwin house at 1707 Esplanade is one of the most important residences in the city. Both the original owner, Cyprien Dufour, and Albert Baldwin were notable figures in New Orleans history, as were architects Howard and Diettel and builders Wing and Muir. The firm of Henry Howard and Albert Diettel designed this Italianate mansion in 1859 for Cyprien Dufour. The lots on which the house was built cost $12,000 and the structure $40,000. Cyprien Dufour was a native Orleanian, a prominent lawyer, state senator and one-time district attorney for Orleans Parish. He and his wife Louise Donnet had four sons, who also were active in local business affairs.

Albert Baldwin and his wife Arthemise Bouligny bought the house in 1869. A native of Watertown, Massachusetts, Albert Baldwin made a fortune in the hardware business with Captain Cuthbert H. Slocomb and by acquiring controlling interest in the New Orleans National Bank. The Baldwins had thirteen children, and these heirs sold the house in 1912 as recorded in Conveyance Office Book 255/392.

Here is one of Henry Howard's more monumental New Orleans residences. Built in a last burst of elegance before the turmoil of war, it is a magnificent example of the late Classic-style. Fifty years ago, the deterioration of a way of life in this mansion and the alteration of its interior were lamented. The house was elegized in a *States* article of April 15, 1923, one of John P. Coleman's series, "Old New Orleans Mansions." Even then he wrote, "time and apparent neglect have had their effect on both its interior and exterior aspect."

From the eighty-year-old son of Cyprien Dufour, the first owner, Coleman gathered the tale of its glories "before its present metamorphised condition":

On the first floor, lake side, is, or rather was . . . a large arched parlor extending the length of the building. The main hall, large and handsomely decorated, occupied the whole length of the river side of the building, giving access to the parlor and dining room, the former of which and the library were embellished in silk. The dining room and the library were in the rear, and back of these apartments was a beautiful mahogany staircase, circular in form and artistically carved, this arrangement putting the stair case in a position where it would neither encumber nor interfere with the apartments which it accommodated on the first floor.

Upstairs was a large room in front and a little reception room looking out on the front porch. There was another large room in the wings, and in the rear of the large front room were two other rooms of unusual dimensions separated by a hall. In the wing nearest to the lake side of the building was a small room and a bath room, and behind these a linen room. The servants' quarters were on the second floor of the annex, and below were the pantry, kitchen, servants' dining room and wine cellar.

Exteriorly the mansion has an imposing front. Massive columns of the Corinthian type, rising from the lower floor of the Esplanade avenue balcony, support the spacious balcony above, and columns of the same type and beauty of construction rise above that to the roof. The furnishings in the parlor were in gold and gray, the decorations being by the celebrated Seabright. The dining room furniture was made to order, as was in fact nearly all the furniture in the more important parts of the edifice.

Lofty ceilings, spacious, well-ventilated rooms, beautiful chandeliers, Italian carved mantels, stained glass windows, beveled mirrors, rich carpets, costly fabrics, exquisite centerpieces and cornices, were a few of the features of the Baldwin mansion. Truly did this old home present the most perfect manifestation of ideal beauty through material forms. . . . Attached to this beautiful mansion was one of the most extensive and highly-cultivated gardens in New Orleans. There nature and art were exuberant, and the whole inexpressibly lovely. In this fair spot seemed to be exerted more than anywhere else that mysterious influence which imparts to the earth the inscrutable energy that tints the flower, shapes the blade of grass and scents the air with the intoxicating odors of the rose.

A recent visit to this house showed a new entrance and stair added to the left; the original entrance was on the right. The service wing at the rear has a curved section, as does the rear gallery. The original curved stair was in the rear of the house, within a curved wall projection containing a stained glass window of a palm tree. The interior woodwork on the upper level is very plain. Decorative cornices and at least one black marble mantel recall detail refinements of this monumental edifice.

Whereas the Esplanade frontage of the property at 1707 Esplanade can be credited to the ownership of free persons of color, Auguste Reynal and Bernard Crokin, via Cultia and Ramis, the back portion of this once sizable property belonged to another illustrious family, the Bernard Duchamps. From the middle of the downriver Esplanade 1700 block and the Roman Street edge of the upriver side, the property belonged first to Charles Morand then the successive Moro, Cultia owners. Although John Lugar is seen on the De Woiserie map as owner of the plot in 1803, Pierre Pedesclaux, the notary, acquired this two and one-half arpents fronting Bayou Road by three arpents in depth soon thereafter.

1707

1707 Wing

1707 Rear

Pedesclaux's habitation was situated there in 1811, having as one of its boundaries that of the Pontalba division across Bayou Road. The Pedesclaux plantation house is also shown on the Pilié 1822 survey just on the left of the projected avenue, which later progressed through and displaced the outbuildings. After the deaths of both Pierre Pedesclaux and his widow, there was an auction to settle the estate of the latter held March 5, 1827, relative to the suit of *F. M. Galez* vs. *Heirs of Pedesclaux.* Pedesclaux's daughter Basilice, first the widow of François David Thomeguey and then wife of Bernard Duchamp, was able to purchase her family plantation, and she and her husband Bernard Duchamp with their children Caroline, Clarice, Adèle and small son Henry lived in the house on Bayou Road. Duchamp died in the 1830s.

In 1841 there was an official family meeting held in behalf of the minor children of Bernard Duchamp. It was established that the amount of property previously sold was barely sufficient to pay the debts of the estate and community. The revenue of the productive property was insufficient in itself for the maintenance and education of her children, and it was absolutely necessary either to sell the remaining unproductive property at the then low prices or to adopt some plan to raise a revenue. Alfred Mercier, Pierre, André, Charles, and Henry Darcantel, cousins of the minors, Pierre Soulé and Louis T. Caire, cousins by marriage, and L. E. Forstall, under tutor, approved a plan of leasing the property as lots and permitting buildings to go up on them "with the reservation however that it shall be stipulated in the acts of leases that the buildings or improvements to be put up on the lots so leased shall be none other than those intended for dwelling houses and dependencies, which buildings and improvements at the expiration of the ten or twenty years as the case may be shall be estimated according to the additional value which they may give to the lot upon which they will be built." Thus about 120 lots not sold in the first sale were to be "leased on ground rent."

The ground rent project apparently failed because on June 28, 1848, before notary Lucien Hermann, the Duchamp children and the widow sold the two-and-a-half-by-three-arpent fronting on Bayou Road, including the land on each side of the Esplanade to their relative Hughes Pedesclaux, also a notary. Eighteen additional lots which conformed to a J. A. Bourgerol survey of April 10, 1839, and attached to the Hermann act of May 18, 1841, were also transferred to Pedesclaux. John McDonogh bought the Duchamp house on the Barracks side of Esplanade for $2,375 and the entire square bound by "Esplanade, Roman, Prieur, Quartier and Chemin de Bayou." Clara and Adèle Duchamp held the Duchamp portion of the 1700 block of Esplanade bounded by Kerlerec, Roman, and Derbigny, selling only when financially pressed. The history of this 1700 block joins the fascinating preamble to the real estate story of New Orleans. It projects from a back field of an eighteenth- and nineteenth-century Bayou Road plantation to the last great and elegant mansions by Henry Howard.

Tremé-Herman House

Eugenie Rousseau's purchase was one of the first "stress" sales from the Duchamp sisters, in 1843, when the present 1725 Esplanade was a bare lot. She soon turned over the property to Charles Munrose, and there were yearly sales including those to owners John Eaton, A. A. Murphy, Louis Gagent, and, finally, in 1851 to Mrs. Adolph Tremé, who purchased the land for $1,600. Mrs. Tremé immediately built the present house at 1725, then sold the following year along with an adjacent bare lot to Anthony Thibaut; the house continued its succession of owners through Julia Seixas, C. E. Allgeyer, and James M. Lapeyre. When the Lapeyres sold the house to Dr. H. Herman in 1921, the act stipulated that three bronze chandeliers were not included in the sale.

This large American townhouse at 1725 Esplanade, with two-story columns extending from the cornice through the second level gallery, is a type seen most often in the Lower Garden District of New Orleans. Its ornamentation is an applied gallery, crowned by a well-molded architrave, with closely spaced dentils and overhanging cornice. A cast-iron rail is set between the paneled box columns, which have elongated necking and rest on piers. This railing complements a fine fence at the banquette, which is partially laid in flagstone. The recessed doorway with pilasters has acanthus carving, traditional in the 1850s. No original mantels remain within this house; however, there are floral ceiling medallions in the double parlors and a cornice molding with relief shell motif. Extending from the rear is a service wing with upper gallery in the mid-century manner.

By 1848 the Duchamp heirs had released another section of their Esplanade Avenue holdings; the site of 1731 was sold to Mrs. Claire Baird, widow of Charles Beirmacki and Cesare Philippi. The buildings constructed and utilized between 1848 and 1895 were removed by widow Philippi when she sold to John Francis del Corral on April 4, 1895, before notary F. J. Dreyfous. The 1915 succession sale of Del Corral to Corrado Giacona for $6,200 included the following description of the spacious house: "The elegant two-story frame residence, #1731 Esplanade, contains halls, ten rooms and bath . . . the house is nicely decorated, in a good neighborhood and a desirable home. In the rear is a servant's room and a garage and an automobile drive on the side." The Giacona family held title to the house until 1931. This property was one of many which was involved in the Canal Bank liquidation.

1725

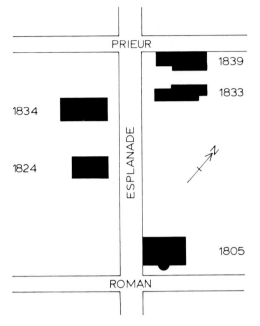

PRIEUR

1839

1833

1834

ESPLANADE

1824

1805

ROMAN

1800 Block

While there remain a number of houses built soon after the original 1841 Duchamp sale along Kerlerec and Columbus, the 1800 block Esplanade frontage remained bare lots until the 1870s, when Henry Millaudon purchased a large portion of the square between 1866 and 1870. It was subdivided for his use in a plan by J. A. D'Hemecourt, August 15, 1872, attached to an act of G. Le Gardeur. Present houses on the former Duchamp-Millaudon property include 1805 and 1824. Number 1805 Esplanade is a large raised six-bay center-hall house built in the 1880s. It combines Classic features such as a Greek Key entrance surround, dentils, and simple cornice. Italianate details blend harmoniously such as the turned balusters, columns on paneled piers, and scroll-edged parapet.

Hughes Pedesclaux kept some of the Esplanade upriver frontages of the 1800 block until he sold to Benoist Oscar Vignaud before Doriocourt, April 6, 1853, for $2,000. Vignaud sold bare lots at auction to A. B. Phillips for the same amount that he had paid Pedesclaux fifteen years earlier. The house at 1824 Esplanade was built for Phillips soon after 1868. His heirs kept the house until 1892 when John May obtained title. May sold it in 1903 to Oliver Canton for $5,950. Canton's widow, Marie Louise Leocadie Lesseps, sold it the following year to Mrs. Albina Maestri Li Rocchi. The P. J. Rinderle family have owned the house for the past forty-two years after purchasing it for $2,400 in 1934. This late-Classic galleried American-style house epitomizes the Esplanade Ridge type. The interior retains its flamboyant murals, millwork, architectural details, and fixtures which contrast with the geometrical Italianate façade. (See pp. 96–97).

Castanedo Habitation

Having approached numbers 1833 and 1839 across the Esplanade it is necessary to again move back into the eighteenth century in order to convey the earliest title holders to the property. Juan Rodriguez, father-in-law of Antonio Ramis, received title to four arpents along Bayou Road, right side, probably the tract from Prieur to Galvez, soon after 1785 via the Moro-Cultia sales. Antonio Ramis acquired the land from his father-in-law and turned it over by purchase and trade to his son-in-law Jose Castanedo in 1800. This became the front portion of the Castanedo habitation, the rear portion of the land having been purchased by Castanedo from Suzanna Caüe Peyroux about the same time.

Joseph Castanedo died in 1819; however, his widow, Marie Rose Ramis, did not dispose of the plantation, but bought out her children's interest on May 29, 1832, before Hughes Pedesclaux. Widow Castanedo received from this sale two parcels of land back of town, as seen on the Zimpel map, from her children and coheirs, Raymond, Joseph, Marianace, Rosa, and Basilice Castanedo, wife of André Castille. Part of her purchase was the Bayou Road frontage running through the projected Esplanade between Prieur and Galvez. She then had a public auction held at Hewlett's Exchange in May of 1833, and had P. Pedesclaux record the sales on May 27, 1833. Essentially, Madame Castanedo sold the lower Castanedo tract, including 210 lots situated primarily in the area bound by Bayou Road, Kerlerec, Prieur, and Galvez.

Other prominent investors among the twenty-five purchasers included Louis Bringier, who bought thirteen lots, and William Israel, who bought fourteen lots, and together in partnership they purchased fourteen more lots. These were prime lots for $80 and $100 each. James Mooney bought thirty-nine lots, some of which sold for $18 and others for $25 each. This land incorporated an edge of the 1800 block and all of the 1900 and 2000 blocks along both sides of Esplanade, which was developed and planted shortly after 1836, with a double row of trees from Villere Street to Prieur. Among the creole cottages that were constructed along Esplanade after this 1833 sale was the creole cottage seen in plan book 99, folio 22. This cottage was built probably as rental income for Louis Bringier.

In an act passed May 23, 1833, before H. Pedesclaux, Michel Doradou Bringier bought from the widow Castanedo the three lots at the corner of Esplanade and Prieur. Within the next three years, on this downtown corner of Esplanade and Prieur at the Duchamp property line, one of the earlier major urban houses was built. M. D. Bringier sold the lots to his relative Louis Bringier, who built the substantial new house which is seen in plan book 14, folio 47, dated 1838, drawn by J. A. Guerard. The house labeled *Bringier* is a large hip-roof mansion beautifully situated on the corner to enjoy the double row of trees planted on the new Esplanade. Louis Bringier mortgaged his substantial new house on September 8, 1836, before T. Seghers. The lot and house were described as "three lots behind the town at the corner of Esplanade and Prieur forming part of the old plantation Castanedo, forty-nine feet along Esplanade by one hundred seventy-seven feet along Prieur by 98 feet to the rear by 183 feet along the Duchamp prop-

1805

1839 and 1833

1824

erty . . . . together with the principal house constructed in brick in two stories and a one-story kitchen of brick between posts and other dependencies of all types which exist on said three lots.''

Just beyond Bringier's property the Esplanade roadway was halted by widow Castanedo, who did not relinquish the land with her own dwelling house, until she had successfully concluded negotiations with the city in 1841. When Bringier failed to make necessary payments on his property, the Citizens' Bank of Louisiana sold the house and lot to Louis Colomb on June 20, 1858. Benjamin Tureaud became the next owner of the site of 1839 Esplanade with the latter completing a sale on May 3, 1870, to Henry Clement Millaudon. Millaudon had purchased a large portion of this square, in 1866, from Victor Olivier, including the site of 1833 Esplanade, as well as the above section, in 1870.

Number 1839, the house on the left in the photograph, was erected in 1872, replacing the Bringier house. The neighboring structure at 1833 was constructed shortly thereafter. Millaudon also financed his investment through the Citizens' Bank, an extract from the minutes of which, dated August 22, 1872, refers to the house ''to be erected'' for Millaudon on lot 23, the site of number 1839. On November 6 of the same year, before notary Felix Grima, the bank management approved a mortgage on the property because ''the said Henry Clement Millaudon has erected new buildings and improvements upon . . . the said lot [site of 1833 Esplanade].'' Three years later Millaudon sold the new house at 1833 Esplanade to Charles Lob ''with gas fixtures, bathtub and apparatus . . . subject to a lease to Rosine Godchaux expiring September 30, 1875, at the monthly rate of $75. In 1898 the Lobs sold 1833 Esplanade to Mrs. L. Ledet, and she sold to

James Numa Larose in 1906.

Calme Lazard, husband of Sarah Godchaux, bought number 1839 Esplanade, designated as old number 285, from Millaudon. Their two children, Rose Lazard, wife of Mayer Israel, and Florence, wife of Henry Block, inherited it in 1887. For the next forty-four years the Attilius Bassetti family owned the house. Mrs. Clothilde de Montrond, widow of Attilius Bassetti, survived her only child by two months. Her brother and sole heir, George de Montrond, inherited the house in 1934.

These two once-identical houses at 1833 and 1839 are brick townhouses designed to have the gallery at the first-level to support and to brace the second-level balcony. A deep cantilevered cornice, supported by large scroll brackets, was a most modern 1870 design feature. It is also repeated in a side balcony. The house at the right has been renovated to appear earlier than its building date of 1872. This was effected by replacing the heavy brackets and balustrade of the second level with the restrained box columns, creating a double-level gallery. Both houses have front doors exemplary of the 1870 decade, though the use of scored plaster, decorative keystones and pilastered doorways was stylish from the 1850s onward.

Seldom do Esplanade Ridge exteriors reflect the decoration and furnishings within a residence. The interiors of 1833 and 1839 are characteristic of the neighborhood at any point from the 1850s. A screen between double parlors is supported by consoles and has a strong plaster centaur face forming the central position. Very large and decorative ceiling plaster medallions appear in a lavish foliated design. Marble mantels with central cartouches and bull's-eye theme are typical of the desired sumptuous effect sought along Esplanade during the second half of the nineteenth century.

1824

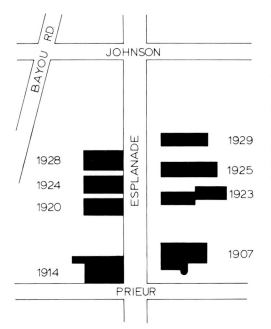

1900 Block

The extant houses on the 1900 block are all Victorian, each exhibiting Italianate features with the exception of 1923 Esplanade. Number 1914 Esplanade was one of the last buildings designed by New Orleans architect Henry Howard. Built in 1884 for August Tête, the original plans are housed in the Tulane University Special Collections. The house was placed on large grounds measuring 120 by 199 feet and was identified as "an elegant residence at old number 298 Esplanade" when August Tête sold it five years later to Hypolyte Laroussini for $11,500.

The turned balusters, rhythmic cornice, balcony brackets, and sweeping spandrels between the paneled box columns are symbolic of the Victorian adaptation of Italianate characteristics. When the Laroussinis sold in 1912, they included "the lighting fixtures, bath tubs, and mirrors." Domingo Brisolara owned the property thirty years; today it is used as apartments. A side entry and addition today obscures the bayed projections.

On the remainder of the even side of the 1900 block are three shotguns with gable fronts, aprons, and spindle bands. The Esplanade has few shotguns, and these are particularly fine expressions of this typical New Orleans house type. They have fan brackets, bayed windows, drop siding, turned colonnettes, and innumerable animated wooden motifs. Portions of an early brick banquette, laid in the herringbone pattern, remain. These houses bear the municipal numbers 1920, 1924, and 1928.

Crossing to the downriver Esplanade side, the house at number 1923 is the exception to the otherwise complete expression of late-Victorian buildings. Michel Doradou Bringier, who owned property all along the avenue, purchased a large portion of the 1900 block of Esplanade in 1836 from Mrs. Harriet Lowe Wooster, wife of Mr. Boswell. In 1867 his heirs

1914

1923

1924, 1926, 1928

had this property auctioned, and Pierre Auguste Pignatel purchased four lots for $4,150 and built the present house at 1923 the following year. Pignatel died in 1892, and his wife Clementine Morant and children were put into possession of the property. They sold most of his estate at auction that same year with the exception of the house, which was retained for three years. It was sold to John Noel Delery in 1895 for $5,000. After Delery died, his widow married Fernand Laudemiey. The Laudemieys sold to Miss Margaret Tessier. In 1918 the property was purchased by Bernard Schott, an enterprising butcher, who occupied stall 15 at the Poydras Market and later built one of New Orleans' largest meat-packing businesses.

This Italianate style, double-galleried, side-hall house contains several apartments and has recently been attractively redecorated. Especially fine storm doors with florid carving in the Baroque manner distinguish the entry. Paneled piers, paired brackets, and a heavy box cornice mark the house in the style of the late 1860s. The hexagonal projections on the sides also

became popular then. On the interior, the bay area is delineated by paired arches, and the lowered arch screen between parlors terminates with a boss serving as the center between these arches. Marble mantels and bronze chandeliers also distinguish the interior.

The pair of late Italianate-Victorian houses at the corner of Prieur and Esplanade, 1925 and 1929, □ were built by Pierre Lanaux shortly after his purchase of two bare lots from black philanthropist Thomy Lafon in 1882. He paid $2,200 for the lots, and his succession sold 1925 for $4,200 in the year 1893 and the second house for $100 more. Both houses were bought by Dolores C. Garcia, wife of Charles Royer. She sold 1929 for only $3,250 at auction in the year 1895, when C. J. Theard was the purchaser. The Theard family retains ownership today. Mrs. Royer married F. E. Davis in early 1895 and sold number 1925, before J. F. Meunier, for $3,500.

Both houses were described at the time of the 1893 Lanaux succession as having halls, front and rear galleries, double parlors, dining

room, kitchens with pantries, servants' rooms, three bedrooms, baths, and sheds. They were once identical houses with movable louvered blinds, which were utilized to shield the rooms from the afternoon sun. The third upper window of 1929 has been replaced by an oval bull's-eye. The fluted columns at the lower level of 1929 have been exchanged for cast-iron supports embedded in foreshortened, inappropriate brick pillars. The house would be immensely improved with full-length columns.

The appearance of the third house in the series, recorded in the Robinson atlas of 1883, would also be enhanced by full-length columns. This building at 1931 could also profit visually by the installation of louvered blinds, which are both practical and attractive. Mr. and Mrs. Roy Troendle recently purchased this house. This trio of buildings, slightly recessed from the banquette behind low iron picket fences, is an extremely handsome group.

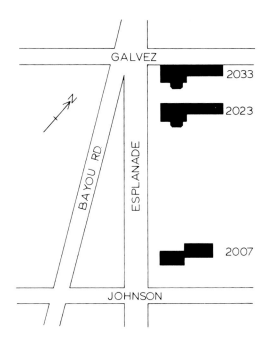

2000 Block

Marie Rose Ramis, widow Castanedo, did not sell all of the Castanedo lots in the auction sale of 1883; she kept eighty-seven feet at the corner of Galvez Street in the 2000 block of Esplanade and sold as late as 1856 a 150-foot frontage in the center of the block to Julien Meffre Rouzan. The corner of Johnson and Esplanade was purchased by Edgar Marin in 1856, and in April of that year he contracted with Nicholas Duru for a galleried center-hall cottage much like the two still standing at 2023 and 2033. Marin was forced to sell his corner house in 1858, and it was purchased by Clothilde Letorey Bertoulin. A description that year confirmed the existence of a "two-story cottage dwelling, with two parlors, dining room, cabinet and large hall on the first floor." The cottage also had two large and two small rooms upstairs, a kitchen with four rooms, a stable, and a carriage house. There was also a fine garden specifying fruit trees. Clothilde Letorey, widow Bertoulin, also purchased sixty feet from her neighbor in 1858 and added it to the lot. When widowed, she remarried, and as Mrs. Pierre Laberie moved to Castres, France. She sold the property to Pierre Lanaux in 1883. The cottage was either moved or demolished, and the present house at 2007 was built for Lanaux. In 1892 the large lot was divided into five sections in the sale of Lanaux's estate.

The present house, which is number 2007, was identified in the Lanaux auction sale of 1893 as a "home recessed from the street, with hall, front and side galleries, double parlors,

2023

2023

2023

dining room, china closet, kitchen, pantry, four bedrooms in the main house, two gallery rooms, servants' room, washroom, shed. It sits on a pleasant portion of Esplanade near all the conveniences accessible by two lines of cars.'' The sale resulted in the $5,900 purchase by F. Couturié, for this and two adjacent lots each with thirty feet fronting on Johnson Street, ''a desirable site for two double cottages in a well improved neighborhood.'' The two additional properties sold were all ''fenced, and have a brick banquette and a gravelled street in front; a splendid building site in a select neighborhood.''

Number 2023 Esplanade occupies a portion of the 150 feet which Rouzan purchased from widow Castanedo in 1856 by act before Theodore Guyol. Since Rouzan was a real estate investor he sold ninety feet of this land in 1859 to Abner B. Charpantier, who hired Alexander Castaing to design 2023 Esplanade and Hubert Gerard to build it in 1860. The cost was $11,000.

The building is similar to many center-hall one-and-one-half-story American-style cottages of the 1860s. The wide front gallery is attached to the gabled roofline, creating a late-Classic-style entrance. Classic motifs of rustication and the dentiled cornice mix with heavier additions such as the pentagonal side bay, triple dormers and ornate cast-iron railing. The rear gallery has Corinthian columns with dentils and modillions; seldom does a rear gallery have a more elegant system of decorative motifs than the front. According to the building contract attached to the records of notary E. G. Gottschalk, January 9, 1860, the house is of wood on a brick foundation. It originally had two cisterns, two wine hollows, a stable, and outbuildings.

The Charpantier estate sold the property in 1866 to Joseph François Avet for $21,000. Avet two years later built the magnificent Baroque mansion at 1120. Judge E. C. Billings owned 2023 in 1870, and in 1875 the Theodore Lanaux family began an extended period of ownership. Today, marble mantels are still in the principal rooms, and the parlor contains a brass chandelier which can be lowered by a system of pulleys. There are lovely plaster ceiling medallions with twisting foliage, and the double parlors are separated by sliding doors with Greek Key surrounds.

Widow Castanedo's House

In 1861 widow Castanedo died at her home, 2033 Esplanade, after living on land owned by her grandfather, Juan Rodriguez, since his purchase in the 1780s from Joseph Cultia. Through the years, she battled the city ad-

2033–35

ministration and prevented the prolongment of the Esplanade. Perhaps fearing a capitulation with the municipality by members of her family, she bought out their interests in 1832. A letter from Mayor Prieur, in 1836, mentioned that the Esplanade would now be opened through the contested Mager, Boisdoré, and Dolliole lands and would cross up to the Castanedo property. The main Castanedo plantation house appears to have been a gabled one with two rear cabinets and a front gallery facing Bayou Road. Four other buildings were visible on a plan of the square, all of which were either demolished for the street extension or moved.

Madame Castanedo could have moved her house, which was in the center of present Esplanade Avenue near Galvez Street, to the lot which 2033 Esplanade now occupies. The Robinson map of 1883 shows the Castanedo house as a squared frame building with detached kitchen. This plot plan possibly relates to an early nineteenth-century house form. By 1896, when the Sanborn survey was made, the house had been enlarged and embellished to its present late Italianate appearance. Now the structure is very similar to its neighbor, 2023, dating from 1860. In Madame Castanedo's inventory, registered in H. Pedesclaux's record of January 10, 1861, there are five newspaper clippings that described property owned by the deceased: "A handsome dwelling house, built of cypress, covered with slates, and bricked between posts, at the height of three feet, divided into four rooms, vestibule in the center front and back galleries, two closets; a kitchen of three rooms, gallery, brick well, privy, cistern, etc. etc." It sold to E. M. Ross for $11,300.

The earlier Castanedo house, if moved to this site, was probably demolished and replaced in the late 1850s when this type of center-hall house reached its height of popularity. Madame Castanedo died without leaving a will, and her five children and many grandchildren shared in her estate of approximately $30,000. There is a complete inventory of the furnishings of 2033 Esplanade, executed for the heirs by Hughes Pedesclaux.

Three years later, purchaser E. M. Ross could not redeem his promissory notes, and the house was sold to Felix Labutut for $7,100. Labutut gave the property to his wife, Angela Urquhart, and she sold in 1880 to William Devlin, who in turn sold five years later to James A. Mackray, founder and president of the New Orleans Stevedoring Company, who had married Julia A. Barnes in 1879. The house is presently owned by Joseph Verderaime. The interior has been remodeled and annexations attached. The lovely cast-iron fence and gallery are of the early 1860 era and add greatly to the street ensemble.

2100 Block

As early as 1718 Marc Antoine Hubert, a Canadian, was granted a three-by-twelve-arpent stretch on the right side of the "Chemin de Bayou" from "Petite Bayou" (one block past present Broad Street) up to the future Charles de Morand's third concession. Baron Marc de Villiers in his *History of the Foundation of New Orleans* (1717–1722) reports that, "A few days after his arrival, Hubert selected a spot situated at a distance of two gunshots from the limits of New Orleans, near the little river of the same name, where he built a very fine house." Within months, however, Hubert went to Natchez with his friend and associate Le Page du Pratz where he established and cultivated several concessions. Hubert was an influential man with the directors of the Company of the Indies, and he opposed Bienville's preference of New Orleans as the site for a capital, preferring a site near Natchez. Hubert apparently had little interest in his concession at New Orleans, and after his death in Paris the land eventually passed into the hands of the Enoul family. Most of the early eighteenth- and nineteenth-century maps retain the configuration of this original Hubert concession, even though titles reveal many subsequent owners.

Antonio Ramis bought from the widow Peyroux a portion of the Hubert concession (Galvez to Tonti) in a three-by-four-arpent sale on the right side of Bayou Road. Ramis sold this land to Paul Cheval, a free person of color, but preserved a lakeward easement strip to his four-arpent stretch, which he had also purchased from the widow. Cheval subdivided the section between Galvez and Rocheblave into eight small habitations and country seats, retaining a two-arpent piece along Bayou Road for his own habitation. The 2100 block of downriver Esplanade crossed the former Cheval habitation.

The purpose of the undated archival drawing, which appears in plan book 9, folio 2, was to survey the plantation immediately behind the Castanedo habitation, that is from the edge of the Galvez-Kerlerec corner through twenty-eight lots of ground situated in the Paul Cheval property, which faced Bayou Road and at that time measured two by three arpents. Much of the Cheval land was carved away by Galvez Street and the wide Esplanade Avenue. At this point, Bayou Road, wending its way in an easterly direction, actually crossed the projected Esplanade. It is the highest point of the natural ridge; some titles at Galvez and Miro refer to homes or preferred sites "at the highest location on the ridge." The Cheval house was removed for the avenue, as was a smaller establishment, probably on land leased by Cheval to a tenant farmer. The Pilié map of 1822 iden-

tifies the latter as a Mr. Wadalis; it could be that Zardais, who owned a small farm further lakeward of the Cheval land, did purchase it by the time of the subdivision into lots.

At the corner of Miro and the downriver Esplanade side is number 2139 which stands as an outstanding example of full-blown Esplanade Ridge style and was recently advertised for sale for $80,000. It is on the site of the edge of the Cheval-Zardais early nineteenth-century property. The large frame two-story house was built for William Chambers of the wholesale grocery firm of Whitehead and Chambers, probably in the decade after the Civil War. In 1899 Louis Monroe purchased the house, where he lived with his family until the 1920s, when Jovite Cau bought it.

The handsome late Classic-style residence has a double gallery with the usual combination of Ionic fluted columns at the lower level and fluted Corinthian ones supporting the traditional deep box cornice having paired brackets and dentils. There are segmental, arched, full-length openings across the front, and a wide, flamboyant entrance framed with paneled pilasters leading to a set of double doors. The house is beautifully situated on a large lot measuring 76 feet front, 105 feet rear by 166 feet on the Galvez Street side, and 104 feet on Miro Street. Large pecan trees spread across the backyard.

The interior of the house is particularly spacious; double parlors are divided by sliding doors with Greek Key frames and have matching ceiling medallions four feet in diameter depicting the faces of the four seasons. Original gas sconces remain, as well as an eight-light gas-electric fixture and one white marble mantel. Another sliding door leads to the large dining room; this handsome room has a dark slate mantel and a bay overlooking the side garden. The former back gallery is now the kitchen, and the large service wing is used for apartments. The master bedroom and sitting room upstairs have slate mantels. The house is presently converted into eight apartments. They are well arranged; no architectural features have been spoiled, and there are no unsightly partitions, added bathrooms, or closets. Unfortunately, one marble mantel has been replaced with a turn-of-the-century type, and the original floors are either removed or hidden beneath narrow oak floors so popular after the First World War.

Among the holdings of Alexander Milne at the time of his death was a two-arpent section on Bayou Road, left side leaving the city, abutting the Dorgenois-Mendez tract; the latter faced Bayou Road and was not affected by the new Esplanade. Milne gave the city land from Bayou Road to the Carondelet Canal for Milne

Road, which ran perpendicular to Bayou Road, following the old French concession property lines. This road between the Dorgenois-Mendez land is seen today from Esplanade touching Bayou Road and ends one block later at Barracks. Several houses face across Bayou Road and the Esplanade at this point, between Milne and Miro.

Only 2176, □ on the river corner of Miro, is now in an acceptable state of preservation. It is a simple Classic-style townhouse that stands on this second Milne Bayou Road property, referred to in his 1844 estate sale as Milne Gardens. Recently renovated for use as legal offices, it was, prior to its renewal, in total disrepair. The site was bare lots in 1868 when purchased for $1,000 by Hubert Gerard, an enterprising builder. Gerard, whose construction credits included 817 and 2023 Esplanade, was haunted by financial problems relative to his real estate ventures. Number 2176 was built within the following year, and in March, 1869, Gerard swore in an affidavit before Justice of the Peace D. P. Montamart and attested that he owed C. L'Hote $860 "for materials furnished and sold" for his property at this site. This was probably for millwork since L'Hote owned and operated a furniture and lumberworking company in the Faubourg Tremé on the Carondelet Canal. It was not until September of the following year that Gerard completed his first lease of the property, which was for three years to Victor Perrilliat at $1,100 per year. The contract signed before C. G. Andry, September 3, 1870, described "a dwelling house corner Esplanade and Miro . . . #348 on the said street, together with all dependencies . . . and the installation of gas." By April of 1871, however, Gerard was back before the justice of the peace to swear in another affidavit; he owed P. Cabiro $360 "for materials furnished and work done on the house corner Esplanade and Miro." The house was then already two years old.

The next year, Perrilliat was gone, the lease failed, and Gerard mortgaged the property for $1,020 to Pierre Francis Nouvet. Another three-year lease was signed when Alexander Adolphe Mouton took the house September 7, 1872, for $1,200 per year. The house was then only three years old, but Mr. Mouton apparently demanded a fairly substantial amount of refurbishing. He advanced the money to pay for painting and materials and made the appropriate deductions from his rent payments.

In 1874 Pierre Francis Nouvet, who held a mortgage on the house, purchased it for $4,000. For the next sixty-five years, this house, present 2176 (old number 348) remained the home of the Nouvet family, and his widow added an adjacent lot to the property in 1883.

2139

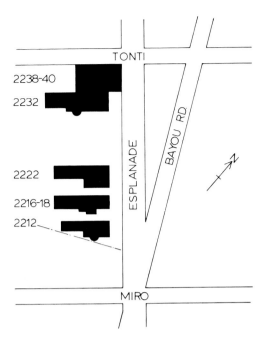

2200 Block

Pierre Darby, a free man of color, owned the next plantation back from the Cheval land on the right side of Bayou Road. Darby, soon after 1834, was to have the rear portion of his land bisected by the continuation of Columbus Street and the lower side snipped off by Miro Street. His own house stood in the center of the projected Miro Street facing Bayou Road. The auction sale of this property in 1860 mentions his immediate neighbors on all sides. The estate of Pierre Darby was probated by the Fourteenth Judicial District Court, Parish of St. Mary, on February 21, 1860, and a public auction, at the New Orleans City Hotel on Common Street, was ordered. For sale was "a certain lot of ground lying and being on the Bayou Road in the Parish of Orleans between Galvez and Miro Streets—bounded on one side by property now belonging to François Coquet, on the other by that now belonging to B. Rodriguez, and in the rear by property now or lately belonging to the heirs of Castanedo, an old one story frame house . . . purchaser to pay Widow Marie Françoise Darby."

The downriver side of Esplanade at the 2200 block is in reality Bayou Road, for the avenue and road have met at their Galvez and Miro junctures; because of this crossover, a beautiful green triangle of land, formerly a part of the Fleitas plantation, splices the two until they separate and spread blocks apart. The small piece of land was dedicated in 1886 to New Orleans historian Charles Gayarré. George H. Dunbar, a resident of the avenue in the 2400 block, donated a terra-cotta base and statue,

Goddess of History-Genius of Peace, having purchased it from the Audubon Park Cotton Centennial Commission. The statue was vandalized in 1938; the present one is a replacement. Formerly, a fountain and ornamental cast-iron shaft graced the area, which has been part of the 1976 relandscaping program by the City Parkway Commission. The houses that face Gayarré Park were formerly on the old properties of Zardais, Tala, Dumaine, Bellanger's Institute, Fleitas (right side), and Abreo; they now face Bayou Road. For Esplanade here is an open vista; there is no 2200 downriver side.

The progression toward the Italianate architectural expression continued along the avenue in the following blocks with the same verve that the early builders once held for the traditional creole cottage. Whether the structure was to be rental property or personal residence, grandiose brackets, rusticated façades with combined parapets and projections were modish. In the 2200 even block of Esplanade, three houses built as investments for Julius Weis are fanciful Italianate townhouses of the 1880s. Weis bought five lots from Nicholas Benachi in an 1881 act passed before Abel Dreyfous on November 14. Benachi had purchased these previously from William Robert Murphy in 1853, when T. Guyol passed the act in June. The Murphys collected this land from B. B. Beauregard in 1836, at which time Louis Bringier, surveyor, had drawn plans for the subdivision of the land that belonged to the heirs of Bernard Coquet, local entrepreneur. Zimpel's survey shows two B. Coquet properties on the left side of Bayou Road with the Esplanade about to cut through both of them. Coquet had purchased this land from Thomas Porée, who owned it in 1822; in 1800, as indicated in the Pintado Papers, it had belonged to Madame Bertran.

Unlike most builders for profit, Weis had each house designed in a different manner. Shown in the center of the photograph, number 2216–18, has the most creative floor plan. The entrances are composed of an enclosed section of the galleries forming a central block defined on the façade by paired windows, a projecting cornice, and quoins.

The house on the right, number 2222, has a standard American townhouse plan with an elaborate second-level gallery. The quoins and projections create strong contrasts of light and shadows. Segmental arched openings and ornate keystones embellish what would otherwise be the same simple townhouse popularized in the city since the 1830s.

Number 2212, also of the American side-hall floor plan, has a front-pitch roofline with

cantilevered balcony. The house is placed on a straight line with Esplanade, but the diagonal and dividing property line between the old Coquet and Milne property cut across the rear, allowing a very shallow side and rear yard.

The Weis family retained the houses until 1892, when 2216–18 sold to Mrs. L. J. O. Plauché Duplantier. Then in the year 1907, number 2222 went to Mrs. H. J. Malochée, whose family had owned property in the 500 block as early as 1821. Number 2212 was sold in 1919 to Mrs. H. B. Sere. This 2200 block of Esplanade, upriver side, presents the building watcher with a varied procession of white frame houses, some shuttered, some galleried, and covering stylistically a period of about twenty years.

Continuing in the same block, 2232 is a late Classic-style house which reflects an earlier decade than that of its three animated neighbors to the left. These New Orleans double-galleried, three-bay homes with superimposed Classic-ordered columns make this type as special to our locale as the creole cottage and the shotgun. Alterations to the front railing and steps, as well as siding, which postdates the construction of the house, detract from the authenticity of this otherwise well-preserved building.

Built about 1859, this house at 2232 was first owned by J. O. Valentin. Within seven years, the Union Insurance Company in 1866 took Valentin into court to force a sheriff's sale in order to recoup defaulted payments. The house sold to Hugh MacDonald in the summer of that year for $15,000. A *Daily Picayune* advertisement for the sale, which ran on May 6, 1866, stated that the chandeliers were not included in the sale. MacDonald held the house only one year before he sold to Fidel Engster; Engster in turn resold a month later to Livingston H. Gardener. In an obvious effort to keep the house out of the reach of creditors, Gardener sold it to his wife in 1880, three years before his firm Keiffer & Gardener filed for bankruptcy. The public sale was advertised in the *Daily Picayune* of March 7, 1883, in which the house was described as an "elegant two-story residence with large well improved grounds #386 Esplanade." Gardener by that time owned $10,000 in mortgages on the house, but his wife's separate funds were not subject to seizure. The house remained in the Gardener family until 1907, when Mrs. Gardener sold to Dr. Angelo Maestri. Subsequent to the Maestri ownership, the Joseph Crucia family owned it for twelve years. The deep lot, which once measured about 200 feet, has now been reduced to 118 feet.

2212, 2216–18, 2222

2232

2300 Block

Fleitas Plantation

The 2300 block of Esplanade traversed the land associated with the habitation of Domingo Fleitas, a Spanish colonial whose property reached from Bayou Road westward (across present Canal Street) to the Jesuit plantation. By the time of the Louisiana Purchase, Fleitas had acquired this Spanish land grant of Carlos Guadioli. Guadioli had received his grant from the Spanish government on May 2, 1801, and had augmented it by purchasing three arpents in depth by two arpents fronting Bayou Road from Madame Bertran, who had just bought this portion of the old LeBreton-Dauberville land grant from Madame Gabriel Peyroux. Alexander Latil had sold to Madame Peyroux, and the story of Latil covers most of the eighteenth-century ownership of this and the Charles de Morand property from Rampart through the 2300 block of Esplanade. By 1826 Domingo Fleitas had died, but his widow remained in the family home on Bayou Road. Since the house was in the way of the projected Esplanade, Domingo's son, Barthelemy, sold most of the plantation in 1836 to Jean Dufour, who in turn sold a section to the Corporation of the City of New Orleans. By 1846, there was a plan signed by J. Communy indicating a subdivision into twenty-five lots of the old Fleitas property.

One of the only houses presented in depth that never faced on the Esplanade is the Chauffe house at 2275 Bayou Road. Research reveals that this dwelling could be the Fleitas plantation house which had been moved from the center of the planned avenue. The house appears to be post-colonial and may well date between 1803 and 1820.

The senior Fleitas had bought from his son-in-law, Louis Aimé Peneguy, before notary Nicholas Broutin on May 20, 1812, this land, which measured 135 feet by three arpents deep on the right side of Bayou Road. There were some buildings, sheds, and cabins on the property at the time of the $2,000 sale. Peneguy had bought the same land just two years before from Broutin. Antoine Frometin had sold it to Broutin in 1805.

Mrs. Fleitas, née Marie Joseph Guesnard, died June 27, 1834. Her will, filed with Theodore Seghers two years earlier, bequeathed everything to her four surviving children, Jean Manuel, Barthelemy, Paulin, and Virginia, wife of L. A. Peneguy. The estate division included the plantation land on the left side of Bayou Road just across from the present site of the house; it was sold within the family and measured only fifty-three toises on Bayou Road but reached back to the Carondelet Canal or approximately seven city squares. The house, situated on the plantation, was described in the inventory and was raised on a brick basement (en briques au rez de chausée), with the upper part half-timbered (haut en colombage). In the basement of the main house, there were "rooms occupied by domestics." The narrow plantation was between two Coquet habitations and contained a kitchen, stable, and dependencies and was cultivated as a garden with fruit trees; the whole was valued at $14,000.

The land on which 2257 Bayou Road now stands was only a garden in 1834. Paulin Fleitas, who lived on a plantation in Plaquemines Parish, sold his interest to his two brothers, and Jean Manuel acquired their interests and that of his sister, Virginia, in 1835. Two years later, in 1837, a master house on the site of present Chauffe house was sold by him before A. Ducatel on January 6: "Buyer is not to begin the enjoyment of master house until the sixth of March next." Either Jean Manuel moved his mother's home to this site, or the present house dates from 1835. Because of the early architectural characteristics—hip-roof, turned wooden colonnettes, cabinet gallery with an original floor plan similar to that of Madame John's Legacy on Dumaine Street—it is proper to entertain the theory of an earlier date. Conclusive proof and archeological findings have not yet been secured.

When Jean Manuel Fleitas sold the house to Frederick Furst, the latter retained it only six years before selling it to B. Poydras de Lallande for $4,300 before J. Cuvillier. De Lallande sold to Charles Gottschalk for $5,000 before L. T. Caire on March 15, 1849, and Mrs. Gottschalk sold to J. R. Powell in 1866. The house had four different owners within the next thirty-five years until Henry S. Chauffe purchased it from Mrs. Joseph Leach on May 20, 1901, before C. J. Theard. The house remains today in the Chauffe family.

Musson House

Only the mid and right sections of an important house at 2306 Esplanade survive. An explanation for the existence of only half of this beautiful frame house, built in 1854, has not been uncovered. The house, which was painted at the height of its beauty by artist Adrien Persac, appears as the cover plate of this volume. In 1852 Benjamin Rodriguez, the builder of 2306, began collecting a series of lots in the square. From the succession of J. B. Guex he purchased three lots, through acts by A. Chiapella. Samuel Moore, who owned entire squares between the Carondelet Canal and Canal Street, sold him a lot in 1853, before

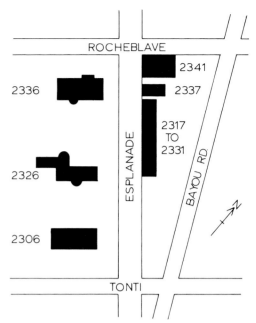

Plan Book 5/18

2306

notary G. Rareshide. Emile Laurent and the city also sold him parts of his property, which finally measured 128 feet, 9 inches, on Esplanade by 199 feet on Tonti.

On May 27, 1854, Rodriguez entered into a contract with entrepreneur William Belly to construct for him a ''wooden house'' for $5,595. The building contract is preserved in the records of J. Lisbony, May 27, 1854, and has been translated and transcribed in part:

Slate roof with English ridge tiles . . . house and stable ''double en voliges'' [roof gable sided] . . . cornice and rear one of wood supported by ''des pilâtres'' [box columns] in best style with double capitals, the whole like Mr. Hebrard's house on Rampart Street. The box columns to be formed by cast iron, the pattern to be selected by Mr. Rodriguez, cost not to exceed 1.50 per foot. Ceilings of both galleries ''planché'' [they are paneled] . . . both levels lathed and plastered inside and finished in white . . . around ceilings of two parlors and two halls cornices of plaster with rosace in parlors and halls . . . four mantels with grates and one in kitchen raised to a convenient level. Two stairs, one in downstairs hall with steps and balusters of mahogany; other stair on gallery [rear, probably] with steps and balusters of cypress. . . . A storeroom under rear stairs with built in shelves. Two other exterior stairs, one to front gallery, other for rear yard . . . two water closets or public conveniences with pipes of ten inch diameter conducting to the privy dug several feet from the house. Marble mantels and fronts to chimneys $80 in parlors; other marble mantels $30. Grates $20. Other wood. All openings with fixed louvre shutters. Windows [double hung] as high as story will permit. All interior doors panelled 1¾'' thick. . . . The four panelled doors at end of both halls will have side lights and transom [imposte]. Sliding doors also panelled, 2¼'' thick. Bottoms of window-closing to be paneled [jib windows] . . . all panelled doors with (decorated) locks. Other openings will lock with whatever lock is convenient. Rear galleries with glazed windows. Three coats oil paint. American glass; shutters Paris green. Six feet of flagstone width all around house also eight foot walk to banquette; part between house and median to rear paved all the length of house. All at level of banquette.

Stable thirty feet long by fourteen feet wide on brick foundation, slate roof, two unfinished floors. Two front openings, one at end large enough to admit a carriage . . . stalls for two horses. Two cisterns of 3,000 gallons on five foot high bases of brick, with door and some shelves. Gutters with pipes to conduct water to cisterns with cornice gutter of copper thirty feet wide. . . . The front on Esplanade with lattice or openwork fence of pickets set on the diamond with a panelled base. A double fold gate, cedar posts, also a carriage gate and three ventilators.

The house was to take four months to build, and there would be a $3 late fee charged for every day after that time. Just six years later Rodriguez sold the house to J. B. Letorey at a public auction on March 24, 1860, before Vignie "with furniture enriching the two parlors of the main house, consisting of two mirrors, two marble consoles; rosewood furniture composed of sofa, armchair, two ottomans, six chairs, two armchairs covered with red velvet, pair of vases, a clock, pair of vases, one jardiniere, pair bronze horses, two tables, pair porcelain, Turkish tapestries, two tapestries (before the chimney), four stores and six galeries gilded and piano." Everything in the sale totaled $19,400.

The house was sold again in 1877 by heirs of J. B. Letorey to B. A. Herman at auction November 15. An ad in the *New Orleans Democrat*, September 28, 1877, describes the house as "that elegant and spacious residence, for many years occupied by M. Musson . . . a spacious two-story frame dwelling, built retired from the street and enclosed by an iron fence, wide central halls with double front galleries; large apartments on both floors; elegantly finished throughout; detached two story kitchen and stable and carriage house; gas, cistern, etc. The surplus ground is beautifully shaded and laid out in walks and planted in ornamental grass, etc. For quiet, spacious and aristocratic residence the property has every requisite. Its neighborhood is one of the most charming in the city."

The house is closely associated with the Degas-Musson families. Michel Musson, a prominent cotton exporter, was the uncle of the artist Edgar Degas and his brother René. He also served as the senior Degas' local agent. The families had common ancestors in the New Orleans Rillieux family. René Degas married his first cousin Estelle Musson. It was an unhappy union that ended in separation. When Edgar Degas visited his sister-in-law and began her portrait (now housed at the New Orleans Museum of Art), it is thought that he occupied 2306. For ten years the Musson family rented this house, and yet it is popularly known as the Musson home, although they never owned it. The Robinson map of 1883 indicates that the Musson-Degas house at 2306 became the Markey and Picard Institute from 1880 to 1891.

A Persac and Surgi elevation and plan commissioned for the Rodriguez 1860 auction sale (cover plate) scarcely resemble the photograph of the house today. The entire left half of the house was sliced away, changing it from a center-hall to a side-hall house. All but one service building has disappeared, and all fences have been ripped away. Crowded between two late houses, the present house is difficult to recognize as the former elegant country seat of 1854.

2326

Sarpy House

The house at 2316 Esplanade was moved to its present location from Dorgenois Street by the Henry Sarpy family. On its original square, which was the 2400 block of Esplanade, Mayor Behrman ordered the removal of all structures. Many buildings were demolished, including the Vredenbergh and Soulé houses. Others were moved, such as the Victor Wogan house, which was placed at 1301 N. Tonti, corner of Barracks. Number 2316, the Sarpy house, was moved to the right sideyard of the Musson house. The roof configuration with its extreme height and slight cant would indicate an early nineteenth-century house. No other architectural details, as seen from the exterior, would give evidence of any architectural style other than an early twentieth-century residence.

Reuther House

The outline of a double-level house with three bays is sketched on the Robinson survey of 1883 approximately in the position of present 2326 Esplanade. Formerly a part of a small plantation owned by Bernard Coquet, title runs indicate a minimum of ten owners before Mrs. Anna Eliza Feitag acquired the property in 1894. In 1903 Mrs. Feitag was the wife of A. F. Markes, and as such sold to Albert P. Noll for $4,000. Noll mortgaged the building and improvements for $7,000, and it is believed that he took an existing structure and remodeled it to the present massive turn-of-the-century home. In 1913, the house was sold for $12,000, by Noll to Joseph Reuther, a New Orleans baker who established a concern known today as "Reising's." The sale included the "fixtures of chandeliers, bathtubs, gas heaters, and entire heating equipment, including instantaneous heaters." The present owners are Robert Tannen and Jean Nathan.

At 2336 Esplanade another fine late Classic-style house was built for developer Benjamin Rodriguez as Esplanade became a mid-century reality. The frame house with gabled side and side bay is in the grand scale of the Esplanade Ridge style. It had no architect but was designed by its builder, Joseph Jouet, who bought it from Rodriguez upon completion.

This lot, like most of the 2300 block, was earlier part of the old Fleitas plantation. Rodriguez collected six lots that formed this large property in the mid-1850s and engaged Jouet to build the house in a private contract still unfound, dated sometime during 1859. While the house and dependencies were in construction, Rodriguez and Jouet met at the offices of notary Abel Dreyfous where they deposited in his ledger their mutual desire to buy and sell the house. The notary recorded that "ils sont tombés d'accord à ce sujet," literally, that "they fell into agreement on this subject." Rodriguez sold the house to Jouet for $6,000. Within a month Jouet sold to James M. Urquhart, who in turn sold to Abraham Haim D'Mexa in 1864 for $12,000. D'Meza lost the house at a sheriff's sale in 1872, whereupon it was bought by Carl Kohn. Kohn sold to Paul A. Poutz in 1878, and the house remained in the Poutz family until 1896. The house was then purchased by Leon Joubert de Villemarest.

Since 1921 it has been owned by the Albert Livaudais family and has been used as three apartments. Several marble mantels, one crystal chandelier, and two pier glass mirrors recall its past grandeur, yet the recent side addition diminishes its original exterior simplicity. Well-detailed bathroom and kitchen annexes can be harmonious and provide the needed space. Most of the early brick banquette remains along the Esplanade and Rocheblave elevations of the house. Oddly, the double iron entrance gates do not line up with the house entrance.

2336

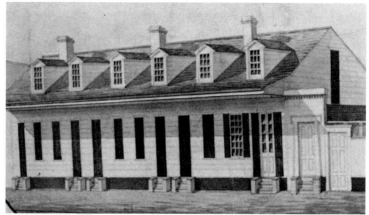

2325–31

Plan Book 73/47

On the same triangle of land formed between Esplanade and Bayou Road, there are two remaining, yet rare, Classic-style shotgun cottages. Their numbers are now 2337 and 2341 Esplanade; they share the history of the Fleitas plantation and Benjamin Rodriguez development. These attractive houses were once identical plastered-front, American side-hall shotguns, but 2337 now has a second story. Rodriguez bought the site of 2337 in 1855 and that of 2341 in 1858. He resold both vacant lots to John Budd Slawson in January of 1858. When Slawson bought these two properties, he also purchased the "Bayou Road Line of Omnibuses" from Rodriguez for a total price of $36,000. The omnibus company operated horse-drawn coaches on Bayou Road and greatly facilitated transportation within the area. By 1862 Slawson had built 2337 and 2341, then sold them to N. M. Benachi for $3,000; four years later Benachi divested himself of the houses, selling them to Abraham H. D'Meza before E. G. Gottschalk for $3,000. D'Meza lost these houses to Miguel de Avendano as well as 2336 in an 1872 sheriff's sale. Stephen D. Pool bought them at another auction in 1883, and they remained in the Pool family until well into the twentieth century.

Architecturally, these two cottages afford a delightful comparison of building types with the creole cottage row immediately adjacent at 2325–27–29–31. Dating from within a year of each other (1859), one group represents the evolution of an early creole house type, while the other is the harbinger of a dominant type of the late nineteenth-century New Orleans architecture, the shotgun. Both have restrained decoration, post-and-lintel openings, symmetry, and strong geometric lines. Each is designed in the urban tradition, set at the banquette, and raised only enough to allow for functional foundation ventilation. Masonry façades together with a projecting decorative ironwork band and iron brackets at the overhang level create a sophisticated appearance for the shotguns, opposed to the simplicity of the creole cottages.

Major differences are most readily apparent

2341 and 2337

at the rooflines, where gable sides in the creole style contrast with the lower hip-roof of the American-style shotgun. The creole row is hall-less with a modest, unadorned façade, while the American shotguns have gracious entrances with wide halls, and are each single-family dwellings. Attic or "garret" space is of enormous importance in the creole cottages, which are equipped with dormers making the upper- or half-story bright, functional spaces. This high-pitched roofline is absent on the shotguns; the roof is so low that the raised parapet most often obscures it. When additional space became necessary, an entire second story had to be added, as at 2337. Unfortunately, this second story spoils the integrity of one of the important houses in the city.

The house on the left, number 2341, retains much of its original appearance within as well as without, having a wide hall opening onto its three successive (shotgun) rooms. The dining room is at the rear of the hall. To the rear left is a two-story connecting service wing forming the effect of a camel back. The ceilings are fifteen feet, and the two front rooms have sliding doors between, with simple marble mantels. Esplanade is a shady and wide avenue at this block, where herringbone brick sidewalks are framed by live oaks and aspidistra.

Benjamin Rodriguez built the creole cottage row at 2325–27–29–31 as an investment in 1859, soon after he bought these and other adjacent lots from Philippe Avegno, Jr., and Theodore Guyol, the notary. An archival drawing in plan book 73, folio 47, signed E. Surgi and A. Persac, illustrates the cottages when they were offered for sale soon after completion March 12, 1860. Nicolas Benachi purchased the new houses at the public auction and recorded the act of sale before Abel Dreyfous on April 5, 1860. Close observation reveals that the drawing is of three common-wall cottages with six apartments while the group is a fourplex today. One of the common-wall cottages has been demolished, and one dormer has been removed from each of the two remaining houses. Louvered shutters were also removed from the windows and doors, and concrete porches and narrow front weatherboarding were added. A series of one-story detached kitchens across the rear of the lot have been replaced by shedlike appendages; where the last cottage and parterre garden were located, there is another house.

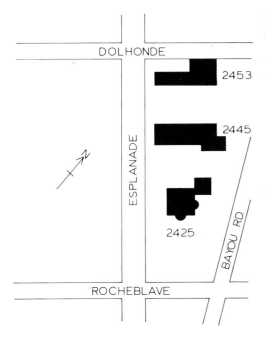

DOLHONDE

2453

2445

ESPLANADE

2425

BAYOU RD

ROCHEBLAVE

2400 Block

The 2400 even block of Esplanade is now a McDonogh school, built in 1911 as Esplanade Girls High. This land was formerly part of the earliest French land grants to Louis Cesaire LeBreton in 1752, and was reassigned to Joseph Suarez in 1800 by the Spanish crown through Ramon Lopez y Angulo, the intendant. The property was then described as two arpents fronting Bayou Road, extending in depth to the Carondelet Canal. Suarez, a Spanish colonial subject, chose to divest himself of the property after the Louisiana Purchase, and Lebreton Dorgenois, Louis Cesaire's grandson, purchased it and built a house on the right of the projected Esplanade. His widow, Marie Joseph Harang, and his heirs, Marie Françoise, wife of Sieur François Morière Fazende; Anne Marie Françoise Geneviève, widow of Dusau de la Croix; Emélie Felicité, widow of Cyril Fazende; Louis Joseph LeBreton de Préfore, and Louis Cesaire LeBreton DesChapelles offered the Dorgenois estate at auction in 1816.

The *Louisiana Courier* of March 25, 1816, advertised the land and home ''on the Bayou Road . . . with a mansion and servants houses heretofore occupied by LeBreton Dorgenois, deceased, formerly marshal of the United States for the District of Louisiana.'' M.

Cauchoix, a lawyer, acquired the habitation and still owned it in 1822, according to the Pilié survey. He sold the Dorgenois habitation to Bernard Coquet after 1822. Coquet was the well-known entrepreneur whose businesses included the operation of pleasure gardens, such as Tivoli on Bayou St. John, and establishments for entertainment. Coquet no doubt lived in the house on Bayou Road between 1825 and his death around 1840. The roof of his house is indicated on a survey commissioned for the subdivision of the Coquet property, dated January 20, 1840. At the time that his heirs were offering sixty-three lots on this property, they were also selling the nearby first plantation owned by Coquet beneath the Fleitas habitation, today marked by the 2300 block of Esplanade.

As late as 1896 there remained on the present school square two major Italianate houses, one brick and one frame. The mansions belonged to W. H. Vredenbergh and to Neville Soulé, respectively. These elegant homes equal in magnificence to the Florence Luling, Wright-Slocomb, and Baldwin houses, were demolished for the school. Henry Howard and Albert Diettel designed the house for William H. Vredenbergh, according to a building contract before W. H. Peters, May 17, 1858, in which Little and Middlemiss agreed to build the ''two story brick house with verandah, Corinthian columns, pilasters, brackets and railing'' for $15,700. The 1896 directory lists Vredenbergh at 2438 Esplanade. Neville Soulé, attorney, was domiciled in 1861 on the adjacent property, old number 396 Esplanade at the corner of Rocheblave. Remnants of one of the homes were removed to Audubon Boulevard and incorporated by Dr. Warren Hebert into his home at number 70.

Brierre House

Adjacent to an inappropriate corner brick building established as the American Federation of Musicians Local No. 174–496 was number 2425 Esplanade. □ It represented the Second Empire frame mansion style and although partially burned, totally neglected in 1975, and demolished in 1976, it recalled with dignity the profusive mid-1870s avenue or main boulevard style. Originally it was the home of Theodore Brierre, a sugar and rice factor, who operated a commercial business with his two sons, Maurice O. and George Brierre. This block had been held in speculation by investors Abraham Haim D'Meza, Archibald Montgomery, and F. E. Duconge before the elder Brierre's 1875 purchase of three large lots. The house was built soon after purchase, and by 1880 Brierre had expanded his holdings

fronting Esplanade all the way to the corner of Dorgenois.

The commodity business was then, as now, highly volatile; by 1888 a meeting of the creditors of Theodore Brierre and Sons was called in the Royal Street office of notary E. A. Peyroux. A statement explaining the financial condition read: ''They [Brierres] have lately met with heavy losses in business resulting principally from the failure of the commercial firm of Philip Hoelzel & Co. on whose notes and drafts petitioners were endorsers for large amounts.'' The business and personal assets of the family were sold in bankruptcy, and an ensuing auction sale by the syndic of the creditors provided the following descriptions of the house:

A handsome and agreeable two-story frame residence, retired from the street, having all the conveniences of a first-class residence. The halls, parlor, sitting room, dining room, and bedroom are papered and are artistically decorated. . . . The ground floor has front, rear, and side galleries, hall, parlor, sitting room, dining room, kitchen, and pantry. On the upper story hall, five bedrooms with dressing cabinets, servants' room, bathroom, and English patent closet.

The garden is beautifully arranged and planted with a collection of rare and select shrubs, flowers and fine orange trees, etc. Also, ornamenting the garden, a fountain with an aquarium; two large cisterns, hydrants in the yard and garden. A fine stable built in the rear of the lot facing Bayou Road, bricked yard, etc. The premises are in splendid order, requiring no repairs whatever; the locality and surroundings are charming. Parties in search of a comfortable home are requested to examine the property. Cards of admission will be granted them; the whole agreeable to plans made by Arthur De Armas.

Unfortunately, the De Armas plan has not been found. It may have contained a watercolor elevation of the house and dependencies. This auction, held three days before Christmas of 1888, was concluded by a sale to Louis Hermann's wife, Marie Emma Lanata, for the modest sum of $9,000. It was a fine investment, for Mrs. Hermann sold in 1894 for $16,000.

The Hermann sale was to Mrs. Maude Elizabeth Tobin, wife of Leon Gustave Gilbert and daughter of John W. Tobin, who was the original owner of a nearby home, 2522 Esplanade. Maude Tobin purchased the house with her separate funds and in 1901 sold to Mr. J. A. Wogan. In 1921 Mrs. Wogan sold to Antonio La Nasa. Fifty years later, the home was still owned by the La Nasa heirs. It was demolished in May 1976, for use as a parking area by the American Federation of Musicians.

Dunbar Houses

Another Esplanade street scene in *Art Work of New Orleans*, 1895, emphasized the neatness of the closely cropped lawns and uniformity emanating from the simple iron picket fences, most often furnished by Hinderer's Ironworks. The view of the 2400 downriver Esplanade shows a side elevation of the now-demolished 2425 Esplanade, before 2435 □ was constructed. A mansard mansion, now demolished, was depicted at 2445, next to an existing mansard twin building identified then as old number 407, presently 2453. The photograph illustrating this Esplanade Avenue pair of rare mansard residences provides a glimpse of their appearance twenty years after their erection.

George Washington Dunbar, his sons and their families, purchased the sites of 2445 and 2453 for their new homes, in the fall of 1873, from Archibald Montgomery. G. W. Dunbar had married Charlotte Zulmé Hacker in 1843 and was in a manufacturing business with his two sons Francis Bird Dunbar and George

Hacker Dunbar when the homes were constructed. In 1879 the elder Dunbar died, leaving his part ownership in the properties equally divided among his children. George Hacker Dunbar married Susie Foucher that same year, and they moved into the corner house at 2453 and had four children, all girls. Francis Bird Dunbar married Anna Tourne. They had three children and lived in the second house, now demolished, at 2445. The interiors were also similar, and both had large entrance halls with side alcoves opening to living rooms with arch screens and decorative consoles. There were inlaid hardwood floors and marble mantels in the main rooms, including the library and dining rooms. Outside, there were greenhouses and service buildings. The deciduous crape myrtles shown in the 1895 photograph are towering trees eighty years later. The Dunbar heirs sold number 2445 to William Lee Hughes in 1910. The lot size was changed in this sale to measure 74 feet by 193 feet, and for the sale the real estate appraiser evaluated the property, including all the mantels, gas and bath fixtures,

window shades and poles, awnings, hall heaters, kitchen stove, even the hall carpet, and outside plants and shrubbery. Hughes held the property for thirty-eight years, until the house was bought by James P. Puig. The George Hacker Dunbars occupied the house at 2453 until 1925.

Englehart's photograph from *The City of New Orleans, 1894*, published by the Chamber of Commerce, conveys all the original similarities and differences of the two houses at that time, and close scrutiny readily reveals the dramatic alterations in the existing corner house at 2453. The front porch with iron railing has been replaced by a concrete landing, a side gallery is gone, and the focal window in the center mansard roof opens only onto a small balcony. The rarity of nineteenth-century mansard-roofed houses, which are proportioned and sensitive to site and surrounding space, makes 2453 Esplanade a very important surviving type, despite these major modifications.

The Dunbar Residences, 2453 (left), 2447 (right) demolished

2453

2453

2500 Block

Between Dorgenois and Broad, the old Girod Canal (now Orleans Street) and St. John Street (Bell), there is a four-by-twelve-arpent tract of land that was bought by speculators from John Watkins in the 1850s. This was a portion of an eighteenth-century French concession to Louis Cesaire LeBreton and Vincent Guillaume Le Senéchal Dauberville in 1752. Both men had abandoned this claim when Joseph Saurez acquired it in 1801 by a Spanish land grant. The Spanish colonial grants in this section ran parallel to the future Esplanade, whereas the ancient French ones had angled back toward Metairie from Bayou Road. In 1809 this land became a part of Daniel Clark's Faubourg St. John via Nicholas Maria Vidal, Spanish civil governor, who had purchased it almost immediately after Suarez' acquisition. This was a small part of the Vidal land which encompassed property from Bayou St. John to Dorgenois Street. This section was described in the sale to Clark on July 24, 1804, before P. Pedesclaux as:

[Vidal's] second habitation, a piece of land to the front of the other plantation on the right hand of Camino Real, leaving from the city for the said Gran Bayou, composed of four arpents front, bound on the city side with Bridge of the Washerwomen and Little Bayou of the Dead, Don Gabriel Peyroux, and by the other part of land belonged to Free Negress Fanchon Montreuil and through the depth with Camino de Gentilly and Pequeno Bayou [Small Bayou, near present Broad] and with lands of Pedro Gueno which before belonged to Don Manuel Ximenes, and with lands of the Deverges ladies; which in diverse portions I bought from Josef Suarez, Fanchon Montreuil, Don Pedro Juzan and his wife and Don Marie Suzanne Caüe, widow of Peyroux before Don Carlos Ximenes, December 10, 1798, and January 26, 1799, and before this notary [Pedesclaux] May 19 and July 3, 1801, as drawn by Carlos Trudeau.

One year earlier, April 16, 1800, Vidal had received a Spanish land grant of vacant lands which were bound on the city side by "habitación de Jose Suarez." The Suarez land became important to Vidal because of its Bayou Road and waterway frontage, both of which he needed. This valuable property was sold along with the other Vidal plantations to Daniel Clark. Five years later Clark had Barthelemy Lafon include this Dorgenois-to-Broad section in his overall Faubourg St. John subdivision and selected that section for the site of his own home.

Daniel Clark, born in County Sligo, Ireland, in 1766, joined an uncle in Louisiana after attending Eton School in England. In 1800 Clark inherited his uncle's substantial business, added to it, and became an important political and commercial figure in Louisiana. Clark's hip-roof dwelling faced the spacious juncture of three future streets, St. John (Bell), Washington (DeSoto), and Gentilly Road at the Halle Bretonne, the site of an ancient Indian market. When he moved to this site from old 823 Royal, his townhouse became the residence of Pierre Baron Boisfontaine, his agent and man of business. Clark died at this Bayou Road house in 1813. His will and events relating to his Faubourg St. John property resulted in a sixty-year lawsuit, longest in the history of American jurisprudence, and one where many primary suits are yet to be computed. In his will of May, 1811, he left to his mother his entire estate with Richard Relf and Beverly Chew, his executors. These executors continued to manage Clark's estate, selling his lots and houses. An ad in the *Louisiana Courier,* March 2, 1814, advertised, "To rent—the beautiful house before occupied by Daniel Clark situated on the Bayou Road. For the price see Richard Relf, executor."

Clark's daughter Myra soon after her birth had been adopted informally by Samuel Davis, a prominent naval official stationed in New Orleans. She was made aware of another Clark will when she reached adulthood, and she began suing the city of New Orleans and the owners of all that part of Faubourg St. Jean and other Clark properties which had been sold by Relf and Chew, making claim to them through a will purported to have been written by Clark in July of 1813, shortly before his death, leaving his entire estate to her. Colonel Bellechasse, Monsieur Dusau de la Croix de Mazillieres and Judge James Pitot were the executors of this lost will. As the court fights proceeded generation after generation, the Esplanade awaited completion. The city had to obtain from Myra Clark Gaines's lawyers "quit claims" in order to acquire clear title to the land that had been part of Faubourg St. John and not sold before Clark's death. Mention is often made of similar claims in order to untangle titles for property transfer along Faubourg St. John and the avenue.

On June 15, 1809, before Pierre Pedesclaux, Clark had sold the Dorgenois-to-Broad land near his own house to Louis Henry Lecesne. The Lecesne brothers were active real estate speculators. Henry Lecesne built a country seat which stood directly in the way of the new Esplanade. The *Louisiana Courier* advertised

2504

this house on April 29, 1811: "In the suburb St. John, a very elegant new house, built with bricks between posts and covered with shingles, divided into five commodious rooms, with back and fronting gallery, kitchen, yard, well, etc., the whole in the best order . . . built upon a lot of about one hundred-eighty feet fronting Orchard Street, by about three hundred-sixty feet on Dorgenoy Street, including in whole nine regular lots . . . has a very fine and well cultivated garden, with a double row of sweet orange trees . . . is every where newly fenced with standing stakes."

The 2500 block, on both sides of the Esplanade, was the rural Lecesne plantation until sold by him in 1825 before P. Pedesclaux to Dame John Watkins. Her son acquired both sides of this block, and he sold them in 1837 before L. T. Caire, February 11, to Joseph Barthet. This land did not actually develop

until it is shown being subdivided into 122 lots, according to a Magny lithograph of a plan dated April 4, 1853. Barthet commissioned a surveyor to subdivide this land and auction it through the office of auctioneer N. Vignie. The lithograph illustrates hip-roof houses along the avenue, then a gravel road, in the 2500 block and along each side of St. John and Washington streets and Gentilly Road.

The Jartoux residence appears facing St. John Street; it had a front-gable roof while that of Bruguière and Clark residences had hip-roofs. The Holland property faced Esplanade at the corner of Dorgenois and Mrs. François' large estate at Broad and Esplanade measured 198 feet by 110; these are two hip-roof structures, one facing the Broad canal, the other the Esplanade. An archival drawing of this house, dated July 8, 1841, by Bougerol in Plan Book 21, folio 18, shows a galleried, dormered

creole cottage surrounded by a split cypress fence enclosing a very long, low stable or outbuilding along Broad. This was one of the first houses facing the Esplanade within the confines of old Faubourg St. John. Katz and Bestoff's modern brick drugstore occupies this site today.

Brugière-Tobin House

The rest of the block remained unimproved except for the Broad Street corner and the Dorgenois corner, until Nicholas Benachi and Benjamin Rodriguez activated interest in the land soon after their purchases from Barthet. Number 2504 Esplanade was built soon after 1855 when Antoine Camille Bruguière bought six lots for $2,400. In 1853 he and his wife lived nearby in a house facing St. John Street. Bruguière mortgaged the improved property for $11,000 in 1857 and sold the house at 2504 to

Isidore Esclapion for $10,700. Esclapion sold two years later to Jacob D. Van Hickle for $11,000. Eclectic details of the mid-1850s, as seen here, were particularized in the Esplanade Ridge style. Capitals on the fluted columns are copied from those of the Tower of the Winds, a Greek order popularized in the city by Henry Howard. The house, although threatened by commercial encroachment and a deteriorating neighborhood, is a credit to the grand period of the Esplanade and symbolizes the hope for its future revival.

The Robinson insurance map of 1883 shows the house of "J. F. Tobin" built on the site of 2522 Esplanade. Captain John W. Tobin, a well-known New Orleans steamboat owner, bought the lot in 1873 before A. Pitot, May 28, after speculative ownership of the grounds by Joseph Barthet, Benachi, and J. S. Meilleur. The Tobin family retained their family home until 1919, when it was sold to Anthony Battistella. Photographs made during the Tobin ownership illustrate the original appearance of the exterior. The original wooden steps at the front and side were replaced with steps of tile and cement in the so-called Queen Anne style. All wooden turned balusters have been removed or changed to cast-iron railings. The method of updating spoils the integrity of the "tout ensemble," which emphasized the use of wooden elements. The front yard was bricked, and garden areas were planted with the traditional camellias and lilies and edged with violets. Aspidistra banked the foundations in a treatment popular well into the twentieth century. Live oak and palm trees, iron urns filled with asparagus fern and a large cistern completed the late Victorian garden scene.

A Tobin photograph affords a view of an "esthetic-period" interior. Matting covered the entire floor with occasional oriental throw rugs. Woodwork and molding were stained dark, and floral wallpaper continued to the ceiling forming a border above the plaster molding. The motif is repeated in the wallpaper medallion above the bronze gas chandelier. Ignoring the busy floral patterns, the late Victorian matron filled the walls with genre paintings, daguerrotypes, and bibelots, and she did not hesitate to drape a blessed palm over grandpère's photo. The furnishings included an elaborate Mallard tufted half-tester bed, with designs inlaid in lemonwood, and matching armoire. New York machine-made dressers, secretary desks, duchesse, and a commode border the walls. An assortment of chairs of various periods and styles includes cane rockers and two 1880s-style wicker rockers. A sewing machine placed near the varicolored marble mantel and a draped chaise lounge complete the decor of the large bedroom.

2522 (Top photo courtesy Edward J. Gay III; middle and bottom photos courtesy Clive Hardy Collection)

2522 (Courtesy Edward J. Gay III)

2522

2540

Meilleur House

Pandea Nicolas Benachi bought the site of the house at 2540 Esplanade from Joseph Barthet in 1858 as recorded by Abel Dreyfous on January 26, selling the lots to Jean Simon Meilleur in 1866, who then built this house. It proved a difficult investment for Meilleur, who lived at 1418 Governor Nicholls, the site of the Charles de Morand brickworks. By 1871 Meilleur had sold the house and its entire contents back to Pandea Nicholas Benachi for a total of $28,000, of which $5,000 was for the contents. Meilleur then immediately made an $1,800-a-year lease for the house and contents from Benachi, and a few months later, in early spring of 1872, he repurchased the real estate and movables from Benachi for the same price. Just six years later Meilleur sold to his neighbor, Roman Forrester Bruguière. In 1920 the Bruguière heirs sold the property to the Third Presbyterian Church. (This congregation built the existing large red brick structure next door.)

This frame, Classic-style house with raised brick basement at 2540 Esplanade is similar to two others on Esplanade, 1251 and 1614. Of the three, 1251 is the simplest and earliest, dating from 1850; and the other two were both built about 1868. The house was raised when it was moved from the adjacent site for the erection of the church building in 1924. Its Tower of the Winds capitals are similar to those of its neighbor at 2504 Esplanade. The present lower level suggests a full two-story townhouse, having a formal entrance.

Deynoodt-Dufossat House

The handsome, rare villa-style house at 2511 Esplanade has been demolished. It was Italianate, with a center hall and side bay, built between 1859 and 1862 for Joseph Deynoodt on land which had contained the François Jartoux rear gardens, as shown on the 1853 Magny lithograph. Deynoodt had bought the lot from Jartoux before Octave de Armas in 1859. On March 3, 1862, in the middle of the Civil War, he sold it to Auguste Reichard, "resident of Alexandria, Egypt," according to S. Magner, August 24, 1864. It was described as an "improved lot in Faubourg St. John" and sold for $14,000. Participating in the sale was Mrs. Deynoodt, Solidelle Legardeur. The Reichard family sold the house two years later to Manuel A. de Lizardi, who owned much real estate throughout the city. He sold this home in 1869 to Theodore and Emma Soniat Dufossat, whose family lived in the house for forty years.

The sophisticated house featured a rusticated façade with a gallery supported by fluted Corinthian columns. The gallery returned to

2511 (Demolished)

the bay with a curving cornice above which was a side gable with decorated pediment. Side gallery supports were box columns, contrasting with the front Corinthian columns. This was one of the finer Italianate villas in the city and had been altered little except for an upper front clerestory. A new, vermiculated, stuccoed foundation also detracted from the original design. The loss of houses such as this is regrettable, particularly when the owners claim they would not have destroyed the house had not the city condemned it. Because there were no immediate plans for its utility or for its restoration, the house was demolished. A photograph in the Tulane University Special Collections Division shows it as it appeared between 1869 and 1908, during the long ownership by the Dufossat family. Notable was a fence across the lot made of square wood pickets of varying heights set between wood pillars above a deep paneled wood base. As was customary with many early wood fences, the entrance gate comprised double doors with cast iron insert panels, topped by a cornice giving the appearance of an arrangement suitable for an interior doorway.

By the time the Esplanade reached deep into Faubourg St. John at the crossing of Broad, it had caused the removal or demolition of the homes of Jean Mager at St. Claude, the outbuildings of the Pedesclaux-Duchamp house at Prieur, the Castanedo manor house, and outbuildings near Galvez, the houses of Paul Cheval, Pierre Darby, widow Fleitas, and the

outbuildings of Bernard Coquet's habitation. Nonetheless, it was a progressive and planned movement and spurred the development of flanking neighborhoods formed from these old habitations behind the city. Most of these were subdivided because of the Esplanade projection, and the developers took advantage of the planned cross streets for the arrangement of lots. The axis of the entire area to the rear of the city was transformed by the city's determination to lay out the area in line with the existing streets of the old city. Heretofore, the axis had been at the angle of the French colonial concessions which fronted on Bayou Road.

Bayou Road, however, did not become obsolete overnight. For example, John Budd Slawson continued the Bayou Road horsecar lines in the 1850s. Pierre Gueno's plantation missed the route of Esplanade by a city block near Place Bretonne, but his widow was able to make brisk sales of the property in 1834. Other prominent families continued to choose the older locations along Bayou Road for their fashionable homes even in the 1850s. Monsieur Benachi had bought part of the Fleitas habitation on the left side of Bayou Road, which made lots on the right side of Esplanade; however, he built his own house in the late 1850s on the site of his earlier house at 2255 Bayou Road. Similarly, the widow Fleitas, it is thought, rather than keep lots along Esplanade carved out of her plantation, moved to Bayou Road.

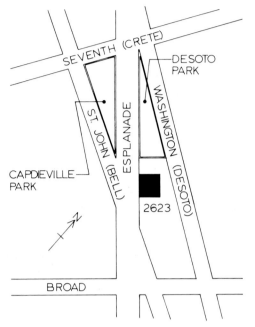

2600 Block

The Esplanade's approach to Faubourg St. John did not create an immediate positive effect. Across the Broad Canal, it entered a community that had been established almost half a century before by Daniel Clark, who sold lots to many individuals in his new faubourg as early as 1809. Clark's surveyor, Barthelemy Lafon, did not utilize a grid pattern for the streets of Faubourg St. John, for the streets fanned out from a focal point at Place Bretonne, creating thirty-five irregularly shaped squares between Dorgenois and Bayou St. John. The plan conformed to property acquired by Clark in 1804 and 1805, bound to the west by swamplands owned by Louis Blanc. The Esplanade's invasive character at this point sliced through the middle of six developed squares between the 2600 and 3000 blocks, all of which had houses facing St. John (Bell), Washington (DeSoto), LePage, Seventh (Crete), Sixth (Swamp or White), Fifth (Sauvage or Dupre), Fourth (Gayoso), Third (Encampment or Lopez), or Rendon (Mystery). This caused the demolition of numerous homes and the necessity of realigning property. The impact presented legal complications in land ownership which continued for generations. A number of houses along the street's route were removed to side streets or relocated along the new avenue.

Ironically, the primary use of the new street for twenty years was as a transportation link to the Bayou St. John and Lake Pontchartrain. The Esplanade and Bayou Bridge streetcar line began in 1863. While New Orleans appreciated this new thoroughfare, the land was not needed for a population expansion until the late nineteenth century. Then, numerous German and creole names appeared as owners of the new houses and shifted from their earlier St. Rose de Lima parish neighborhood. The French names are of old New Orleans creole families, for although the Americans through the generations congregated generally upriver in Faubourg St. Mary and beyond, the creoles left the French Quarter to move along the Esplanade Ridge toward the Bayou. A few suburban country seats were built in the late 1860s and 1870s on large lots along the new avenue; most houses, however, date from the turn of the century through the 1920s, and today the general impression of Esplanade, architecturally, from Broad to the Bayou, is one of large single-family homes built in various eclectic styles, set back on spacious and deep lots. There remain homes in the City Beautiful and mission styles. These examples, as early as

1910, featured stucco, red tile roofs, and several Moorish and Spanish decorative details. Neo-Tudor motifs, along with stick-style detailing and some art nouveau designs, may be seen. Bungalow-style houses, popular in the 1920s and 1930s and prevalent in the Gentilly Terrace area, appeared with Egyptian-style pillars on piers. While few of these houses on the avenue are noteworthy individually, collectively they reflect the history of the city as new suburban development. The entire atmosphere was new; numerous pocket parks opened vistas to the right and left of the avenue. Older homes along Grand Route St. John, DeSoto, and LePage are visible through the parks. The neutral ground narrowed, and the sidewalk oaks grew into an arc forming an inviting wide corridor. Large front gardens, unfenced and free, further spread the spaces, creating a rural aura.

Faubourg St. John had been rural, and its eighteenth-century history included the development of many farms and chronicled the life of famous French and Spanish colonials. The history of this land as concessions and habitations stemmed back to the founding of New Orleans. The great area between Bayou St. John, Dorgenois, and the Carondelet Canal (Lafitte) is most clearly associated with the names of Louis and Evariste Blanc, Daniel Clark, and Nicolas Maria Vidal. Other characters appear as the history of the land unfolds, most notably Louis Cesaire LeBreton, who had a concession there in 1756, the Brasilier Tourangeau family, and Vincent Le Sénéchal D'Auberville. Joseph Chalon and his wife Elizabeth Desruisseaux and Andrés Almonester y Roxas, all active in real estate behind the city, were owners of a habitation eventually comprising Faubourg St. John.

In the 1770s Andrés Jung acquired the land from Broad to the Bayou along the future route of Esplanade. This was done through purchase and inheritance via his wife Pelagia Lorreins, whose first husband was Jean Baptiste Brasilier dit Tourangeau. Andrés Jung sold sixteen by twenty-two arpents to Joseph Chalon and his wife Elizabeth Desruisseaux. They in turn sold them to Andrés Almonester y Roxas on May 7, 1781. The act of sale before L. Mazange describes the property.

We sell to Andrés Almonester y Roxas a habitation that belongs to us for having acquired it from Andrés Jung according to a retrocession of the land, before the present buyer [Almonester was also a notary], with the rest of the habitation [part was also acquired from Magdalena Brasilier, widow of Enrique Desprez, eight arpents by twenty-two arpents before J. B. Garic, October 15, 1774]. It is situated in the parish which they call the Bridge of the Bayou St. John, a half league distant from New Orleans, composed of sixteen arpents of land front and twenty-two arpents depth, with various buildings fabricated of wood and brick, bound on one side by the Camino Real, and by the other with vacant lands. We also sell three negroes, twenty-four head of cattle, one horse, three wagons and all the pigs and other animals which we bought. . . . We sell it for 6000 pesos.

This was a plantation, the proceeds of which Almonester, a patron of the new Charity Hospital of St. Charles, offered in 1783 for the support of the hospital. He specified that an abundance of lime and lumber were to be had on the place. However, Almonester did not pursue such use of the land too long since he sold half of it to Louis Antoine Blanc in 1793 and five years later in 1798 relinquished to him the remaining half.

Nicolas Maria Vidal came to the Bayou during the last years of the Spanish colonial period and purchased from Louis Blanc a portion of Blan's habitation near Bayou Road. It measured "six arpents facing the Camino Real of which was measured a half arpent in the figure of a triangle bound by lands of Joseph Suarez and on the other side lands of the seller L. A. Blanc." Immediately afterward, Vidal appealed to the king of Spain for additional lands contiguous to his new habitation. This was land toward Carondelet Canal from Bayou Road, and his concession was granted April 16, 1800, before Roman de Lopez y Angulo. A third tract assembled by Vidal from various purchases referred to in the 2500 block completed a large contiguous area with waterways and roads.

Then in 1804 Daniel Clark came to the bayou, purchasing lands from both Vidal and Louis Blanc, putting together a parcel between 1804 and 1805 out of which he made Faubourg St. John. On July 24, 1804, Clark purchased Vidal's three tracts, described in part:

Know that I Don Nicolas Maria Vidal promise to sell to Daniel Clark of Natchez a plantation of my ownership, with buildings and utensils of labor, situated on the Camino del Gran Bayou, titled San Juan, leaving from this city for the Bayou on the left side of the Camino Real, six arpents fronting on it . . . lined on one side with lands which Josef Suarez possesses, and on the other side with lands of Don Luis Antonio Blanc, and behind extends in depth to the Canal Carondelet, and outside the parallel line continued behind the habitation of said Blanc to the Bayou, which belongs to me from having bought it from Blanc before this notary January 30, 1800, and the rest in depth which I acquired by a concession that the Intendant made me on April 16, 1800.

2623

2623

The following year Clark purchased from Louis Blanc before N. Broutin, January 25, 1805, "six arpents facing Bayou Road with the depth it is able to have joining on one side the lands of the seller and on the other the lands of the acquirer, for $5,000."

Louis Lecesne had bought from Clark much of the former Vidal land in the 2500 and 2600 blocks, including the intendant's own country house between Broad and Crete (Seventh), which was the first to obstruct the route of Esplanade across Broad. This was offered for sale in 1811, along with the Lecesne house between Dorgenois and Broad, according to a *Louisiana Courier* ad:

Another property contiguous to that above described [Lecesne House], and occupied by the proprietor undersigned, measuring about 14½ regular lots, at the corner of the Broad street of the Canal, and St. John St. [Bell] running back to Orchid St. [Live Oak]. Upon which stands a substantial brick Dwelling-House, divided into two large rooms, with back and fronting galleries. On the left hand from the principal gate stands in the first yard, a building erected with bricks between posts and covered with shingles, of one hundred feet in length, divided into a kitchen, two large rooms for servants, pantry, cellar, rooms for the dressing maids, and two other rooms to receive travellers.—On the right hand stand a coach-house, a lodging for the ostler, and a stable behind, with a hen roost erected on square brick pillars. In the second yard stands a building of eighty-three feet in length, by twenty-three in width, which is used as a store for provisions, and an ox-stall with a spacious hay loft. The said property has also a well cultivated garden, yielding a pretty good income, with a pump of irrigation, and a very fine double row of trees. It belonged formerly to the Spanish auditor [Vidal]. The subscriber will also sell the furniture of the house, and some negroes attached to said plantation, as well as twenty or twenty-five milk cows, 80,000 northern bricks of the best quality, and a great quantity

of boards, planks, timber, etc. Those last articles will be sold separately if required.

The house is shown in a drawing in plan book 22, folio 20, by L. Bringier, April, 1837, when a "plan for 27 lots in Faubourg St. John" was commissioned. The Vidal house is seen in the projected route of Esplanade. The plan indicated that many of the outbuildings described in the 1811 sale have been removed for the subdivision into lots of the grounds. Part of the double row of trees leading to the house from rue Washington and an isolated hip-roof cottage set back from Seventh Street are seen in the drawing. The hip-roof main house with wings of similar roof treatment was no doubt built for Vidal soon after his acquisition by grant and purchase of the property at the turn of the eighteenth century.

Jung House

The former Vidal corner at the Broad Canal presents a disastrous twentieth-century commercial encroachment into a substantial residential area. Unplanned buildings glut the intersection: a doughnut shop, Martinizing cleaners, drugstore, and filling station. However, the green oak tunnel provides relief leading to the Classic Revival house at 2623 Esplanade, which is painted yellow and adjoins the tiny DeSoto Park. Situated on speculative property acquired by the Marquis de Pontalba of France after the extension of the Esplanade, it passed through several owners until 1887, when Mrs. H. J. Rolling sold the large lot to Mr. and Mrs. Louis A. Jung. They built the present house at 2623 around 1896.

The comfortable two-and-a-half-story house reflects the Classic Revival taste which followed the late Victorian flamboyant period. The projecting façade with its pediment and fluted Corinthian columns "in antis" illustrate the Classic taste and contrast with the wooden balcony fretted in a Chinese pattern. The low

fence fabricated by Hinderer's Ironworks includes two unusual art nouveau gates. Handsome heavy posts may be seen along the side of the lot where one of the fine gates opens onto DeSoto Park.

In 1896 the Jungs gave part of this land to the city of New Orleans, through act of donation. The donated triangular plot measures approximately 4 feet on Crete, 140 on Esplanade and DeSoto, 50 on the Broad Street side. The donation was contingent "on the condition that the property . . . shall be forever kept and dedicated to the uses of the public as a park." J. J. Woulfe notarized the gift, on August 31, 1896, and DeSoto Park remains today one of the small parks that enhance the Esplanade between Broad and the bayou.

The Jungs were a French colonial family who appeared in the Bayou St. John area early in the French colonial period, when the name was often written *Juen*, according to superior council records. Coincidentally, almost two centuries later Louis A. Jung built this house on land subdivided from the plantation of Louis Blanc. Mrs. Jung was Marie Azelie Le Dossu d'Hébécourt, whose family were prominent owners of a plantation adjacent to City Park toward Carrollton. She was an heir of Joseph Chalon, an eighteenth-century settler of the bayou. Louis Jung left the house to his three daughters and three sons. An inventory of his estate dated July 31, 1918, before W. W. Young, illustrates the furnishings and lifestyle of the period.

Capdieville Park across from DeSoto Park is also a triangular space; both parks were originally part of Lafon's square 8 until the Esplanade intersected it. When Paul Capdieville was mayor, 1900–1904, the Esplanade Avenue Gentlemen's Association bought the triangle and donated it to the city for use as a park dedicated to the mayor.

2700 Block

The present houses that line the 2700 up-river block □ postdate 1883. The Robinson map of that year shows just one house on the irregular square bound by Seventh (Crete) and Sixth (White) streets. The present school site across the street contained the home of Cyprien Dufour, which was described in an 1871 inventory of his estate taken on February 15 before P. C. Cuvellier," a dwelling house and outhouses just completed and the late residence of the deceased, on property acquired the thirteenth of May, 1870, before P. C. Cuvellier from B. Abadie." Dufour also obtained a quit claim from Myra Clark Gaines, and to finance the new house he signed a promissory note, dated March 15, 1870, with Albert Baldwin before the same notary. This was the third and last Esplanade residence of Cyprien Dufour whose family owned property in the Vieux Carré area of Esplanade at number 820 from 1816 until 1914. Dufour built the elegant mansion at 1707 Esplanade which he sold to Albert Baldwin, who was the financier of his third and final home, at which Dufour died soon after it was completed. McDonogh 28 □ now occupies this land and is an attractive building that continues the tradition of educational institutions along the Esplanade.

2800 Block

Cresson House

One of the more decorative of the late Victorian homes on the avenue is a turreted Queen Anne-style center-hall house at 2809 Esplanade. □ Although the steps and railing have been changed, the house retains nearly all of its fanciful jigsaw work, spindles, corner blocks, and skirtings. The asymmetrical, angular lines formed by turret, gables, and portico are typical of the turn-of-the-century style and achieve the builder's intended animated effect. Multiple projections contrast with recessed forms, turret with pediments, solids with voids, and light areas with dark ones. The multicolor pattern of the original turret creates texture, as does the applied design on the double gables. Further texture is achieved with quoins and drop siding at the main level. An old photograph illustrates that further contrast and color were provided in the original paint scheme. While such houses abound in most southern towns, they are unusual in New Orleans, predominating in the Bayou St. John area with some modest examples uptown.

A stark contrast to nearby classicism on the avenue, this fanciful building provides variation. Built about 1902 by an Irish real estate speculator, W. James Hannon, who purchased three lots in 1901 from the widow of Henry Communy before C. T. Soniat, December 17, the house cost approximately $10,000. The owners boasted that the hall was the longest and largest in a private residence in town. A photograph of the parlor, made soon after the house was built, illustrates an "esthetic period" interior. Mantels, sliding doors, and bronze chandeliers remain. The massive carved wood entrance is of cypress. Hannon's son intended to build a moviemaking company in New Orleans during the infancy of the industry, but his efforts failed and along with his demise went the family fortune. The Hannons sold to George Mulé in 1914. The home, divided tastefully into apartments, is owned by William Cresson.

The frame American-plan cottage at 2841 Esplanade □ was built for Mrs. Marie Rosella Deslonge, wife of Pierre Amedée Guyol, who purchased the bare lot in 1878 for about $800 from Hypolyte Laroussini before T. Guyol on May 11. When Mrs. Guyol sold at auction to Mr. and Mrs. Louis Palms in 1882, a newspaper advertisement described the house:

Elegant recently constructed cottage, corner Esplanade and Dupré, near the splendid residences of A. E. Bignon and E. Forestier, Esqs. Improvements comprise an elegant, newly built one story and attic cottage, slated, containing a piazza [portico] hall, parlors, dining room, two bedrooms and large vestibule; two large rooms with halls and cabinet in the attic and two-story frame slated kitchen containing four rooms and side galleries; gas throughout the property; shed, privies, cistern, etc. The lots are the highest on the ridge, the property combines all the comforts of a pleasant home and those in search of a good home should not fail to visit it before the sale.

The house as it appears today is extremely chaste and simple for the period in which it was built; it continues in floor plan and decorative style traditions popular from the late 1840s in the city. The pilaster-style entrance with deep cornice also reflects a Classic-style tradition popular in New Orleans from the late 1840s. The door with its large pane of glass, however, was new and in vogue when the house was built. The lines of the widely-spaced dormers reflect Classic Revival proportions and motifs although aluminum screens spoil their effect. The portico with two champfered columns on piers may have been added with a twentieth-century reroofing and guttering.

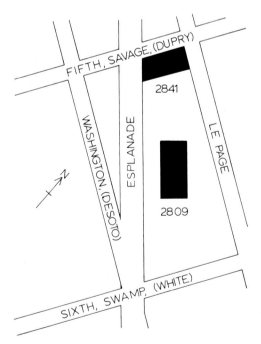

2809 (Courtesy William Cresson)

2809

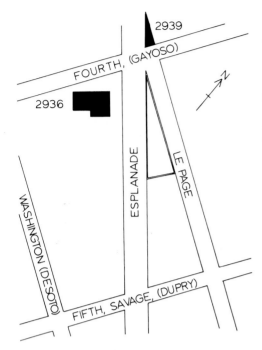

2900 Block

The Mission-style house at 2917 Esplanade □ was the home of Franny Hinderman when an old photograph was made showing the house as it originally appeared in the early twentieth century. Closing of arched openings, removal of iron railing, and alteration of steps and porch along with monochrome painting has spoiled the effect of the architectural style intended by the builder. The Mission and Spanish colonial revival styles are now recalled by the red tile roof, rafter extensions, and projecting blocks, and the fancy brickwork in the Moorish style.

The Gothic villa, like the one at 2936 Esplanade □ was popularized by Andrew Jackson Downing's 1849 publication on country houses. It is a decorative style and building type unusual to New Orleans. The lot on which the house stands was bare in 1874 when François Briou sold the property to Mrs. Henry G. Martin before E. Grima on July 30. The house was probably built by Charles J. Bier, who bought the lots in 1882 from Mrs. Martin, née Jeanne Communy. The house stood on the lot when Bier sold it to Louis Ruch for $4,500 in 1888. The frame house has the American center-hall plan on a raised basement.

The wide, gabled front with deep overhang and the floor plan recall the similar house at 3627 Carondelet built much earlier in the mid-century. The square tower which is, unfortunately, not easily seen from street level, is one of the handsome architectural features of the house. The coherence and sophistication of the tower design reinforces the reality that the present alterations spoil the integrity of the house. The steps, porch, and porch railing are new, and the latter should be replaced with turned balusters. The simple molded window lintels must have been more elaborate with jigsaw crestings. The present double screens obscure the entrance, which was probably etched glass doors with carving and a surround more in keeping with those of the tower. Even though it is presently the home of the International Society for Krishna Consciousness, the organization obviously lacks awareness of architectural reality. The house is painted powder blue with canary yellow trim. Careful study of 3627 Carondelet Street and of Andrew Jackson Downing's nineteenth-century illustrations of similar houses would make possible correct restoration although, unfortunately, the interior has been stripped and the exterior mutilated.

Another triangle park on the downriver side of the 2900 block of Esplanade was formed by the continuation of Esplanade and the subsequent prolongment of Sauvage (Dupré) and Fourth (Gayoso) streets. The land was part of square 32 on Barthelemy Lafon's 1809 original plan of Faubourg St. John. The park itself stems from an 1895 donation before notary J. D. Taylor whereby Blanche Claudette, divorced wife of John Claverie, Jr., donated the triangle "to the City of New Orleans, John Fitzpatrick, mayor, on the condition that it forever be used as a park." The land was part of a larger portion she received from her husband in the divorce settlement recorded on March 12, 1891, before C. T. Soniat. It extended roughly from Washington Street all the way to Grand Route St. John on which Claverie had established a dairy farm that he still owned as late as 1890.

By the terms of the divorce Claverie gave his wife: "eighteen cows, three horses and three carts comprising part of a dairy attached to said

2936

2939

real estate and valued at $1,000." The dairy farm had "a splendid cottage house" on it, facing Grand Route St. John in 1861 when Jean Louis Mouler sold to Henry Duviaud the large parcel described as bound "by the late Fortin Plantation [Faubourg Pontchartrain], Esplanade Avenue." Jean Claverie, Sr., bought the property from the estate sale of Henry Duviaud at auction with the act passed August 6, 1877, before A. D. Doriocourt. Like many other lots in Faubourg St. John, these large portions of two squares were claimed by Myra Clark Gaines, who gave up her title to it to Duviaud before A. E. Bienvenu on February 7, 1877. In addition to the dairy there was also a rope walk near Esplanade and Fourth (Gayoso) in an 1890 illustration attached to an act of M. T. Ducros on May 10, 1890. The late development of this property, therefore, was because of its farm activity and legal entanglements from the heir of Daniel Clark. The history of this tiny park indicates the difficulties wrought by street extensions into a previously existing neighborhood. Fourth Street or Gayoso was continued across Esplanade long after Esplanade became a reality. The land formed as a result was an isolated side yard of the house at 2939 Esplanade. Edward W. Smith had to buy from Mrs. Claverie another triangle which today gives the house a deep front yard. At the time of the construction of the house, there was little front or back yard, but considerable property on each side.

The house at 2939, which Edward Smith built in 1888, is an American-style center-hall cottage. Smith bought the property from John R. Fell in June of 1887 before notary Sidney Beck; later that year he mortgaged the lot for $500 to raise money to pay for the construction of the house seen on a plan dating from 1888, annexed to the inventory of Smith's estate. When Smith died, June 3, 1924, the subsequent inventory of his estate recorded before notary T. Dreyfous on June 10, 1924, refers to "the late residence of the deceased at 2939 Esplanade" as having "three bedrooms, hall, parlor, library, dining room and kitchen." The house remained in the Smith family until the 1950s and is much as it appeared at the time of its construction. Double-fold louvered shutters at the segmental arched entrance open onto a recessed door with transom, leading to a wide center hall flanked by two rooms on each side. Double parlors on the left are divided by sliding double doors. There is one wooden mantel of the 1880s period, a type readily available by order number from local mills, as was the millwork throughout the entire house. Lovely plaster ceiling medallions are also an interior

feature. The chimneys are situated at the frame gable ends, and a side porch with deep overhang is supported by handsome steamboat scroll brackets.

3000 Block

At the 3000 block, the Esplanade crossed Grand Route St. John, entering into Faubourg Pontchartrain, another established suburb dating from 1809. This faubourg just two blocks wide and six blocks long was hewn from the original habitation of an early French-Canadian family who arrived at Bayou St. John in 1708.

The Canadian Antoine Rivard dit Lavigne bought out the other farmers and concessionaires at Bayou St. John and cultivated seventeen arpents facing Bayou St. John running to Bayou Gentilly on land approximating twenty arpents in depth. This successful habitation was held by the Rivard widow and his family until 1771, and the subsequent owner, Santiago Lorreins (Jacques Baptiste Lorain alias Tarascon), kept it until 1807. At that time Lorreins sold what remained of his former Rivard Lavigne holdings to Elie Beauregard, father of Pierre G. T. Beauregard, the Confederate general, before Pierre Pedesclaux on September 26.

The sale describes the property sold to Beauregard "retired captain of His Majesty's Service, a habitation with all the buildings, etc. . . . situated on Bayou St. John facing one side of the Bayou, two hundred-four arpents and fifty-four feet surface, joining on one side Mr. Daniel Clark [Faubourg St. John across Grand Route St. John] and on the other Petit Bayou of Gentilly and lands of Gabriel Peyroux, bound in the rear by lands of the succession of deceased Sieur Hilaire Boutet and on the west by that of the Succession of John W. Gurley, also deceased." Beauregard paid $15,000 for this tract, from which emanated the future Faubourg Pontchartrain, the St. Louis Cemetery III, the Luling mansion complex, and the Fairgrounds. Beauregard acquired funds for this important purchase from Daniel Clark, who held the mortgage for the property. In 1809 he still owed Clark $14,000 according to acts of Pierre Pedesclaux March 6, 1809. This may have been the purpose of Elie Beauregard's sale of the entire property except for his own house and grounds (site unknown) to Louis Fortin and Jean Blanque for $16,000 on March 6, 1809, in an act before P. Pedesclaux which states that Beauregard was "habitante de Chemin de Bayou St. Jean."

Blanque and Fortin immediately established Faubourg Pontchartrain and deposited a plan in Narcisse Broutin's office on June 10, 1809. The streets were laid out parallel and perpendicular to Grand Route St. John into nine rectangular areas. Parallel to Grand Route St. John were Florida (Ponce de Leon) and Fortin. Perpendicular were rue Percée (Vignaud), Mystery and Encampment (Lopez). Following the formation of Faubourg Pontchartrain, Blanque and Fortin partitioned the new subdivision between them before Pedesclaux on June 6, 1809. Each took ownership of half the lots.

By 1813 Jean Blanque was dead, leaving enormous debts which the estate could not cover, and on November 14, 1816, an auction of the estate was held by François Dutillet, auctioneer. Many of Blanque's lots in Faubourg Pontchartrain were sold to speculators and individuals. Fortin himself died in 1819, and notary Carlile Pollock recorded the details of his Faubourg Pontchartrain holdings in an act of November 25, 1819. Widow Fortin sold a large part of the land beyond Faubourg Pontchartrain toward the lake to Evariste Blanc, who, having sold most of his family holdings on the left side of Grand Route St. John to Daniel Clark and the city, reinvested on the right side. He built his own house, now the Holy Rosary rectory on the Bayou, buying a strip of the Rivard plantation via John McDonogh and David Olivier. Another strip was sold by widow Blanc to Florence Luling. On May 31, 1859, before T. Guyol, the Luling site was described as "part of a larger portion of ground owned by the said community for upwards of twenty years before the death of Evariste Blanc."

Just inside the boundaries of Faubourg Pontchartrain is Alcée Fortier Park, created by a triangle left when the Esplanade cut into the first square bound by Grand Route St. John. The Parkway Commission is in charge of the upkeep. Nearby, across Esplanade, another triangle has not fared so well. A garish quickfood stand occupies it. □ A creole cottage on this triangle continued in private ownership after Esplanade was cut through as indicated in the archival drawing in Plan book 47A, folio 56, by P. N. Judice in 1866.

3300 Block

At 3330 Esplanade is a galleried, frame creole cottage currently being renovated by architect Ashton Smith as his residence. The house is characteristic of the 1840s in type and style. There are Greek Key surrounds and mantels. One of the cabinets contains a stairway, and there is a floored attic and a detached kitchen parallel to the house at the rear of the lot. Title research reveals that this lot was bare in 1873. The land belonged to Louis Fortin as part of his share of the Blanque-Fortin partition. Joseph Klar, a carpenter and one of a large contingent of Germans who settled in the Gentilly Road-Bayou Road area in the 1830s, bought seven lots in the square at the succession auction; each lot, according to notary H. Pedesclaux, May 13, 1834, measured 60 by 150 feet and faced Ponce de Leon (Florida). In

1873 Joseph Klar sold four lots to John Hager, but by then the lots had been reorganized and resurveyed to front the new Esplanade Avenue. The Hager family kept the lots until 1906 when Mrs. Hager's heirs sold this lot and house at 3330 Esplanade. A side-gabled creole cottage presently occupying this lot could date from the 1834 Klar purchase; it would have been moved at some time to this site.

The modest frame shotgun nearby at 3356 Esplanade ☐ was built in the rear field of the home of Evariste Blanc at 1342 Moss Street, now known as the Holy Rosary rectory. The grounds of the mansion were subdivided in 1892 at a public auction which settled the estate of Mrs. Fannie Labatut, deceased widow of Evariste Blanc. This lot was bare then and sold for $540 to Mrs. Sylvanie Blanc, daughter of Evariste and widow of J. D. Denegre. Soon thereafter widow Denegre sold the bare lot to Robert E. Saucier for $700. Saucier built the

3330

shotgun house in the early years of the twentieth century. When Saucier sold to E. B. Guenard in October of 1911 for $3,400 he certified that he had been assessed $174 by City Council Ordinance Number 10,511 in 1895 to pay his share of a $19,083.43 bill from Charles Spinks and Son for "vitrified brick pavement with concrete gutter bottom and blue stone curbing." This paved the entire block, which is the longest block along the Esplanade, and the longest one in the city.

Luling Mansion

The elegant mansion of Florence Luling once faced Esplanade Avenue with formally landscaped grounds, including part of the present New Orleans Fairgrounds. The present houses facing Esplanade were built in the front garden of the Luling home after Labatut and Ducayet streets were renamed Leda and Verna. This is alleged to have occurred during the 1920s ownership of George W. Soulé, whose wife's name was Leda. The mansion may now be seen hidden away at 1438 Leda Street. The grounds of this impressive suburban mansion had been part of the Nicolas Fortin estate and comprised a part of the early-eighteenth-century holdings of Rivard Lavigne. Florence Luling purchased the large tract, eighty acres, fronting on Esplanade Avenue, from the heirs of Evariste Blanc on February 24, 1864, before S. Magner, notary. Luling had left his native Germany prior to the Revolution of 1848 and had acquired great wealth in cotton factoring, making numerous business contacts in England. He contracted with the architectural firm of Gallier and Esterbrook to design and build the house in 1865. It is the largest and most elaborate of the remaining residences designed by James Gallier, Jr. One of the city's most unusual and lavish examples of the Italianate style, the house reflects the universal attributes of the period and decorative style rather than the more regional and particular aspects of the Italianate style as seen on most of the Esplanade or in other sections of the city.

The house was raised on a terrace surrounded by a dry moat and progressed three and one-half stories in height including a raised basement with deep rustication and arches with keystones in the Baroque manner. A square cupola was placed at the fourth level. The sophisticated design includes a diminishing of proportion for each level, with galleries and balconies on three sides on two levels and a deep overhanging entablature or cornice. The main two levels are of plastered brick-with-stone trim around arched openings, stringcourses, and quoins which animate the

surface in color, texture, and design. Abstract two-dimensional forms of the building surface originate as a result of these design techniques. Plasterwork, stone, and brick contrast and complement one another. The cross muntins of the arched windows meet a course of molded banding across the house on three levels, creating a horizontal emphasis as do the deep cornice and the balustraded balconies. Great scroll brackets support the second-level balcony; many of the original wood-turned balusters have been replaced with hollow half-metal replacements. An arcaded gallery on one side of the main level and a handsome octagonal bay occasion the diversity of shape and scale associated with the Italianate style. Two fine two-story flanking pavilions, with bridges between them and the main house, have been destroyed but may be seen in the elevation prepared by James Gallier, preserved in the Labrot Collection, Tulane University Special Collections. The huge earth mound upon which the foundation was placed necessitated a two-level staircase. Wide granite steps progressed to the entrance upward in the grand manner of European villas of the seventeenth and eighteenth centuries. There were three other homes along Esplanade which may have equaled the Luling mansion in scale and concept: the Wright-Slocumb house at 1205, the Vredenbergh house in the 2400 block designed by Henry Howard, and the Avet house in the 1100 block designed by Jacques De-Pouilly. They have all been demolished.

The notarial records of S. Magner, March 13, 1865, preserve a letter that Luling wrote James Gallier, Jr., which indicates the expense of the mansion during its day, and it specifies luxurious interior details, also giving specifics as to the granite steps and other materials:

Dear sir, your favor of 9th inst. giving your estimates of the cost of putting my building in a habitable condition, is before me. The extraordinary variations in your former estimates and the large amount of work to be left temporarily undone, forbid me to prosecute the work except on some basis satisfactory to me.

For such basis I embrace your recent estimate of $23,000 and $1,000 more for unforeseen extras, making $24,000, for which sum you then agreed to finish the main building, wings, granite steps, iron fence and banquettes in the proposed and complete style. In this estimate of $24,000 was included the hauling of the necessary dirt or sand for the banquette, terrace etc. at a valued expense of $3,000, which I proposed to have done with my own teams, leaving therefore $21,000 for the entire work and materials to be furnished by you. I presume you are willing to abide this, your own recent proposal.

On these $21,000, I paid $3,000 and again on Saturday $3,052 = 6,052, leaving $14,948.—and deducting your present estimate for necessary work say $10,283 for the future and final completion of Granite entrance, steps, terrace walk, iron fence, and banquettes in the proposed and complete style, leaves $4,665.

If then I am to enter into your proposal to have the main building finished for occupation and enclose the wing buildings, dispensing for the present with the granite entrance steps, terrace walks, iron fence, banquetting and cistern for the stated sum of $10,283, I must exact the condition in the shape of a regular contract, that I may at any time call upon you for the completion of the work now dispensed with, for the sum of $4,665 to be paid by me.

And further in granting the $1,000 for extras and considering the fact that the building in a complete state will cost me from 75% to 100% above your original estimate which induced me to commence the building, I understand it that a building, banquette etc. shall be completed by you in the most approved and finished style; that the exterior and basement inside walls shall be amended throughout, the remaining exterior walls of wings painted in oil; the building shall be supplied with pantries, kitchen and cellars properly shelved and partly glass doored with drawers underneath, linen closet to be cedar lined, all the interior arrangements, such as waterclosets, bowling alley, stable, cistern and sinks shall be completed in the best workmanlike manner. The painting of all woodwork shall be done in the most approved style—white gloss inside, hall and stairs oiled, pantries, etc. grained as may be indicated by myself or representative. The plastering, cornices and ornaments to be executed in the proposed style. The outside walls of the wing building, shall have a row of flagstones at the base and the yard shall be flagged in the proposed dimensions. . . . The ceiling of main roof or attic shall be roughly floored over. The chimneys supplied with tops if found necessary. The garden wall shall be water colored and the iron fence oil painted, with bell apparatus. The banquettes shall be bricked and flagged in the best manner and supplied with iron bridges at the three entrances.

Great sadness struck the Luling family soon after they moved into the magnificent home; two young sons drowned in nearby Bayou St. John. This, combined with reverses in the cotton factoring business during Reconstruction, caused Luling to move to England. On July 12, 1871, he sold the house and a large tract of land on which it stood to the Louisiana Jockey Club, G. A. Breaux, president for $60,000. The Jockey Club was chartered May 15, 1871, "to establish a race course." Edgar Degas, the French painter, visited the new race course in 1872 and commemorated it with paintings of activities there. The twenty-two-room Luling house with its Italian marble mantelpieces, frescoed ceilings and walls, and formal gardens in the romantic style provided an elegant clubhouse for subscribers or aficionados of the races.

Jewell's Crescent City of 1879 describes the Fair Grounds, as the race course had been dubbed since the Louisiana Agricultural and Mechanical Fair had been held there in 1871; "Race course is an ellipse exactly one mile in measurement . . . within it are the Club House, platform for music and dancing, and a base ball park. The Public Stand, built by the Jockey Club on the south side of the course, is considered the best stand on the continent, being an enormous three story pile of graceful and substantial carpentry, two stories high, with comfortable seats for more than five thousand people, with ample promenades, broad and easy staircases, roomy saloons, and commanding a view of the whole course and enclosure. Lofty cupola. Also exhibition buildings, deer park, stables for more than 100 horses, flower gardens and nurseries." The elegant chandeliers designed for the Jockey Club are now in the center hall of Oaklawn plantation, Franklin, Louisiana.

Late in the 1870s, Florence Luling returned to the South, settled in Mobile, Alabama, and purchased the Dawson home in Springhill. The latter had been built in the 1840s. Luling was probably responsible for the Italianate alterations and additions to this home, which remains today with etched glass double doors having the engraved initials F. L. installed there for Florence Luling. □

Adjacent to the Luling house is the St. Louis III Cemetery, □ which predates the Luling house. It was established on land which Evariste Blanc's son-in-law and heir, Felix Labatut, sold to the Cathedral wardens, June 8, 1849. The land was "two arpents wide by fourteen arpents deep" and cost $15,000. Blanc had acquired this land, also part of the Rivard LaVigne ancient holdings, via Lorreins, Beauregard, and Fortin. It is notable that Luling would establish his country mansion in close proximity to the cemetery. The broad central aisle and main cross alleys of St. Louis III provide visitors with a deceiving concept of great space. Crowded along their way are many thousand family tombs and society vaults. As many as 100,000 individuals have been buried within these architecturally significant edifices. These include many Esplanade Ridge families, such as Cyprien Dufour, who, like General Beauregard, is recalled along the avenue from the river to the bayou.

Luling Mansion

City Park

The grand Esplanade culminates at Bayou St. John facing City Park of New Orleans. It is symbolic that the street began and ended at the bodies of water that caused the city to be founded at its present location. This brings the route of the street from the formal old city of 1718 across numerous early plantations to the site of the first French settlement of 1708, which preceded the founding of the city. While the route of the Esplanade to the bayou was purposeful, it is a happy accident that the street leads straight into the large park. The park site was a working plantation that belonged to Louis Allard when the Esplanade prolongment was designed in 1822. Esplanade Avenue had been completed by 1850 when the owner of the Allard plantation, John McDonogh, died and left the land to the cities of New Orleans and Baltimore, and New Orleans conceived the idea of a park. In 1858 the city employed a parkkeeper for the site, putting him on the municipal payroll. McDonogh's recommendation had been to subdivide the plantation into lots and sell them for city revenue. The city compromised and retained eighty-five acres and sold the additional land only to repurchase it many years later.

The Allard Plantation bordered both the Bayou St. John and the Bayou Chapitoulas, providing waterways on two sides. The personalities associated with the land are French and Spanish colonial figures important to the development of the settlement at the bayou and the city of New Orleans.

A large tract of about eighteen arpents facing Bayou St. John, bound on one side by the Bayou Chapitoulas (City Park Avenue), was owned by François Héry, called Duplanty, according to a map dating from about 1723 in the Newberry Library collection at Chicago. Duplanty was married to Magdeleine Brasilier, daughter of Jean Baptiste Tourangeau, called Brasilier, who owned vast tracts both across the bayou and also on the Duplanty side toward the lake. Duplanty was an active contractor in the colony, and energetic farmer; he cultivated his own property at the, bayou and leased an adjacent plantation from widow Elizabeth Desruisseaux in 1770. After five years the lease was canceled on May 2, 1775, probably due to Duplanty's death. Duplanty is best known as the contractor for the first Cabildo, built under Governor Alexandro O'Reilly.

After Duplanty's death Magdeleine Brasilier, his widow, married Enrique Desprez, once of Opelousas and a lieutenant in the Spanish army. She sold the plantation in 1772 to Jacques Lorreins Tarasçon. Jacques Lorreins Tarasçon and his wife Marie Louise Baudon had two daughters, Suzette Francisca and Pelagia, who married J. B. Tourangeau Brasilier. Francisca married Louis Allard, who was born in France in 1749, son of Louis Allard and Doña Ana Rolland Pendozi. Sometime between 1781 and 1784 Louis Allard acquired by donation and purchase fourteen arpents front of the Lorreins-Tarasçon plantation on the site of City Park. Twenty years later, in 1811, Allard was able to purchase four more arpents frontage lakeward from his plantation to reassemble the original Duplanty holdings. (See *American State Papers,* Nos. 82 and 83, Vol. VII, p. 687)

This lakeward part of the Duplanty-Lorreins holdings belonged to Pelagia and her second husband Andrés Jung in 1781, when Jung describes his plantation as backed by Santiago Tarasçon (the Allard tract) on one side and St. Maxent on the other (Mazange, November 6, 1781): "A plantation on the Bayou measuring eight arpents front by eighty arpents deep, adjoined on one side by Mr. Allard's lands on the other by Mr. Maxent's place. A brick dwelling house has been built on this plantation together with a frame kitchen, three cabins for the negroes, a new store room which serves as a cooperage and an old one where utensils are kept." This was sold by Jung's estate and Mateo Osten bought four of the eight arpents in 1802, selling them to Francisco Riano. Allard bought them in 1811, thus putting it back in the traditional bayou ownership clique. The rear part was sold eventually to Zenon Cavelier. The Allard children, Louis, Jr., and Lise, who married J. F. Robert, inherited the tracts henceforth referred to as the Allard plantation.

On March 23, 1829, a mortgage before notary Felix de Armas by Louis Allard, Jean François Robert, and Madame Lise Allard, his wife, to the Consolidated Association of the Planters of Louisiana for $27,500, describes the Allard tract:

A plantation situated on the Bayou St. John being eighteen arpents front by forty-three arpents in depth bound on one side by the Metairie Road [City Park Avenue] and on the other by the property belonging to the succession of the late Francisco Riano (his remaining four of eight arpents), and in the rear by that formerly belonging to Zenon Cavelier, the area of which plantation is 774 arpents, of which 168 are today planted in corn, garden, orchard, rice, hay and sugar cane, the surplus being in standing timber and savannahs.

All the buildings generally whatsoever that are on the said plantation, principally consisting in a master house with an upper story, the lower one in brick, a stable for forty milk cows in the same building, a stable for the

City Park

City Park

sheep and a large chamber with fireplaces for the shepherds; in a house of several rooms serving as a hen house; in a building divided into three parts serving as stable, coach house and servants rooms; another building on sills divided into two serving as warehouse for provisions; another building divided into six chambers with double chimneys for negroes; a warehouse on sills of forty-five feet by twenty serving as a work shop, containing also a workshop for workmen; another warehouse of fifty feet by twenty-two for the grain and the corn with a gallery serving as stable

for horses . . . a new building furnished with hangers and racks for twenty mules, the said building being forty-eight by twenty-two, a building of posts in the ground of sixty feet in length by twenty-five for lodging the carts etc. in the roof a large pigeon house, a new cabin of twenty-five feet by fifteen with chimneys divided into three rooms.

As a result of this mortgage the Allard property was seized by the sheriff and sold on June 11, 1845 (Mortgage Book 38/377). John McDonogh was the purchaser of this 654 acres

along with 19 slaves, 10 horses and mules, and 140 head of cattle for $40,500. McDonogh died October 6, 1850, and A. Mazureau, notary, recorded an inventory of his estate that year. New Orleans acquired clear title to the Allard lands before notary Eusebe Bouny as recorded in Conveyance Office book 78, folio 615, wherein Baltimore "abandoned and transferred their undivided half" to the city of New Orleans. The city held a sale of McDonogh's estate, and acts are recorded before notary Bouny in Volume V.

The city sold much of the Allard-McDonogh property, including the Bayou St. John frontage. By the time the park was established, some 654 acres, referred to in Allard transfers as 18 arpents by 43 arpents, had been reduced to 85 acres, and the boundaries, established in a plan by B. F. Nicholls, ran from "Metairie Road [City Park Avenue] to Monroe Avenue, St. Louis to Ursulines" and included 55 squares of ground. Subsequently, the original Allard tract was reacquired for City Park. This tract ran roughly from City Park Avenue to the railroad bridge near Harrison Avenue reaching back beyond the Orleans Canal for two miles.

In 1872, with the city expansions toward the lake, under the prodding of Mayor Crossman and surveyor Louis Pilié, the city contracted with Bogart and Cutler, designers of New York's Central Park, to draw plans to landscape the grounds under the supervision of George H. Grandjean, United States deputy surveyor. According to the March 13, 1892, *Daily Picayune*, however, the city only paid half of that $5,000 and the "other half was sued for"; with the plans going to "a safe, if obscure, resting place among the archives of the Supreme Court." After that, the article continues, "Nothing more was heard of the park. People forgot where it was. . . . Then the weeds grew higher . . . the City Park stood abandoned, desolate, and mysterious."

Finally, in 1891, Victor Anseman, known as the "father of the park," interested the citizens in its development. A permanent group designated as the City Park Improvement Association (CPIA) was formed. The CPIA was and is a private nonprofit corporation with a self-perpetuating board, having legal status acquired from the state in 1896 for complete private management of a public park. The CPIA embarked upon a program of continuous land expansion and improvement. A fence was built, 3,000 feet long on City Park Avenue, and painted bright red. Subsequent land augmentations were accomplished through more than fifteen purchases, major and minor, and ranging from $50 to more than $106,000. From its original 85-acre area in the 1850s the park had expanded, by 1896, to 213 acres with a depth of 1,780 feet, and today it covers 1,500 acres bounded by Bayou St. John, the old Orleans Canal, City Park Avenue, Robert E. Lee Boulevard, and two areas of 16 acres extending to Lake Pontchartrain, all complete with lawns, lagoons, buildings, concessions, amusements, and athletic fields and structures.

Just beyond Bayou Bridge, in front of the park entrance, is the equestrian statue of Civil War hero General P. G. T. Beauregard, designed by Alexander Doyle and erected in

City Park

1915. Beyond it is the stately Monteleone Gate, twenty-five-foot marble pylons, from which extends tree-lined Lelong Avenue. This culminates at New Orleans Museum of Art, in front of which is the Jahncke Fountain dating from 1912.

In 1910 Isaac Delgado, a prominent New Orleans philanthropist, donated $150,000 to the park for construction of a museum. That same year fifty-nine architects submitted plans for the design of the museum, and the Chicago firm of Ledenbaum and Marx was selected, with James Koch of New Orleans as contractor. According to its designers, the building was "inspired by the Greek, sufficiently modified to give a subtropical appearance." There are six Ionic columns across the portico, and the limestone walls are bare, save where terracotta panels have been set in. On either side of the portico there are terra-cotta sculptural decorations set in panels below the entablature. In 1971, under the leadership of the director James Byrnes, plans to enlarge the museum were undertaken. These were further increased and reorganized to incorporate the Wisner Education Wing and the Stern Auditorium by the present director, John Bullard, and the name of the complex was changed from Delgado Museum to New Orleans Museum of Art. Architects for the additions, which tripled the space of the original building, were August Perez and Associates, with Arthur Feitel, associated architect.

Behind the museum in Grandjean Bridge, built in 1909, commemorating the civil engineer who supervised the building of the park waterways. Originally built of iron, the bridge was rebuilt by the Works Project Administration.

To the right of Lelong Avenue lies Big Lake, an eight-acre replica of Lake Pontchartrain, and just beyond begins the thirty-acre chain of interconnected lagoons, designed to simulate a typical Louisiana swamp and bayou scene, and routed so that one may glide through much of the park on them. Within the chain lies, among many others, the distinctive Isle of Pines and in its depth, a concealed iron pavilion donated in 1904 to the park by F. Dunbar.

East of the museum stands the McFadden house, for many years the only private residence in the park. The original five-bedroom, two-bath home was built for Fred Bertrand in 1909. In 1919 William Harding McFadden purchased the Bertrand house, which was then just beyond City Park's limits. McFadden completely rebuilt and enlarged the 1909 structure

into its present configuration of a Spanish revival style. Representative of a complex designed in the grand manner reflecting luxury and wealth, the grounds included four acres used as kennels for forty hunting dogs, a stable, green houses, and three custodial houses. There are remnants of a Japanese garden replete with bamboo teahouse and bridge. Arranged around an open atrium the house included a trophy room, conservatory and interior marble swimming pool, having murals of outdoor scenes on the walls and ceiling. Characterized by its Spanish tile roof, stucco-covered towers, and projecting wings, arched openings, wrought iron, walled-in terraces and patios, the house is remembered during the McFadden residency as having a picturesque, fairy-tale atmosphere. In 1942, McFadden sold the mansion to City Park for $40,000; it was leased to Samuel Barthe for a private boys' school from 1948 to 1958. Following that, it was leased to the Christian Brothers, also for a boys' school.

On the west side of the museum, the attractive Dreyfous Bridge crosses the lagoon and leads to the casino building, built in 1913 at a cost of $36,000. This building, with its arched gallery, red tiled roof, and roof garden, serves today as the park refreshment center.

Popp Music Stand, designed by Armstead Brothers, architects, between 1924 and 1928, is an open granite rotunda with twelve Ionic columns supporting a weathered bronze dome in the Classic Revival style, near Marconi Drive. "Tribute of John F. Popp to Music, 1917" is inscribed on it. The structure is set on a raised podium which projects on one side to form a bell-shaped porch, which is inscribed to Alexis Ribet and was dedicated in 1916. The Bandstand as it is often called, was designed by Emile Weil, New Orleans architect, as a replica of the Temple of Love at the Trianon at Versailles. John Philip Sousa played on this podium when he visited the city.

Near the Dumaine Street entrance stands the elegant Peristyle, a granite pavilion built in 1907 at a cost of $16,000 after designs by Andrey and Bendernagel executed by Pedro Ghiloni. The City Beautiful style structure is set on a slightly raised stylobate, rectangular in basic shape with circular or half-rotunda ends. Neoclassic motifs are combined in an interpretive manner inspired by the Columbian Exposition in Chicago in 1893. The hothouses were designed by Julius Koch at a cost of $12,000 and were rebuilt in 1976. In 1933 the Chicago architectural firm of Bennett, Parson, and Frost

provided overall plans which have served as a continuing guideline for the City Park.

Improvement Groups

Many private neighborhood groups and politically appointed commissions have been responsible through the years for the appearance of the Mississippi River levee, Esplanade Avenue, and City Park. In the 1790s Governor Carondelet responded to the need for an aesthetic promenade along the levee by arranging for orange trees to be planted. Today responsibility for the safety and appearance of the levee belongs to the Orleans Parish Levee board. The avenue itself was planted by the two municipalities to which each side belonged until 1883 when:

[A board of commissioners] was created by the City Council charged with "the improvement and embellishment of Esplanade Street and middle ground thereof, from the river to Bayou St. John, and that the said commission is hereby invested with all the necessary powers to improve and embellish said avenue, as well as to replace the decayed and missing trees on said middle ground and to trim and place in shapely condition those now standing thereon . . . that the following named be and hereby constituted the said Board of Commissioners and are hereby duly authorized to raise by voluntary subscriptions the necessary amounts to carry out their designs." Among the appointees were residents of the Esplanade including Albert Baldwin, George Dunbar, L. Godchaux, Aristide Hopkins, A. Delvaille, J. M. Seixas, Captain J. W. Tobin, August Tete, Dr. John H. Pike, Pierre Lanaux, Jules Aldigé and Armand Pilié.

These names will be recognized as inhabitants of the Esplanade. Their trust was augmented in the 1890s by the Esplanade Avenue Gentlemen's Association and interested property owners. Just before the turn of the century, momentum was gained with the City Park Improvement Association, but their aggressive participation had been taken over by the City Park manager's office. The Board of Commissioners, however, eventually forfeited their responsibility which has been picked up by the Parkway Commission established as a city department on May 5, 1909. The last quarter of the twentieth century must see public demands that the tax-supported commissions perform efficiently and responsibly, be it the Levee Board, the Parkway Commission, or the City Park management. The private sector, however, must reassume responsibility to their community with vigilant interest and spirited participation.

New Orleans Notarial Archives

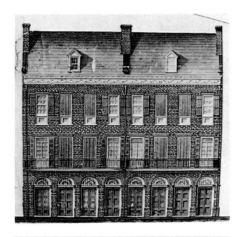

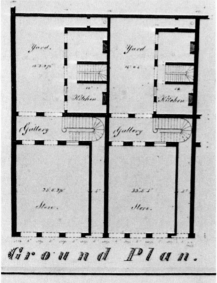

Plan book 11, folio 43, signed and dated, "April 19, 1845, M. Harrison, civil engineer." This is **1331** Decatur or **504–508** Esplanade. The brick was painted red, penciled white; the shutters were green. The ironwork was black and the roof gray slate.

The New Orleans Notarial Archives is a major repository of primary information concerning New Orleans architectural history. Notaries' books preserve the building contracts and specifications for many of the city's public, private, and religious structures. In addition, plan books are available, showing the elevations, floor plans, and positions on the municipal square of over two thousand New Orleans houses and buildings. These contain invaluable information for the scholar, architect, builder, and house owner.

It was customary for the city, under the auspices of the sheriff's office, to commission an elevation of any building that was to be sold by that office at public auction and to have these displayed in the auctioneer's office for examination by potential purchasers. The persons commissioned to make these drawings included well-known architects and builders, yet the city engineer and city surveyors were the most available draftsmen, receiving for their renderings approximately twenty dollars for each elevation. Signatures on the elevations include a number of popular landscape and portrait painters, as well as sign painters and those who were advertised in the city directories as decorators of interior walls or muralists. Renowned architects such as James Gallier, Sr., J. N. B. de Pouilly, and L. E. Reynolds also contributed their talents to this documentary art form in watercolor and gouache on paper.*

The remaining drawings date from 1802 through 1918, after which photographs were used. Some are embellished with street scenes, including brick banquettes, flagstoned tree-lined avenues, lampposts, and trade signs. Lagniappe for the illustrations was provided in picaresque scenes showing children playing and running with hoops, as well as ladies with reticules and umbrellas, riding in carriages or strolling along the streets. The drawings indicate the exterior colors and paint combinations in vogue for each house type and style. In most, the exact measurements are recorded with the floor plans. Variations of fence and gate styles are defined, and gardens are often delineated.

A structure built in 1810 may not have been recorded until 1830, at the time it was to be sold. Buildings sometimes were sold immediately upon completion; others, long after original occupancy, were sold two or more times and are illustrated on successive occasions. Houses or commercial structures can be studied as they were originally designed and also with later alterations.

Included in this selection of archival drawings are all the known illustrations pertaining to Esplanade Avenue. Many of these original houses may have been demolished, but their inclusion herein contributes to the overview of thirty recorded buildings on the avenue from 1836 to 1876. Beneath each archival drawing is a cross reference by page number to inform the reader of an existing house or one which once occupied a known address site.

* Most renderings are "elephant" folio size. Since they are bound in 24" x 29" books and folded, most of them are damaged and are in need of repair.

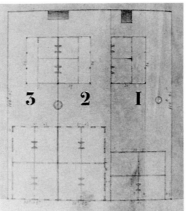

Plan book 58, folio 6, signed and dated, "March 17, 1837, C. Crozet." These cottages once stood on the site of **529** and **533** Esplanade, having been built by François Sel; they burned in 1837. The weatherboards were painted light green trim, off-white, and shutters darker green. The wooden steps, brick foundation, and chimneys present pleasing warm highlight shades. These cottages have an existing avenue counterpart in **2325** Esplanade.

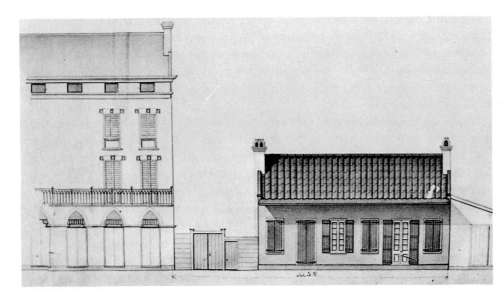

Plan book 22, folio 32, signed and dated, "July 24, 1844, J. A. Pueyo." In square 52, this ochre-colored red-tile-roofed creole cottage stood next to **608** Esplanade which is sketched in next to the carriageway. This cottage was a double, with each side having two windows and a door closed by painted green shutters.

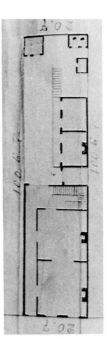

Plan book 53, folio 10, signed and dated, "April 1, 1836, Fr. Jacob Rothaas." Another of the demolished 1830s creole townhouses which once abounded in the area between **400** and **1000** Esplanade. This one was very similar to others in the same **600** block of square 155, bound by Royal, Chartres, and Kerlerec. It was painted a salmon color with white trim and dark green shutters.

Plan book 65, folio 39, signed and dated, "March 21, 1852, Adolphe Knell." Plan book 73, folio 25, signed and dated, "May 13, 1875, G. Pirenter, architect and civil engineer." Demolished. Two archival drawings show the same 1830s house formerly at **623** Esplanade before and after a mid–nineteenth-century renovation. As built, the creole-style townhouse had three full-length openings with transoms at the first level. Sometime after the 1852 date of the first drawing the house was "Americanized" and the first-level façade was changed to have a Greek Key entrance surround and a single-fold paneled door painted in two tones. French doors were shortened to two double-hung windows. The simple wrought iron balcony at the second level was removed and replaced by a second-level gallery of cast iron also applied to the third level and painted a bright bronze, and the exterior painted a mauve rather than the blue in the 1852 watercolor.

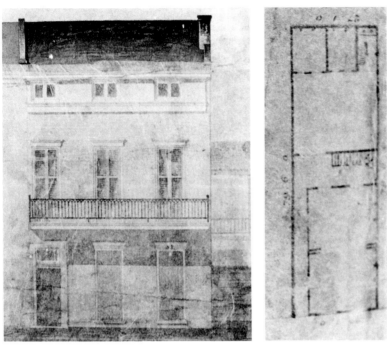

Plan book 35, folio 63, signed and dated, "February 8, 1866, de Pouilly." Number **611** Esplanade, built in 1847, as it appeared before the addition of cast iron galleries and an ornamental cornice with parapet. Note the similarity to **714** Esplanade which was built about the same time. Painted a light ochre to imitate stone. Stairs in rear foyer behind the double parlor, not at the end of the narrow side entrance hall.

Plan book 31, folio 27, unsigned and undated drawing of the house at **714** Esplanade (see text). Discovery of this archival drawing offered evidence that the house was built for Jonathan Lord Warner between 1843 and 1846 rather than for A. R. Brousseau in the late 1850s as previously published (Volume IV, *New Orleans Architecture*). The façade epitomizes the New Orleans traditional Greek Revival townhouse: Greek Key entrance surround with cornice above two short, matching windows below and three full-length double-hung openings above. This decorative motif continues in the carriage entrance frame. The frieze of the applied wood entablature has three attic openings with cast iron grilles, painted black.

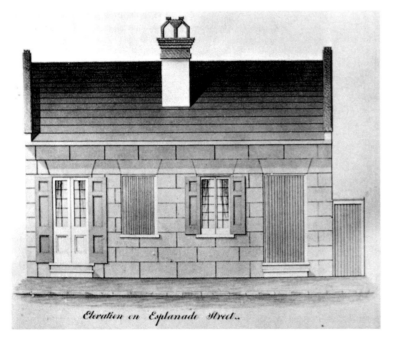

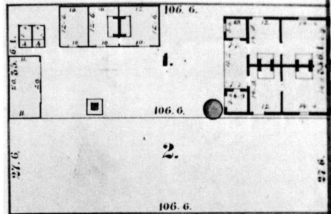

Plan book 57, folio 6, signed and dated, "May 5, 1845, Henry Moellhausen." This demolished creole cottage at the site of **730** Esplanade illustrates the prevalent cottage type along the Esplanade. The floor plan indicates that the plastered-front brick creole cottage had double cabinets in the rear gallery. No stairway is indicated. A two-room kitchen with a servants' room and a storehouse along with a privy, cistern, and third outbuilding were part of the complex. Of note is the chimney pot of brick, a prominent part of the roofline esthetic.

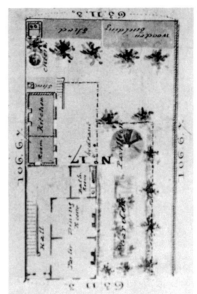

Plan book 78, folio 36, signed and dated, "September 27, 1866, Charles A. de Armas." This two-story Classic-style townhouse remains at **817** Esplanade. The façade was originally lathed and plastered then scored as indicated on the archival drawing. The façade was painted gray, the trim white, panel base was tan, and the ornate cast iron was a rich bronze. Shutters were green.

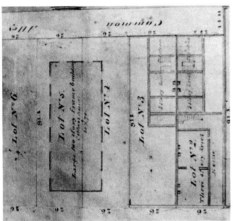

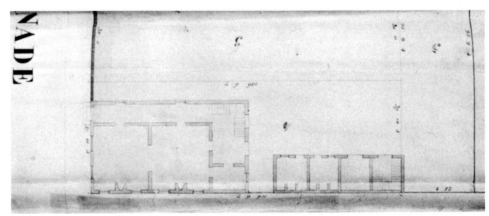

Plan book 79, folio 16, signed and dated, "March 18, 1857, C. A. de Armas." A row of common-wall townhouses dating from the 1830s stood in the **900** block of Esplanade. Now **919** remains and this archival drawing illustrates one of the row and would serve as a guide for the restoration of **919.** The original color scheme was tan with green shutters; the side is brick.

Plan book 28, folio 17, signed and dated, "April 5, 1848, Hemecourt." This corner creole townhouse stands at **938** Esplanade. When it was built in the 1820s it was one of many such houses to be found on corners of the creole faubourgs. The original color scheme was tan plastered brick with dark tan baseline under first-level windows. The roof had brown-toned slates, the window trim was white but the shutters dark green.

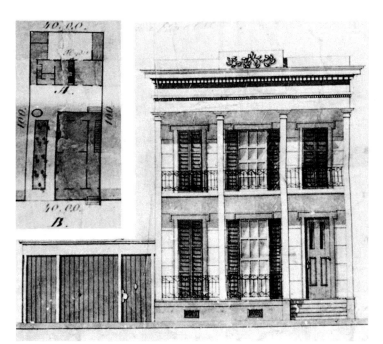

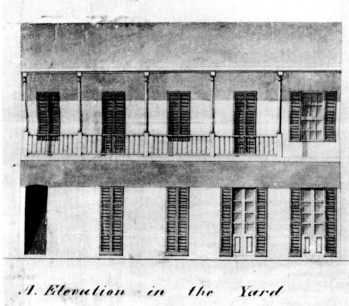

A. Elevation in the Yard

Plan book 21A, folio 40, signed and dated, "March 27, 1851, Adolphe Knell." The elevation of a demolished detached kitchen building at the site of **1016** Esplanade was part of the Pierre Roup complex of 1827. It served until after 1876. The main house, probably a creole cottage, was demolished and replaced by the three-bay townhouse built for Freeman Annabel. The house was white with green shutters and had an oak faux bois door. The present house at **1016** is incorporated into this 1840s house.

Plan book 104, folio 8, signed and dated, "December 3, 1839, J. A. Guernard, Jr., surveyor." This Esplanade and Rampart intersection remains in the **1000** downriver block with the exception of the hip-roof corner creole cottage. Third-floor alterations to **1037** have caused the loss of a roof terrace; the elegant three-level double had access to the upper level through the narrow side alleys to the rear circular stairways or directly through the double parlors. The creole cottage on the right is presently **1029**. This is a pen-and-ink drawing rather than a watercolor.

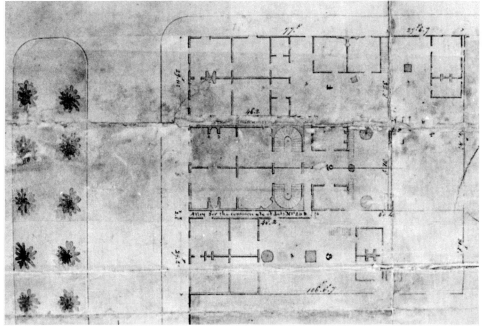

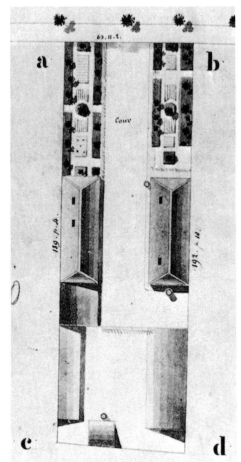

Plan book 65, folio 32, signed and dated, "June 21, 1855, P. Gualdi." This is Felix Pinson's house, built as his own residence in 1826 (see text, **1100** block downriver side). This brick building was plastered on all elevations and shaded a golden ochre. The shutters were the usual green, but the window trim, dormers, and pilasters were white. The service building and garden wall were the same ochre, and the carriageway paneled door was two shades of green. The front entrance door was faux bois.

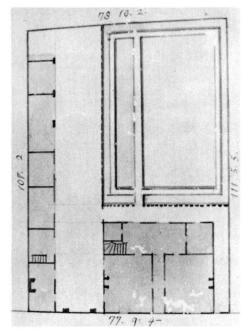

Plan book 61, folio 39, signed and dated, "February 11, 1837, Volquin." In the **1100** downriver block on square 380, Felix Pinson erected two houses; both were demolished. This house consisted of two equal-size hip-roof structures facing one another across a walled court. Of brick, plastered, scored, and painted ochre with dark tan base trim, the main buildings with green window shutters were connected to gray frame stables. This dwelling was replaced by a late Victorian house (see text, **1137** Esplanade) demolished in the 1970s.

Plan book 76, folio 14, signed and dated, "December 18, 1863, A. Castaing." This demolished corner grocery store at Rampart and Esplanade was painted pale ochre with paris green shutters at the time of this 1863 sheriff's sale.

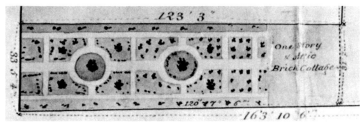

Plan book 26, folio 36, unsigned and undated. This archival plot plan of a one-story-and-attic brick cottage indicates the site of **1120** Esplanade. The house and garden that ran along Esplanade for 120 feet to the corner of Rampart were probably built for Mercelite Hazeur soon after her acquisition of the property in 1812. The cottage was replaced by another major house designed by J. N. B. de Pouilly, soon after 1868. It too was demolished.

Plan book 46, folio 2, signed and dated, "March 15, 1855, A. Castaing." This two-story brick hip-roof corner dwelling at **1236** Esplanade was painted brick, penciled white, with white trim, green shutters, black iron railing, dark gray slate roof (see text for full description).

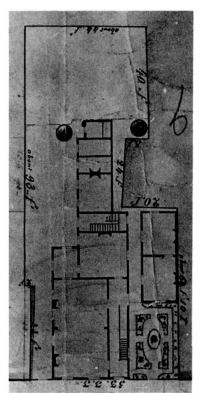

Plan book 85, folio 20, signed and dated, "June 17, 1864, A. Castaing and J. S. Celles." This mid–nineteenth-century side-hall townhouse, now demolished, once stood adjacent to **1120** Esplanade. Notable features include the relatively high level of the entrance and first floor of the house. Seldom are New Orleans townhouses raised five steps off the banquette. The second-level gallery is also exceptionally deep, necessitating slender iron colonnettes for support set into the curb. Observe that the shutters are vertical board below, and louvered above. A parterre garden faced the side service building. The acorn-pattern ironwork had a bronze finish, while the house and service building were painted tan, with a gray base.

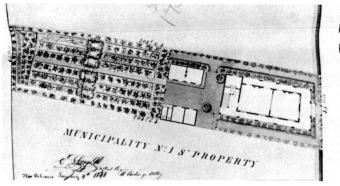

Plan book 65A, folio 63, signed and dated, "January 4, 1848, E. Surgi." The house at **1244** Esplanade as seen in 1847. This is a rare two-bay house with galleries on three sides and rear stairways. Less than five examples appear from fifteen-hundred archival drawings. In 1847 it was painted white with green shutters, as were many houses along the Esplanade. One-half the depth of the 204-foot lot is laid out as a garden with an arbor between the rectangular beds.

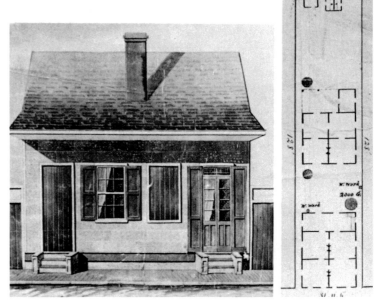

Plan book 7, folio 7, signed and dated, "March 26, 1862, Ch. de l'Isle." This demolished creole cottage stood on the Milne estate in the **1400** block of Esplanade behind Milne's own home which faced Barracks. It dates from the late 1830s and was included in Milne's estate sale in 1842. The gable sides of the house were weatherboard, but the scored plaster façade was painted and dappled gray to imitate stone. This is a sophisticated touch as are the elegant transoms above the casement openings and the french doors grained to resemble oak. The floor plan indicates that behind this main cottage was another structure having four rooms and a rear gallery with cabinet. This building was as large if not larger than the main house at the street, reflective of the mysteries often found in the complex behind creole housing.

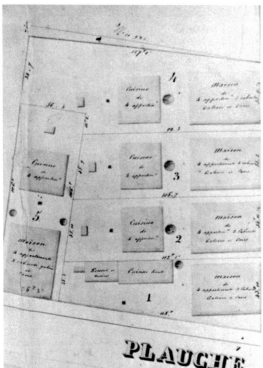

PLAUCHÉ

Plan book 21, folio 25, signed and dated, "May 11, 1844, E. Surgi." Four cottages as they appeared soon after completion, described as Passebon Row. Number **1308** Esplanade, second in the cottage row, survives. Originally, the cottages had an abat-vent beneath the roofline and a row of bricks laid in a sawtooth pattern beneath a row of dentils; both were replaced in a mid–nineteenth-century renovation in which the roof was raised and the overhand incorporated. The cottages were frame with plastered brick facades painted white. Vertical board shutters with interior panels and strap hinges were painted paris green and hung between splayed lintels and sills. Note detached kitchen arrangement. The artist, Surgi, has made a genre painting of this elevation reflecting something of the life style of the Esplanade in the 1840s. Note the light fixtures and newly planted trees on the Esplanade, the grassy neutral ground on which soldiers are marching, and the plank walkway across the neutral ground from Plauché (Marais).

Plan book 16, folio 27, signed and dated, "May 3, 1850, E. Surgi." These two demolished creole cottages at the corner of Esplanade and Claiborne on the square backed by Derbigny and Bayou Road in the **1600** block are the result of the subdivision following the 1836 projection of Esplanade through the Curval habitation. The muntin arrangement of the dormers, the proportion of the casement doors and transoms, as well as the low positioning of the house to the ground near the banquette level would indicate a building date between 1838 and 1848.

Plan book 47A, folio 46, signed and dated, "March 6, 1860, Charles A. de Armas." Square 1042, at Esplanade and Bayou Road intersection between Galvez and Miro, backed by Kerlerec. Two frame cottages, one with box columns and front gallery, the other with front cabinet gallery. Both are recessed behind garden fences, one of strip boards painted white and green, the other, a gray split-cypress palisade.

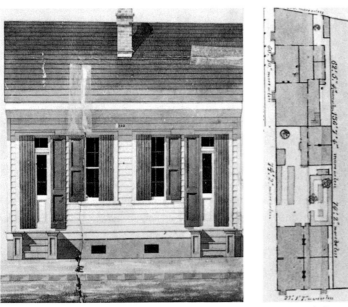

Plan book 99, folio 22, signed and dated, "May 10, 1876, A. Toledano." When this demolished creole cottage on **1800** Esplanade was drawn, it was on property formerly belonging to widow Castanedo. Bound by Bayou Road and Johnson, the plot plan indicates that this modest dwelling extended seventy-four feet, two inches, on Prieur; it hides an intricate complex with kitchens, service buildings, parterred gardens, and stables to the rear.

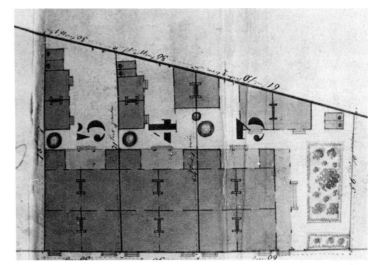

Plan book 73, folio 47, signed and dated, "March 12, 1860, E. Surgi and A. Persac." Two of these three common-wall creole cottages with cabinet galleries, built by Benjamin Rodriguez in 1859, remain at **2325** and **2331** Esplanade. Comparison of the archival drawing with the extant houses illustrates that alterations have diminished the esthetic impact of the four-room double cottages.

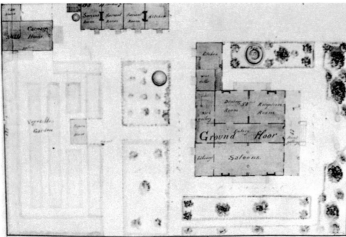

Plan book 21, folio 18, signed and dated, "July 8, 1841, Bourgerol." demolished house, once situated at the corner of Esplanade and Broa the square bound by Dorgenois and Barracks in the **2500** block, w galleried creole cottage with four front casement openings indicative of standard four-room creole cottage plan. An extensive stable faced B Street; the complex was surrounded by a vertical board picket fence.

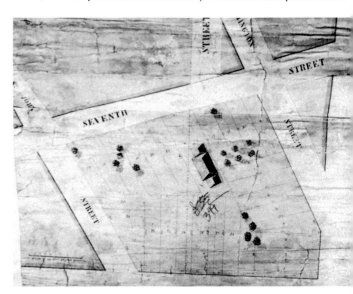

Plan book 22, folio 20, signed and dated, "April 11, 1837, Louis Bring The 1800 habitation of Spanish Colonial Lieutenant Governor Nicolas V is shown in the route of the projected Esplanade, indicated by dotted l on each side of the house.

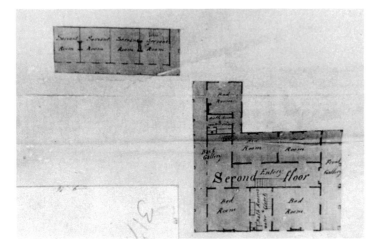

Plan book 5, folio 18, signed and dated, "March 12, 1860, E. Surgi and A. Persac." White frame two-story Greek Revival house with extensive garden, stables, and outbuilding partially remains in **2306** Esplanade (see text for complete description).

Plan book 47A, folio 56, signed and dated, "February 24, 1866, P. N. Jud architect." A frame creole cottage (demolished) painted white with p green shutters and a detached slant-roof kitchen built after Esplanade enue was cut through this square of Faubourg Pontchartrain in the 18 Note cast-iron cistern, flag post at the corner of Mystery and Esplana Open post and picket fence met solid palisade on side. Banquette ho and-buggy rail tilted up to the covered walkway supported by woo posts, indicating that this cottage was a commercial establishment. **3300,** photo index.

PHOTO INDEX

This index completes the record of the appearance of the Esplanade in 1976. Photographs illustrate structures that range from the fine to the terrible. Elegant nineteenth-century homes presently in bad condition are recommended for restoration, and ill-designed, unsuitable modern buildings are condemned. Original, attractive features of mutilated buildings are highlighted as are acceptable features of mediocre architecture. Similarly, unacceptable alterations spoiling the integrity of houses are decried. Recommendations for the entire street are presented, and attention given to the despoiling of all important intersections as well as most corner locations. All references to Volume IV refer to the Friends of the Cabildo's *New Orleans Architecture: The Creole Faubourgs, Architectural Inventory*. Cross references within the text may be found at the address number identified by the square symbol mark.

427. On this site, Felix Pinson designed a creole townhouse dating from 1834; it burned in 1895. The present replacement should have correct texture of rustication and appropriate placement of fenestration. See text.

503. Built as part of a complex between 1846 and 1867 for Julien A. Lacroix, free man of color, grocer and real estate investor. Rusticated façade, with bracketed, pedimented windows, pilasters, and mansard roof, added in the late 1880s. Formerly had cast-iron-covered walkways on two elevations. See text.

435. A two-story side-hall, mid–nineteenth-century brick townhouse with original fenestration, second-level cast-iron gallery. Became commercial at the first level by 1882 when J. B. Clovis Cadot's estate sold it. See text.

510. Three-story townhouse dating from the late 1830s. See text.

511. Ill-defined spatial conceptions, large pavement parking areas, square, sprawling, low-level design—entire complex unsuitable for Esplanade. Old brick, sham louvres further insult the architectural integrity of a nineteenth-century avenue.

520. Early twentieth-century raised-basement house. See text.

533 and 529. Lucy Cheatham houses. See text herein and Volume IV.

530–32 and 534–36. The turn-of-the-century six-bay double house on the left was probably raised after the advent of the automobile. The alteration has clean lines resulting in a raised-basement effect not harmful to the scale of the house. 534–36 presents a fine late Victorian interpretation of a double two-story house, continuing the late 1870s tradition of gallery at the first level combining with railing and deep bracketed overhang above. See text.

547. Sophisticated plastered brick Italianate detached townhouse designed in 1879 by William Fitzner, architect, and built by P. R. Middlemiss for Andrew Johnston. See Volume IV.

601. Twentieth-century church, now used as apartments. See text.

606. Built for Henry Raphael Denis, 1834. See text.

611. Gable-sided, semidetached townhouse built in 1847 as rental property for Marie Rambaus Journu, the widow of Claude Journu by Etienne Derepas, using specifications for a house previously built by him for Mrs. Journu on Chartres Street. See Volume IV. 613 and 617. (far right) Two common-wall plastered brick townhouses with gabled sides and elongated attic windows below a saw-tooth cornice. Square-headed openings with flat lintels and twin Greek Key entrance architraves suggest a building date in the 1830s, prior to René Beluche's sale to Joseph Sauvinet in 1841. See Volume IV. 621. The

Lamothe family owned this property during 1829–1860; the two present common-wall, three-story brick houses and service wings built about 1839 for Jean Lamothe. Paul Rivera, co-owner with Henry Parlange, contracted with builder Louis Folliet to make radical changes in 1860, which resulted in the Classic-style continuous façade having an unusual arrangement of two and three openings. See Volume IV. **627.** This townhouse once had a common wall with a demolished building, which stood at 623. Built for Joseph Sauvinet probably by 1847, when he sold the property to J. A. Montgomery, the house typifies the American-style townhouse with gallery projecting over the banquette at the second level. See Volume IV. **633.** (left) Side-hall, three-story townhouse probably built after Joseph Sauvinet sold the property to J. A. Montgomery in 1847. Hallmarks are the fine cast-iron galleries at the second and third levels, great chimneyed, gabled sides, and Classic entrance. See Volume IV.

623. In Pops Whitesell's photograph of 1920s tobacco shop is seen through the neutral ground sycamores. Shows an originally side-hall, three-story townhouse of the early 1840s which was demolished by the time Henry Morris Hobbs penciled a sketch of Lamothe House and **627** in 1938. The space is now a driveway. Both photo and sketch are housed in the Historic New Orleans Collection.

637 and **639.** This twentieth-century bungalow-style double is not a successful example of this style. The adjacent Edwardian-style house at **639** blends with the galleried single and double family dwelling vocabulary of the street.

622. A stick-style frame dwelling. See text.

632 and **634.** Second Empire, two-level, mansard-roofed frame houses. See text.

713. Such red-tile-roofed twentieth-century multiple-family houses illustrate a decline in architectural aesthetics. The low iron fence, the existence of a gallery, and the traditional scale are the only contributions to the street scene. It is better, however, than the shelled parking lot surrounded by high "Page" fence on adjacent corner.

719, 723, 727. These three late-Classic two-story frame houses were designed by architect Benjamin M. Harrod and built by Leonce N. Olivier for Aristide Hopkins in 1873. All three houses were formerly identical. See Volume IV.

716–18 and **720.** Well-designed single- and double-galleried shotguns with jigsaw work fit well; as individual compostions they are well designed in a traditional format of the early twentieth century.

735. Built for Mr. and Mrs. Achille Chiapella by Nicholas Duru, 1856, this detached Classic-style townhouse is set at the banquette with side yard enclosed by a high iron fence set on a granite base with granite piers and gateposts. Features: great chimneyed, gabled ends, large octagonal side bay, fine millwork in the recessed entry with granite threshold. See Volume IV.

741. Monumental in style and proportions, this masonry detached townhouse was designed and built in 1859 by William Freret, architect for Adrien Barbey at a cost of $10,000. The house resembled its neighbor at **735**, which had been constructed three years earlier. See Volume IV.

807. In 1859, Little and Middlemiss, builders, constructed this three-story plastered brick Greek Revival townhouse for Captain William Whann at a cost of $18,750. Its twin across the street at **806** was demolished. See text herein, and Volume IV.

817. Frame Greek Revival townhouse. See text and archival section herein and Volume IV.

823. An ornate frame two-and-one-half-story house with central hall built in 1856 for Stephen LeGardeur de Tilly by Barthelemy Courcelle at a cost of $9,950. The refinement of Classical exterior detail is of special interest, as is the composed centrality of design. The principal floor is at the second level as indicated in the building contract; accordingly, the façade at the second level has received emphasis in the creole fashion. See Volume IV.

832. The traditional townhouse floor plan here is presented with a façade formula popularized in the 1870s, having full-columned gallery below, with an upper balcony and turned wooden railing, the whole crowned with a deep bracketed overhang. Designed by Fourchey and Fourchey, architects, for Dr. J. N. Charbonnet, in September, 1893.

833. Earliest documented Esplanade house, this brick-between-posts cottage in the colonial style, originally with porte-cochère entry, was built about 1810 for John Gourjon, Jr. In 1811 it was described as "a main house 36 feet long, built of colombage," shingle-roofed, divided into three rooms "with galerie on the street, cabinet, and rear dependency." See Volume IV.

835–37. Only "dog-trot" style house on the avenue, has a narrow central passageway leading through the building to a courtyard. The brick creole-style double dwelling with two outer entrance doors in the present façade which are not original, but were formerly french-casement openings which opened into double parlors on either side. The house was built as a double in 1833 for François Girod by Charles Thompson at a cost of $6,500. See text herein and Volume IV.

836–42. Frame corner dwelling. See text.

839. The architect or contractor and owner of this once adequate corner store-house in the late Victorian style lost sight of community responsibility with this remodeling effort. It is aesthetically wrong to brick up a lower level or brick in windows, doors. Hip-roof, chimney, and building shape suggest the original type and style.

905. This is the only raised plantation style on the avenue. Brick, central hall with Greek Revival characteristics that include a two-level front gallery. Built soon after 1831 for François Gardère and known as the Gardère-Claiborne House. See text herein and Volume IV. (La. State Museum photo)

935. Site of early nineteenth-century New Orleans College. 1920s bungalow-style single-family dwelling replaced an earlier house. Inappropriate to avenue style. See text.

900. The Vieux Carré Commission failed in its community responsibility here. Site overbuilt. There is more to compatible design than the use of old bricks and inclusion of mansard roof. Site and design are incompatible to historic area, ruinous effects extend to **906** (right) and all neighboring buildings.

917 (right). François Gardère had this 1830s hall-less creole townhouse built at the same time as his neighboring building at **905**. The brick was originally painted and penciled, and the roofline embellished by sawtooth and dentil rows beneath a brick cornice. See Volume IV. **919** (left), one remaining of two common-wall plastered brick creole townhouses built by Edward Grastour for La Compagnie des Architects in 1833 for $10,226 each. The two houses were large in scale for the era of the 1830s. The Architect's Company first sold this house in 1835 to Pierre Soulé, lawyer and statesman, who sold within months to the nephew of Napoleon Bonaparte, Achille Murat. Two years later, creditors nearing, Murat auctioned it for $16,000. See text herein and Volume IV.

937. This Victorian mansion, featuring a square turret tower set at an odd angle to the façade, was built for G. A. Lanaux in 1884. Slightly altered by enclosure of the upper gallery, the design nevertheless retains the Baroque animation of a decade inspired by Second Empire, Victorian Gothic, and Victorian Italianate styles. See text.

922. See text.

1009–11 (right). A plastered brick townhouse probably built between 1829 and 1833 for Pierre J. Baron Boisfontaine, who also owned Daniel Clark's townhouse on Royal. Architecturally, the house fits the 1830s, and the rectangular attic windows, simple post-and-lintel openings, and door and window arrangement could be original. Other details, like the recessed entrance, probably post date the Civil War. See Volume IV. **1015** (center). This two-story frame house was built 1881, James Freret, architect, for Estelle Musson. The house exemplifies the 1870s interpretation of the detached townhouse type popular along Esplanade. Deep bracketed overhang and balcony at the second level, tall recessed segmental arch entry, drop siding, quoins, modillions, and window cornices characterize the style. The interior is traditional Esplanade Ridge style. **1017–21** (left). The present façade siding, moldings, and cornices as well as the attached two-story service wing postdate the building date of this creole cottage. Recent analysis of this house coupled with title research indicate a possible building date as early as the 1840s rather than the 1880s. See Volume IV.

1029. Creole cottage built for Petronille Bordrier Monsignac, a free woman of color, before 1832; dormers are a later nineteenth-century addition; central chimney has been removed. The original well-proportioned plastered façade, with clear surfaces, is now altered by twentieth-century bricking over. **1037**. This four-bay creole double house was built about 1833–36, also for Petronille Bordrier Monsignac. The plastered brick house has three full stories without the dormers, although today the top one may appear to be a half story. This third story once was recessed and had flat roof terraces to its front and rear sides formed by extensions of the brick walls of the house in the Spanish colonial style. Archival section, plan book 104, folio 8. See Volume IV.

1039. An early twentieth-century version of a two-level New Orleans double house. Each side has two bays, no hall, and a rear stair leading to a second level. Hallmarks of the style are the use of three neo-Classic columns widely spaced across the façade at each level. Remnant of first-level balustrade remains with one base pier. The wide dormer with its muntin arrangement in the Gothic manner was popular in 1920s. The house might be called an extremely modest version of the City Beautiful style with very few vestiges of the original inspiration.

1004. Frame house on site of two masonry townhouses. See text.

1026. An Edwardian-style residence set behind an iron fence is compatible in scale and style to the Esplanade. Dormers, bays, galleries, columns, and balcony railings continue a familiar idiom.

1038 and **1040**. Demourelle property. Intersection destroyed by former filling station, present used car lot. Billboards crowd area more than is indicated in photograph. Intersections create external moods which infiltrate all four surrounding adjacent neighborhoods. Introduction of commercial buildings not reflective of surrounding architectural scale or type destroys entire neighborhoods. See text.

1137. The 1970s demolition of this 1880s center-hall mansion replete with galleries, bays, mansard roof, and decorative dormers was a major loss to the Esplanade. The Second Empire-style building continued the mid–nineteenth-century traditions in center-hall floor plan and a spacious interior reflective of the Esplanade Ridge style decoration. A photograph made during demolition illustrates medallions, bracket-supported screen, and moldings with plaster work in deep relief. All are indications of the luxurious decor which by its scale and grandeur had served as an important architectural expression on the Esplanade.

1208. Jean Mager house remodeled many times. See text.

1214. Frame early twentieth-century double town-house. See text.

1222, 1224–26, 1234–36. Originally two residences and two kitchens. See text.

1244, 1252, 1262. Street scene depicting a typical group of double-level mid–nineteenth-century Esplanade Ridge homes. See text.

1219. A New Orleans interpretation of the bungalow style of architecture, continuing the traditional raised basement, deep front gallery, center-hall American floor plan, and hip-roof. Queen Anne-style steps illustrate the popularity of cement; paired columns on heavy brick piers are a stylistic hallmark. Replacement of the original wood porch railing with modern iron is unfortunate as is the installation of a window where the basement ventilator once was. Such houses are complemented by tropical planting, like the palms seen here, and lavish use of greenery.

1227. See text.

1233. A building should be considered as a compositional section of the street scene—as an area with spatial relationships and part of an architectural and environmental complex. None of these considerations are evident in this structure.

1247. Two-level frame early twentieth-century house incorporating front gabled roof with pediment treatment popular in New Orleans "stick-style" architecture. Front porch is tiled and stairs have Queen Anne turn. House is pleasantly located behind large magnolias; it was part of the old lands of Morand-Moro-Mager holdings.

1265 and 1261. Double galleried townhouses; 1261 demolished 1973, remains vacant lot. See text..

1302. This corner store-house replaces one of the Passebon Row creole cottages (see text herein and archival Plan book 21, folio 25). Note the late Italianate entrance leading to the second level, the second-level wood railing on both street elevations and bracketed overhang to the hip-roof. Original turned wood columns should be reinstalled on the banquette to support the deep balcony.

1306–08. Only remaining of four creole cottages of Passebon Row. See text.

1310. Probably one of the first twentieth-century international-style houses along the Esplanade. Its success cannot be analyzed because the house fails to fit into its visual and historic context along the Esplanade.

1332. Ill-conceived, this nondesign was probably built to last only as long as the mortgage. Ideally, a mid–nineteenth-century building should be moved to the site

1342. See text.

1313. Three-bay frame townhouse on former Plauché plantation. See text.

1315. St. Anna's Episcopal Church, 1956.

1337, 1333, 1327, 1323. Number **1323** paritally shown. Row of late nineteenth-century frame double-level Esplanade Ridge houses. See text.

1400. Continues the corner store-house tradition most often observed in surrounding Faubourgs Marigny, Tremé, New Marigny. The brick chimneys, second-level overhang, from which brackets have unfortunately been removed, and the wide cast-iron balcony on two sides are pleasing architectural details. Such balconies with their cast-iron colonnettes placed in the edges of the banquette make a covered walkway, a hallmark of New Orleans corners for a century and a half.

1423. Aldigé House—former Alexander Milne plantation. See text.

1341. Perhaps the side galleries with iron supports and railing and brackets as well as the narrow vertical stripes of bricks alternating with the fenestration panels were an attempt by a planner to adapt modern brick, metal windows, and post-1950 architectural design to the Esplanade vocabulary. If so, it failed.

1432. This perfectly chaste Classic-style frame townhouse, which once had double galleries supported by box columns like the ones remaining at the second level, could be restored to its original mid-nineteenth-century appearance. Removal of the lower level gallery, the unfortunate facing in old brick, and the modernizing of lower level windows was an ill-conceived alteration.

1501. A masonry corner commercial site at Villere is an ineffective building which replaces a one-time creole cottage store-house.

1518. 1840 creole cottage moved to present location on lot in 1880s. See text.

1347. Raised four-bay cottage. See text.

Esplanade and Claiborne intersection. Intersection has been desecrated by four filling stations, an elevated expressway, and constant filth fluttering from the dry dirt beneath the roadway.

1614. Raised-basement three-bay Italianate house. See text.

1632. A fine gable-sided, three-bay side-hall townhouse with balcony in the Italianate style. See text.

1722 and **1730**. Corner sites seem to be the first to be demolished; these two houses are the second and third buildings on their historic sites. Both houses, had they not been distastefully remodeled, would have fit into the street scene in scale and context.

1737. A Spanish Revival version of the New Orleans center-hall raised cottage with gallery. Reflective of the decorative style after the turn of the century. Compatible in scale.

1809. Considerable money was unwisely spent here on awnings and cast iron, both unsuitable to this type and style of bungalow.

1819. A traditional center-hall raised-basement villa-style house with gable sides, its decorative style is neo-Classic Revival. The present expensive fence, platforms, steps, brick piers, and box columns do not complement a house of pleasing design. Early photograph of house exists at Tulane University Library Special Collections.

1829–31. A bungalow is ruined by awnings, paving of the yard, and four gas meters set where flower beds once softened the façade. Foundation planting, even a small green lawn with shade trees, could aid this Carrollton- or Gentilly-style home.

1800 and 1808. Awnings, modern ironwork, false shutters, enclosures, and alterations of fenestration spoil the integrity of these two early twentieth-century homes.

1822. Makeshift adaptation of this single-family dwelling into apartments is detrimental to the restrained Eastlake characteristics of this turn-of-the-century home.

1832. A modest version of the City Beautiful decorative style. Dormers, galleries, balcony, lavish planting, and a fence across the front are continuing characteristics of such dwellings which make them compatible to the street scene.

1834. The photograph has captured the potential charm of this late Classic-style residence. A pilastered entrance with dentiled cornice, deep reveals, and a recessed door with a transom are clues to the one-time elegance of this house. A well-proportioned gable side is supported by box columns of a recessed side gallery. These attractive characteristics reflecting New Orleans mid–nineteenth-century building traditions go unnoticed from the front. The recessed side gallery was a popular method of creating a passageway without enclosing it and is seen in houses dating from the late 1840s to the turn of the century.

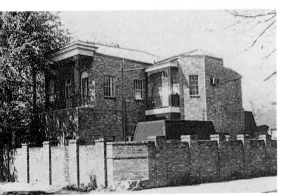

1907. A fine mid–nineteenth-century townhouse with an Italianate bay has been devastated by ill-advised brick facing. At one-half the cost, the fine house might have been restored and made convenient for modern living. Brick facing completely covering a frame house is expensive and architecturally inaccurate.

1913. An Edwardian-style family home has traditional iron fence, galleries, and balconies, which blend with the Esplanade architectural vocabulary.

1931, 1929, 1925. Three once-identical frame townhouses. See text.

1931–33 (right). Rental property has approached slum conditions at the former three-bay townhouse in the late nineteenth-century style. See text. **1937.** (left). Possible parapet restoration on bay and minor improvements would improve this early twentieth-century dwelling. Note Italianate decoration beneath the verge board.

Corner Esplanade and N. Johnson. Both of these corner store-houses have been mutilated. Vestiges of cast iron, some well-proportioned doors and surrounds, an attractive gable end, and hip-roof are clues to the original attractive buildings. The decline in comprehension of architecture during the third quarter of the twentieth century is seen here. See text.

2007–11. Frame double-level house, altered on first level. See text.

2014. This hip-roof, three-bay frame house with wide Greek Key entrance behind an original recessed door and sidelights is somewhat unusual arrangement. The Sanborn map of 1894 illustrated several houses on this triangle facing Bayou Road.

2015. Early twentieth-century restrained example of City Beautiful style having three Ionic evenly distributed columns, with decorated facia. Front gable simple brackets. Iron fence would complete the setting.

2127. An Edwardian version of the New Orleans raised-basement, galleried, and dormered cottage recalls the continuing tradition of a popular New Orleans house type on into the twentieth century. Louvered windows in the dormer, an unsightly plate-glass window in the center façade with its adjacent airconditioner, could easily be removed and with minor repairs and paint, the house would reflect its suitability to the Esplanade ambiance.

2200 and 2206. To the left is a traditional example of the City Beautiful aesthetic as seen in New Orleans simplified version. The Ionic columns, diamond-shaped small window and the low, wide dormer are indicative of this type found throughout midcity and uptown. The cottage at 2206 on the right is almost identical in fenestration and entrance arrangement, but the house is built lower to the ground, and the decoration is Victorian in flavor with a high shingled front gable, deep gallery supported with irregularly spaced colonnettes having decorative applied work spandrels and brackets. This house probably predates its neighbor by a decade. Note the louvered shutters in front of the recessed front door.

2024. Sam Wing Cleaners and Ticket Tick Inc., out of place on a historic, nationally recognized city avenue.

2164. Two twentieth-century double houses: one on the left retains its original woodwork and appearance is far more suitable than the one on the right which has suffered added ironwork, awnings, and a portico.

2201. Downriver corner Galvez. A hip-roof with corner emphasis, an animated verge decoration, and repeated french doors with louvered shutters opening onto a deep second-level gallery recall the days when this traditional corner store-house fit well into its neighborhood and street scene. Brick facing with cliché pilaster motif and dripping arches are unsightly, with no architectural precedents and should be ripped away.

2115. A very fine townhouse with large hexagonal bay in the idiom of the Esplanade Ridge style as translated in the 1870s and 1880s has been transformed by unsightly additions, enclosure of the first-level gallery, and ungainly brick piers. Subsequent application of asbestos siding and makeshift openings has altered the integrity of the house. The bay with its second-level balcony and the second-level deep bracketed overhang, segmental arch fenestration and turned baluster balcony railing are suggestive of the possible charm of the house.

2176. Remodeled frame townhouse. See text.

2213. A twentieth-century example of a galleried double house at 2213 (right) replaces an earlier nineteenth-century home. The house has not been altered and is representative of a modest City Beautiful or midcity type that comes into view as one approaches Broad Street. 2221 (left). It is difficult to imagine that a sign advertising "luxury apartments with pool and patio" for this Esplanade address could refer to this address. A second-level bay, supported with brackets, and some Greek Key surrounds as well as a hip-roof and the boxlike shape of the structure indicate that a Victorian example of the three-bay townhouse is disguised here.

2238. Gable sides, an overhang, and the proportions indicate that beneath this improper brick facing and openings lies a neat creole cottage.

2316. See text.

2317. Another example of misguided alterations is seen on this frame gable-front house which was once probably a six-bay double shotgun with front porch beneath the overhang. The present façade is an uninformed attempt at improvement.

2435. Another modest City Beautiful incorporating three columns, porch, Queen Anne steps, and front pediment. Well proportioned to site.

2535. Buildings such as these give a good appearance on the modern architect's drawing board, replete with landscaping, curved walkway, beautiful blue sky, and green grass. The unknowledgeable client may become convinced his structure will be a credit to the grounds and neighborhood. The structure is out of scale and context and does not complement the street environment. The application of a segmental arch overlight to the entrance, the modern adaptations of box columns, and the lowered arches on a portico are unsuccessful.

2700 Upriver block. See text.

2826. Beyond Broad toward the Bayou there appear twentieth-century versions of the galleried shotgun which are recognized by wide front entrances. This one with the traditional spindlework band above colonnettes with appliedwork spandrels has had the wooden porch railing removed.

2733. McDonogh 28. See Introduction.

2801. Leaded glass and stained glass along with projecting gables are features of this comfortable early twentieth-century residence built within the confines of old Faubourg Pontchartrain. Unfortunately, remodeling caused the removal of the original wood columns and decorations at the first level. Perhaps the woodwork there matched the interesting railing at the second-level balcony along the side, which could serve as a pattern for renovation of the front.

2809. Early photographs loaned by William Cresson. See text.

2821. Neo-Tudor interpretation within 1920s residence. Timbers and brackets should be stained dark to emphasize style. Early photograph is in Tulane Library Special Collections.

2841. Modest late nineteenth-century frame cottage.

2907 and **2909**. The redevelopment of the areas of Faubourgs Pontchartrain and St. John after the cut-through of the Esplanade in the 1850s was not completed until after World War I. These two commodious frame residences resemble many found uptown in the areas which developed after the great 1883 Audubon Park Exposition. The house on the right with its succession of three wide gables with shallow overhangs and brackets had a stick-style inspiration while the one on the left expresses an interpretation of the City Beautiful aesthetic.

2914, **2918**, **2926**. A street scene comprised of similar-sized early twentieth-century type cottages set beyond the tree-lined sidewalk provides a tranquil street scene of similar architectural types.

2917. Mission-style house; early photograph in the Tulane University Library Special Collections.

2936. Gothic villa. See text.

3018, 3020, 3024. The architectural firm of Toledano and Wogan is traditionally responsible for many of the early twentieth-century houses along the Esplanade. One of that firm's trademarks was the shield seen as decoration here on the piers of the central house. On the right and left are two interpretations of the early twentieth-century bungalow style, of which there are more examples between Broad and the Bayou in midcity than in any other neighborhood.

3023–25, **3027–29**, **3031**. To the right is a relatively pretentious example of a double shotgun given a twentieth-century interpretation. To the left and the center are two of the many examples of the Neo-Classic Revival architecture seen along this segment of Esplanade involving many decorative elements of that style.

3102, 3108, 3112—14. To the left of two City Beautiful houses is a raised house with Italianate woodwork and lowered arches across a front cornice. House has a center-hall floorplan. Earlier history is indicated than present modernizations reveal.

3200. Derby Place is a restaurant unfortunately situated on one of the triangles that remained in private ownership after Esplanade cut it off from the rest of the square. The palm tree and the light standard are the only suitable furnishings here. The city should acquire the property for another small park site. See archival, Plan book 47A, folio 56.

3336. A three-bay, frame shotgun house with rusticated façade has late-Classic-style entrance and two full-length casement openings. Twentieth-century alterations of the gallery and side additions have disguised the character of this once pleasant shotgun with hall. Restoration by analogy would be simple.

3354. Appears today as a 1920s-style camel back with side hall. It is likely that the front-gable house dates from early twentieth century; the present massive steps, gallery flooring, piers, and paired pillars are later additions. These might be removed and replaced with four turned posts, jigsaw railing, and steps of smaller scale.

Cabrini High School. At 3400 Esplanade is a large institutional building constructed as the Sacred Heart Orphan Asylum in 1905, Robert Palestina, architect. The building was financed by Captain Salvatore Pizzati. It is presently part of the complex of Cabrini High School and Convent. □

3333, 3335–37, 3339–41. To the right is an impressive example of the late Victorian multilevel house featuring a rounded gallery, projecting and bayed blocks contrasting with squared segments of the large home. Beside this are smaller scaled double shotguns, the three unified by the symmetry of spacing of the oak trees lining the street.

3356. A fine three-bay, side-hall 1900s shotgun with gallery, as indicated by the front gable. Full-length surrounds for segmental arch openings are a handsome variety featuring bull's-eyes and molded cornices. The original steps, gallery floor, and lower portion of the box columns have unfortunately been replaced with masonry, spoiling the façade proportion intended by its late Victorian style.

Luling Mansion. Jewell's Crescent City. J. W. Orr lithograph.

3342. A rural-style two-bay shotgun featuring a hip-roof and gallery on two sides. Casement opening provides entrance and egress from this passageway gallery. The original wood steps, gallery flooring, and jigsaw supports have been replaced. Replacement of the jigsaw gallery railing and wood posts would be an essential part of correct renovation here.

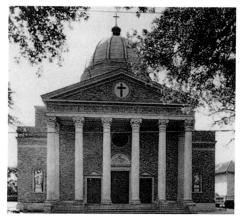

3400. Our Lady of the Rosary designed by Rathbone de Buys, 1924.

St. Louis Cemetery III, designed in 1854, is despoiled by this overscaled, ill-designed apartment house facing Bayou St. John and City Park. This prime location was recently purchased from the Catholic archdiocese of New Orleans.

EPILOGUE

The future of this historic corridor, the Esplanade Ridge, after 125 years of predominance in the city, is poised at the crossroads of changing social patterns. For years, pressures have mounted against the peaceful residential character of Esplanade. Lest it go the way of lower St. Charles, equal pressures must be extended to enforce zoning, curb the crime proliferating from adjacent neighborhoods, and deal with the increasing blight caused by commercial interests, transients, and absentee landlords.

In the last ten years, demolitions have all but eradicated both sides of the 1100 block. The lovely 1849 Castera house at 1261 was torn down by the Episcopal church; the massive Wright-Slocomb mansion at 1205 was destroyed by the Catholic church. At number 1707 Henry Howard's extraordinary Dufour-Baldwin house stands deteriorating, a noteworthy monument sadly neglected. Another major residence designed by Henry Howard and Albert Diettel dating from 1858 stood on the site of a McDonogh School in the 2400 block. The building contract before notary W. H. Peters described it as a two-story brick residence with galleries; the *Daily Crescent* of September 15, 1859, referred to it as an "Elizabethan style residence, unique in this city." The true Second Empire mansard roof type, once well represented along Esplanade, has become a "rare and endangered species." One remains at 2453; its twin at 2445 was demolished in 1972; 2425 was demolished in 1976. The beautiful 1850s American-villa-style residence at 2511, with its graceful curving gallery, has bowed to Ricca Wrecker's demolition. Deterioration of the Esplanade Ridge can be halted by an infusion of dedicated new owners interested in single or multiple dwellings within walking distance of the Central Business District, and close enough to bicycle to the lakefront university.

Mansions too large for single-family use can be preserved as apartments and retain interior and exterior details; they can be economically profitable ventures. An enormous Queen Anne-style mansion built in 1900 at 2809 Esplanade is a case in point. Counting its carriage house and raised basement level this building has fifteen well-kept, adequately spacious apartments. Each apartment has two entries, but all are scarcely noticeable. Primary architectural features throughout have been kept and restored.

Prohibition of commercialism along Esplanade was a consideration as early as 1841 when a family meeting was held on behalf of the Duchamp heirs for the disposition of property along Esplanade in the 1800 block. A stipulation was made as to the residential character of the area when major New Orleans business and professional men, Pierre Soulé, Louis Caire, L. E. Forstall, and the Darcantel brothers approved a plan to lease property as lots and permit buildings to go up on them "with the reservation however that it shall be stipulated in the acts of leases that the buildings or improvements to be put on the lots so leased shall be none other than those intended for dwelling houses and dependencies." Through the records of the entire street, mention is made of dwelling houses—with few references to stores or commercial edifices.

Rank unplanned commercialism without residential code restrictions is another negative force here and on other main New Orleans avenues. Intersection ugliness is detrimental to rehabilitation. Zoning weaknesses are also a primary danger to Esplanade, where 15 percent of a home may be legally used as a commercial outlet without a zoning waiver. Only modest controls are possible since zoning restriction waivers are constantly granted. Individual buyers should understand that adaptive reuse is preferable to replacement. Citizen awareness—interest and determination—is the only safeguard for the Esplanade or any other main thoroughfares.

SELECTED BIBLIOGRAPHY

Bibliographic sources, both primary and secondary, used for *New Orleans Architecture,* Volumes I–IV, were also employed in the production of this book. Notarial acts and records from the Conveyance, the Mortgage, and the Will books were the basic tools used in property research. To those were added court records, council records, and colonial judicial documents preserved in the Louisiana State Museum and recorded in issues of the *Louisiana Historical Quarterly.* The Tanesse maps of 1810 and 1816, along with the John Pilié surveys of 1818 and 1822, dealing with the development and prolongment of Esplanade, were invaluable aids from the city engineers' office. The Charles Zimpel map, 1834 (endsheets) was a major resource tool. The following list completes the bibliographies published in the previous volumes:

Barron, Bill. *The Vaudreuil Papers.* New Orleans: Polyanthos, Inc., 1975.

Bezou, Henry C. *Metairie: A Tongue of Land to Pasture.* Gretna: Pelican Publishing Co., 1973.

Gilmore, H. W. "The Old New Orleans and the New: A Case for Ecology," *American Sociological Review,* IV, 1944, pp. 385–94.

Giraud, Marcel. *A History of French Louisiana.* Vol. I. Baton Rouge: Louisiana State University Press, 1974.

Hennick, Louis C. *The Streetcars of New Orleans.* Gretna: Pelican Publishing Co., 1975.

Holmes, Jack D. L. *Honor and Fidelity: The Louisiana Infantry Regiment and the Louisiana Militia Companies, 1766–1821.* Birmingham: n.p., 1965.

Huber, Leonard V. *New Orleans: A Pictorial History.* New York: Crown Publishers, Inc., 1971.

Insurance Maps: Sanborn, 1876, 1894; Robinson, 1883.

Latrobe, Benjamin H. B. *Impressions Respecting New Orleans.* edited by Samuel Wilson, Jr. New York: Columbia University Press, 1951.

McDermott, John Francis, ed. *Frenchmen and French Ways in the Mississippi Valley.* Urbana: University of Illinois Press, 1969.

———. The Spanish in the Mississippi Valley, *1762–1804.* Urbana: University of Illinois Press, 1974.

Toledano, Roulhac, Sally Kittredge Evans, and Mary Louise Christovich, comps. *New Orleans Architecture, Volume IV: The Creole Faubourgs.* Gretna: Pelican Publishing Co., 1974.

Vieux Carré Survey, Historic New Orleans Collection.

De Villiers, Marc. *Histoire de la Fondation de la Nouvelle-Orléans, 1717–1722.*

Wilson, Samuel, Jr. *The Vieux Carré, New Orleans: Its Plan, Its Growth, Its Architecture.* New Orleans: Bureau of Governmental Research, 1968.

INDEX